HOW TO READ THE FINANCIAL NEWS

HOW TO READ THE FINANCIAL NEWS

TENTH EDITION

C. Norman Stabler

~~~~~~

BARNES & NOBLE BOOKS

A DIVISION OF HARPER & ROW, PUBLISHERS

New York, Hagerstown, San Francisco, London

HOW TO READ THE FINANCIAL NEWS. Copyright 1932, 1933, 1936, 1937, 1938, 1941, 1949, 1951 by New York *Herald Tribune*. Copyright © 1959, 1965 by C. Norman Stabler. All rights reserved. Printed in the United States of America. No part of this book may be used or reproduced in any manner without written permission except in the case of brief quotations embodied in critical articles and reviews. For information address Harper & Row, Publishers, Inc., 10 East 53rd Street, New York, N.Y. 10022. Published simultaneously in Canada by Fitzhenry & Whiteside Limited, Toronto.

First BARNES & NOBLE BOOKS edition published 1972.

STANDARD BOOK NUMBER: 06-463327-6

83 84   20 19 18 17 16 15 14 13 12 11

CONTENTS

PREFACE

A HIGH SCHOOL OR COLLEGE STUDENT, UPON ENROLLING for a new course, finds the earlier days of his semester devoted in large measure to learning the terminology of his subject. A cotangent, an amoeba, a short story, a verb, an atom, a kilowatt, or capital gains distribution must mean exactly one thing, and nothing else. It must be thoroughly understood by the student and the professor. Otherwise, classroom discussions might approach, in their confusion, conversations between people speaking different languages.

The field of finance has its lexicon as surely as do the old and new sciences of metaphysics, biochemistry, and atomic power. Articles, discussions, and news items which one sees in his daily newspaper concerning economic, business, and fiscal developments are far less complicated than are similar articles about breakthroughs in the numerous scientific fronts.

The fact remains that the financial section of a newspaper is thought by many, perhaps unjustly, to be too technical and to use a jargon all its own. The accusation is partly true. It is becoming less true as the number of those who own securities increases.

This growing group has a stake in what is printed in the financial sections of newspapers here and abroad. Its members are acquiring a degree of acquaintanceship with day-to-day stories of business and finance through a process of osmosis.

The mere fact that some 17 million individuals in the United States now hold shares of common or preferred stocks, and that the number is rising steadily, is proof enough of the growing need for authoritative financial news. In 1955 the number was only 8 million. Neither estimate includes the vast number of holders of bonds or of those indirectly concerned through their ownership of life insurance policies and savings accounts in commercial banks, savings banks, and other thrift institutions.

In 1955 the New York Stock Exchange sponsored a survey designed to discover the extent of public knowledge of financial and business affairs. It learned that a large part of the public had only a vague knowledge of financial terms and operations.

Surprisingly, 77 per cent of the adult population could not adequately define a common stock. Even in households that owned some shares of common stock, there were 39 per cent that could not do so. Gratifying, however, was the discovery from this survey that in 16 million households where no shares were owned, there was a desire to learn of financial matters.

The students are willing. They want to know. There is a large and ever-expanding group that seeks to increase its knowledge in this fascinating field.

This book is designed to be of assistance in that endeavor. I have sought to make it simple and easily understood. There is no "gobbledegook."

Kenneth L. Calkins, of the Boeing Company, certainly a leader in his field, asked once why a man must write, "man-machine requirements in this system environment impose several visual acuity problems," when all he means to say is, "he can't see the instrument panel."

No one group has a monopoly on such "gobbledegook." Let there be none of it in this edition of *How to Read the Financial News.*

This is edition number ten. The first was written in 1932, in the depths of the depression which made everyone acutely aware of economic forces. This newest edition is revised and enlarged, and brought up to date to include discussions of the more recent developments one sees discussed in his daily newspaper.

Like earlier editions it is designed to acquaint readers with the services performed by a comprehensive financial section, of which there are many in the leading newspapers and magazines of this country and of the free world.

Earlier editions have been used by educators to familiarize school and college students with financial terms and to help them properly to interpret stories, statistical tables, charts, and features.

This is not a book on how to invest, how to make a killing in Wall Street, or what to do with the family's income. There are many excellent books on these subjects. I do not give financial advice; rather I hope to make the financial section of your newspaper come alive so that you may better understand it and profit thereby.

As with the previous editions I have leaned heavily and profitably on authorities in Wall Street and in Washington.

I also wish to thank the *Wall Street Journal,* the *New York Times,* and the *New York Herald Tribune* for permission to use illustrative material.

C. N. S.

New York City
September 1964

HOW TO READ THE FINANCIAL NEWS

1

~~~~~~

INTRODUCTION

AN ADVERTISEMENT THAT HAS BEEN PLACED FRE-
quently in major newspapers by a trust company which gives tender
care to well over a couple of billion dollars worth of securities of its
clients, carries a slogan to the effect that: "NOW"—is always the
hardest time to invest.

It continues with the explanation that no day is a simple day.
Always something is happening, not only on a day-to-day schedule
but on an hour-to-hour basis, and even a minute-to-minute one.
The word "status" is in the dictionary. Its application to the vast
panorama of business and finance that affects the livelihood of each
of us is one of constant change, for we are all consumers. Most of us
are members of the production section of our economy and, directly
or indirectly, we are all investors in the general welfare of society.

As such we have the benefit of the improved mediums of communication, the newspapers, periodicals, radio and television, and other
electronic marvels. In this edition we are concerned with the desire
of a good portion of our population to learn how better to understand, through these media, the wealth of information that is made
available to each of us.

There are readers who become appalled by the wealth of statistics they encounter in the financial section of their newspapers. I recall visiting a friend on a rainy night, and when his daughter entered the house with muddy overshoes her father directed her to "put those overshoes in a piece of newspaper; don't track mud all over the house."

"All right," she replied. "I'll use the financial section. Nobody will want to read that."

But a growing number of people are demanding more and more from the financial sections of all forms of communication. They want those long statistical tables, spot news about companies and industries, opinions of economists and business leaders, and explanatory articles on individual companies. Within this expanding group there is a vote of dissent to the old saying that economics is the dismal science.

Yet many who wish to understand the financial news admit quite frankly that the financial section of the newspaper is, to them, too technical.

Actually, it is not. But personal conversations with a number of doubters indicates they believe it is. They know that a leading newspaper in any of our major cities accords more space to the general subject of our economic welfare than to any other single subject. Frequently these stories are printed on the front page. Only a portion of them are in the financial section. Subjects covered include the gamut of taxes, cost of living, droughts, legislation, wages, court decisions, and a host of other subjects which touch the welfare of those within the body politic. That is all of us.

Stories of this nature share a newspaper's columns with those of international moment, local happenings, crimes and accidents, the doings of the social set, sports, and obituaries, to name a few classifications. The reader of the average major daily is presented with twenty-four hours of world history, highlighting principal developments. He has enough reading matter to fill three average-sized novels. To read everything, his task would encompass 100,000 to 300,000 words, not including advertising, pictures, cartoons, or special features.

Approaching the end of his reading he would come to the financial and business section, where he is offered a running account of a day's developments in the world of business, finance, and industry, and a statistical record that normally covers two to three thousand prices of such varied things as stocks, bonds, money loaned for different periods of time, basic commodities and futures, textiles, and the cash prices of farm produce.

This is the section in which the science of economics, with all its ramifications, is accorded full sway. It is packed with up-to-the-minute information. Accuracy is paramount, and a staff of specially trained newspapermen strives to give the reader the economic story in easily understood terms. This effort frequently imparts to the financial section a kaleidoscopic appearance, because the influences that may affect one's pocketbook are myriad. Developments of economic importance are recorded and weighed, and their possible repercussions on world markets noted.

Such stories form but one phase of the wealth of material. Great though their significance may be, they occupy only a part of the entire financial section. A larger part is devoted to statistics, the figures of the markets where securities, commodity futures, and goods are sold and the figures which are essential to the kind of news story which characterizes the modern financial section. Unquestionably there are many avid newspaper readers who feel that because of the mathematical appearance of this section, it must be tedious and complicated, that therefore they had better not attempt it. It is my hope that by describing this section, I can allay this suspicion and show the reader how he can use the financial section of his newspaper to his enjoyment and advantage.

It is far from being limited to news of a mathematical nature as can be seen from a quick perusal of the headlines on any one day. One edition chosen at random contains accounts of meetings of the boards of governors of the World Bank and the International Monetary Fund, a noisy meeting of stockholders at which they voiced dissatisfaction with a management proposal to sell a unit of the company to a holding company, a possible shortage of sugar, a nine-figure antitrust and breach of contract suit, the sharp rise in the stock of a certain company which manufactures one of the long list of new scientific instruments, and a congressional argument on the value of futures trading in Irish potatoes.

These reports were in addition to the usual stories of an obviously financial nature, such as earnings statements, the weekly sale of bills by the United States Treasury, the stock market, dividend declarations, and an account of a study by the Federal Reserve Board.

Events of the last few decades have combined to make a growing part of our population financial minded. The emergence of the United States from its position as a debtor nation a few decades ago to that of the world's greatest creditor, the establishment of our financial and banking community as the world's leading money market, the diffusion of ownership of our corporate securities among small investors, including customers and employees, the vast growth of mutual funds, and the impact of greater governmental direction and participation in the economic affairs of its citizens are among developments that have made financial news must reading.

The reader cannot pick up his newspaper without being confronted with stories on prices, taxes, strikes, crops, profits, and myriad other things that affect his welfare. He has come to make growing demands on his newspaper as a consequence, and the financial section has had to keep pace.

2

BAROMETERS OF BUSINESS

THE BULK OF THE SPACE AVAILABLE IN THE FINANCIAL section is devoted to markets. Readers want to know the prices. But in keeping with the higher standards of today's modern financial section, an increasing amount is being devoted to news of all industry.

It is no longer a case of keeping the investor informed of the price at which his stocks and bonds are selling, but of telling the story behind his companies; a story that starts with the raw materials of the farm or the mine, goes through the stage of manufacturing, the transportation of the final product, its distribution to the public, and its financing throughout the entire trip.

The stock market is but one phase of the journey. It commands the attention it gets because, in the final analysis, it is the mirror in which is reflected the degree of performance of all other branches of industry. It is a market place devoid of sentiment, where the play of economic factors and the opinion of hundreds of thousands of investors are measured objectively in dollars and cents. It is the first to reflect confidence or nervousness, prosperity or depression, and the general state of health of our complicated economic organism.

A large portion of the reading matter in the financial section is of routine nature, appearing at regularly recurring intervals. The American businessman has come to rely more and more on the statistical compilations made by industrial trade organizations and government bureaus as guides for his activity.

The number of these compilations runs into the hundreds, and no newspaper could publish all of them. The twenty to thirty more important ones are published, however, as soon as they become available. In this category fall stories of crop reports; financial indexes such as bank clearings and life insurance sales; trade barometers such as the production of electric power, steel ingots, copper, paper, and crude oil; business barometers such as store sales, wholesale and retail prices, and failures; and other important yardsticks of activity such as carloadings, building construction, and foreign trade.

A complete list would include any compilation that helps present an over-all picture of changes in the field of investment. Frequently an aid to measuring the ups and down of industries is supplied by the application of a reliable index.

Aside from regular statistical reports made by various government bureaus, trade associations, and trade publications, figures are frequently brought together in tabular form by banks, investment organizations, and newspapers. These are designed to provide the student of economic affairs with a quick but comprehensive picture of the major indexes of business. Such compilations take different forms, but usually they give the latest available figures, a comparison with the previous period, and a comparison with a year ago. Frequently they show the percentage up or down.

An example of the subjects covered may be seen from the following compilation.

Total Economic Activity—Annual Rate in Billions of Dollars
1. Gross National Product
2. Personal Consumption Expenditures
3. Government Expenditures
4. Private Capital Investment
5. Total Personal Income

Employment, Production, and Trade
6. Employment

  7. Unemployment
  8. F.R.B. Index of Production
  9. Manufacturers' New Orders
10. Manufacturers' Inventories
11. Automobile and Truck Production
12. Steel (Net Tons)
13. Freight Car Loadings
14. Electric Power Output (K.W.H.)
15. Department Store Sales
Commodity Prices
16. Wholesale Price Index
17. Consumer Price Index
18. Basic Commodity Price Index—Weekly Average
Interest Rates
19. Discount Rate—New York Federal Reserve Bank
20. New Bill Rate
21. 4–6 Months Commercial Paper—Weekly Average
22. Corporate Bond Yields Aaa
23. U.S. Treasury Securities
Money and Credit
24. Demand Deposits and Currency—All Commercial Banks
25. Total Investments—All Commercial Banks
26. Total Loans—All Commercial Banks
27. Consumer Credit
28. Business Loans—Reporting Member Banks
29. Federal Reserve Credit—Weekly Average
30. Excess Reserves—Weekly Average
31. Member Bank Borrowing—Weekly Average
32. Free Reserves—Weekly Average

BAROMETERS OF BUSINESS

ADVERTISING—*Media Records* issues a monthly report on newspaper advertising by classification.

AUTOMOBILE PRODUCTION—A compilation frequently seen in the financial section is the weekly one of *Ward's Automotive Reports*. It gives the weekly production of passenger cars and trucks in units, for the United States and Canada, with a comparison.

The Automobile Manufacturers Association issues a yearly review in which it gives vital statistics on the industry, covering production, number of employees, parts production, taxes, registrations, and exports.

As in most industries there are a number of trade publications which issue reliable industrial compilations, and these are frequently reprinted by the newspapers.

BANK CLEARINGS—Dun & Bradstreet, Inc., issues a weekly compilation of bank clearings for principal cities, individually and combined. It is published in the newspapers Friday mornings.

BILL RATE—The rate of interest at which the Treasury sells its short-term bills, published Tuesday, is an important index of the money market. The weekly report covers the amount of bills applied for, the amount accepted, the average price, and the approximate yield.

BUILDING CONSTRUCTION—The F. W. Dodge Corporation issues monthly figures on construction contract awards for the thirty-seven states east of the Rocky Mountains. The report gives the number of projects and the dollar volume, as well as the number and value of alteration projects, for residential and nonresidential buildings.

The Department of Commerce reports on privately financed residential construction by month, about a week after the close of each month.

The volume of engineering contracts awarded is compiled weekly by *Engineering News-Record*, and is reprinted in the newspapers Friday mornings. It covers the United States and gives comparative figures for previous periods.

BUSINESS FAILURES—Dun & Bradstreet, Inc., reports every Tuesday on the business failures for the week ended the previous Thursday. The report is broken down geographically, by industries, and by the amount of liabilities involved.

CARLOADINGS—The Association of American Railroads issues once a week an estimate on the number of freight cars loaded with revenue freight. It is issued Thursday afternoon and covers the week ended the previous Saturday. The report is broken down to show loadings by districts and also by freight classifications, such as coal, grain, livestock, and the other major kinds of freight.

COPPER PRODUCTION—The Copper Institute reports monthly on

the production, deliveries, and amount of refined stocks of its members, usually about the tenth of the month.

CROP REPORTS—The United States Crop Reporting Board issues twenty-one reports a year on wheat, corn, oats, barley, rye, and soybeans. These give acreage under cultivation, farm stocks on hand, amounts in interior mills, elevators, and warehouses, the condition of the crops, and estimated yield per acre. They are carried by the newspapers as issued. In addition there are reports covering miscellaneous crops, such as hay, grain sorghums, fruits, and vegetables.

There are twenty reports a year on livestock and wool, giving cattle, sheep, and lambs on feed, total livestock on farms, wool and mohair production, a spring pig report and its total production at the close of the year, and the cattle and lamb feeding situation.

CRUDE OIL AND REFINED PETROLEUM PRODUCTION—The American Petroleum Institute issues a comprehensive weekly report on oil statistics. It is published Wednesday mornings. Daily average gross crude oil runs to the stills of refining companies and the production are shown by states or fields and comparisons noted, as well as the Bureau of Mines calculated requirements by states and the state allowables, in those states where these restrictions are applied.

This report also gives the production of various refined products, and stocks of finished products at these refineries, at bulk terminals, in transit, and in pipe lines.

The Bureau of Census issues an annual report on the production of crude petroleum and natural gas, by states. It gives total production, the number of operating companies, number of wells being drilled and producing, and the expenses and value of products.

DEPARTMENT STORE SALES—Department store sales on a country-wide basis and for each of the twelve Federal Reserve districts are compiled and made public weekly by the Federal Reserve Board. Department store and apparel store sales for the larger cities in New York State are released by the Federal Reserve Bank of New York for each week and each four weeks' period. The dollar value of store inventories is reported once a month, usually about the middle of the month following the period covered.

Total retail store sales are issued by the Department of Commerce by months, about six weeks after the close of each month.

The large mail order and chain store systems report their sales monthly to the newspapers, and they are published as received. Usually they are available between the fifth and tenth of the month, and cover the previous month.

In New York City the United Parcel Service reports weekly on its deliveries of packages and furniture. The report covers more than 400 stores.

ELECTRIC POWER PRODUCTION—Weekly figures are compiled by the Edison Electric Institute and are issued each Wednesday, covering the previous week. These reports give the kilowatt-hour output for the country by districts, with comparisons with preceding periods. Individual public utility systems also issue weekly reports on their own output.

EMPLOYMENT—The United States Department of Labor issues monthly figures on employment, usually about the middle of the next succeeding month. This is broken down into agricultural and nonagricultural workers, and then further subdivided into industries. It also reports on payrolls and wage rates, and on the labor turnover, by industries.

FOREIGN TRADE—Imports and exports of the country are compiled by the Department of Commerce, with the figures broken down into various major groups of commodities or merchandise. They usually appear about the middle of a month, six weeks after the close of the month covered.

The principal studies released to the newspapers cover six subjects and all give monthly data. They are: Over-all total export and import data, exports and imports by economic classes and leading commodities, exports and imports by countries of destination and origin, foreign trade by United States customs districts and areas, and entrances and clearances of vessels through United States customs districts and areas.

IRON AND STEEL PRODUCTION—The American Iron and Steel Institute compiles several valuable sets of trade statistics, two of which

Sales of Big Stores In New York Area Soar 19% in Month

Department store sales in the New York metropolitan area soared in February as leap ~~~ provided retailers with five ~ in the month.

~rvey made yesterda~ ~w York Times disc~ ~les of the area's s~ 19 per cent ahead of the 1963 month.

volume of stores in alone, or "downt~ also advanced 19 ~m the total in Febru

gain was the sha~ ~area stores register~ ~ increase in March. ~ of city stores at ~owever, rose by 13~

incidence of five s~ ~aturdays in the m~ ~ prominently in the ~onally, there are ~ays in February.

~eather Helped Sales

~ weather was als~ The temperature fel~ ~~g~~~s from the average ~perature of 33.4 degrees. A earlier, the temperature 5.1 degrees below normal.

There were 25 shopping in February, compared wit~ last year but the additional~ was the all-important Satu~ Retailers also were hamp~ last year by the 114-day n~ paper strike here. Lack~ promotional advertising sharply into retail sales, ~ chants said.

February was the second secutive month in which vol~ rose sharply from levels o~ year earlier.

The February gain was ~formly distributed as all partments participated in advance. No weak s~ were reported. Gains range~ high as 83 per cent in a dep~ ment of one outlet.

In the metropolitan area, advances for the reporting stores were 29.3, 23.5, 21.8, 19.5, 14.5, 14.4, 13.3, and 12.9 per cent.

Gains among downtown stores weer 30.5, 24.8, 21.4, 18.9, 17.5, 15.9, 14:5 and 12.4 per cent.

Wholesale Price Index Fell 0.1 Point in Week Ended Dec. 3

WASHINGTON—The Labor Department's index of wholesale prices declined 0.1 percentage point in the week ended Dec. 3 to 100.1% of its 1957-59 base.

An advance of 0.1 percentage point in the industrial commodities sector was more than offset by a 1.4-point decline in farm products and a 0.1-point drop in processed foods, according to department figures. Lower steer and hog prices led the farm products decline; the processed foods drop reflected in part lower prices for most grades of beef and for fryers.

The index, with 100 equaling 1957-59 prices:

	Dec. 3	Nov. 26
All commodities	100.1	100.2
Farm products	92.9	94.2
Processed foods	101.0	101.1
Meats	87.2	88.8
All commodities other than farm products and foods	100.9	100.8

Bank Clearings for Month Show 14 Per Cent Decline

Bank clearings in 26 leading cities across the country dropped 14 per cent to $139,306,948,000 in February, from the record $161,961,219,000 in January, according to Dun & Bradstreet, Inc. The seasonal decline was expected in the short month of February. Check transactions last month were up 13.6 per cent from the $122,586,431,000 total for February, 1963.

Transactions in New York City totaled $79,089,298,000 in February, 13.1 per cent below January, but 14.6 per cent above the $69,036,940,000 of last year.

Rail Carloadings Fell Last Week From 1963 But Topped 1962 Pace

By a WALL STREET JOURNAL *Staff Reporter*

WASHINGTON—Rail carloadings last week declined from the year-earlier level but rose from 1962, the Association of American Railroads reported.

Loadings totaled 529,476 cars, down 3,341 cars, or 0.6%, from year-earlier volume but up 922 cars, or 0.2%, from 1962. Compared with loadings in the previous week, which included the Washington's Birthday holiday, volume was up 13,358 cars, or 2.6%.

On a ton-mile basis, the association said, volume was about 12.1 billion, up 3.3% from the year-earlier level and up 9.6% from the level two years before. A ton-mile is one ton hauled one mile.

Through last week, 1964 carloadings rose 4.9% to 4,689,471 cars from last year's pace but were down 0.4% from 1962's.

Piggyback loadings of truck trailers on railroad flat cars totaled 16,236 cars in the week ended Feb. 22, up 2,007, or 14.1%, from the year-earlier level and up 4,254 cars, or 35.5%, from like 1962 volume.

In a separate report, the American Trucking Associations said intercity truck tonnage in the week ended Feb. 29 rose 1.3% from the like week last year and 3.6% from the previous week this year.

Rail loadings as follows:

	Feb.29wk Cars	1963wk Cars	%	Prev. Wk Cars	%
Miscellaneous	298,506	+ 7,554	2.6	+ 9,474	3.3
Coal	101,118	− 2,546	2.5	+ 3,732	3.8
Coke	8,162	+ 814	11.1	− 158	1.9
Ore	15,338	+ 1,814	13.4	− 54	.4
Forest products	39,253	+ 1,005	2.6	+ 612	1.6
L.C.L.	14,018	− 5,132	26.8	+ 287	2.1
Grain	51,207	− 6,268	10.9	− 353	.7
Livestock	1,874	− 582	23.7	− 182	8.9

are regularly published in leading financial sections. One gives the rate of operation of the industry for the current week. The rate is expressed as a percentage of the industry's total capacity. The other is a monthly report, showing the industry's production of steel by tons.

LIFE INSURANCE SALES—The Life Insurance Agency Management Association reports monthly on the amount of life insurance purchased in the United States. It is broken down into industrial, ordinary, and group purchases.

LUMBER PRODUCTION—The National Lumber Manufacturers Association issues a weekly report on lumber production, shipments, and unfilled orders, with comparisons with the previous week and the previous year. It covers 491 lumber mills.

PAPER PRODUCTION—The American Paper and Pulp Association reports weekly on production and the percentage rate of mill operations. Output and stocks of newsprint are reported monthly by the Newsprint Service Bureau.

RAILROAD EARNINGS—The Association of American Railroads issues a monthly recapitulation of the earnings of the Class I railroads, usually in the second week of the second month following the period covered. It issues weekly reports on the number of locomotives and freight cars on order and in good condition. Earnings of the individual roads are issued by the roads themselves and are published in the newspaper, in abbreviated form, every month.

TIRE PRODUCTION—The Rubber Manufacturers Association reports monthly on the production of automobile tires, usually about three weeks after the close of each month.

WHOLESALE PRICE INDEX—This is published weekly by the Bureau of Labor Statistics and appears in the newspapers on Fridays or Saturdays. It is an index of prices, not volume of production. It covers the most important divisions of farm products, food, fuel, building materials, household goods, raw materials, metals, and textiles.

Dun & Bradstreet also issues weekly an index of wholesale and retail prices.

3

THE CAPITAL MARKET

IN OUR SYSTEM OF FREE ENTERPRISE, THE CAPITAL market plays a vital part. This market contains the mechanism whereby loans are floated for the monetary needs of the United States government, the states and cities, numberless corporations, and foreign borrowers. Corporate stock issues, which represent ownership of the companies concerned, also move through this market, which centers in New York.

Much of the economic development of the nation can be attributed to the ready access to new capital enjoyed by industrial organizations and the transportation and communication systems. It is noteworthy, moreover, that every single stock and bond quoted in the voluminous tables of daily dealings on the New York Stock Exchange, the American Stock Exchange, the over-the-counter (OTC) market, and other markets was at one time a "new issue."

In general, it is the investment banker who acts as the intermediary between those who need long-term capital and those who have funds to invest or to risk. These investment exports tend to specialize. Some handle only bonds or other evidences of indebtedness; some originate stock issues exclusively. Most of them, however, handle both senior and junior securities (see Definitions of Terms), with a tendency in one direction or the other, and also with distinct predilections for types of financing with which they are familiar.

The capital market is a highly complex affair, responsive not only to the needs of borrowers and lenders but also to the requirements of many federal and state laws. The issues of the United States Treasury need no underwriting by bankers and are offered directly to the public. In underwriting state and municipal loans, institutions may vie with investment bankers.

In the regulatory sense, a vast change was effected in the capital market mechanism by the Banking Act of 1933, which directed commercial banks to divest themselves of securities affiliates. Previously, such affiliates played a large part in underwriting corporate flotations. The Securities Act of 1933, as amended, also affected the mechanism profoundly, for under it corporate issuers, with the exception of the railroads, must file voluminous registration statements with the Securities and Exchange Commission. The railroads were required under earlier laws to file information on their financial activities with the Interstate Commerce Commission. Federal, state, and municipal issues are exempt from registration, but many state commissions require corporate issuers also to file information with them.

The federal securities laws are far-reaching. They were designed for full disclosure to investors of all facts relating to new issues, and sometimes are referred to as the "truth in securities" enactments. The enormous registration statements, however, seldom are consulted by investors, who rely more on the "prospectus," which is a condensation of the main statement. Under the law every purchaser of a new corporate issue subject to registration must be supplied with a prospectus.

To these complications of the capital market are added many others, some of them fundamental to economics, others merely matters of meeting the needs of applicants for funds and of those who have them to lend or risk. Thus, the basic economic interest rate is all that the federal government needs to pay on its borrowings; but that rate appears to be subject to some extent to governmental edict,

$50-Million Debenture Issue Offered by Beneficial Finance

A $50-million issue of Beneficial Finance Company debentures was offered to investors yesterday at a 4.58 per cent yield through an underwriting syndicate headed by Eastman Dillon, Union Securities & Co.

The underwriters reported the issue got an "excellent" reception from investors. One described it as "almost all placed."

The debentures, which carry a 4½ per cent coupon and mature in 1992, were offered at a price of 98.75.

Proceeds from the sale will be used to reduce short-term bank loans and commercial paper outstanding, incurred and sold to provide funds for subsidiaries.

Beneficial Finance is a holding company with subsidiaries engaged principally in small loan, merchandising and sales finance businesses.

Potomac Edison

A Lehman Brothers syndicate won $16 million of Potomac Edison Company bonds yesterday in the week's largest competitive corporate underwriting.

The group bid 101.457 for the bonds as a 4⅝ per cent issue and reoffered them at 102.046 to yield 4.50 per cent to maturity in 1994.

Bond dealers estimated the issue was "something under half sold" late yesterday.

Other managing underwriters for the issue were Eastman Dillon, Union Securities & Co.; Harriman, Ripley & Co., and Merril Lynch, Pierce, Fenner & Smith, Inc.

Other bids for the bonds, also as 4⅝s, came from Equitable Securites Corporation, 101.429; Halsey, Stuart & Co., Inc., 101.40; Kidder, Peabody & Co., 101.267; Salomon Brothers & Hutzler and Blyth & Co., Inc., jointly, 101.10999; W. C. Langley & Co., 101.07; White, Weld & Co., and Shields & Co., jointly, 101.05; and First Boston Corporation, 100.919

New York Central

The New York Central Railroad awarded $5,175,000 of equipment - trust certificates yesterday to an underwriting group led by Halsey, Stuart & Co.

The syndicate bid 98.70 for a 4½ per cent coupon and reoffered the securities to yield from 4.10 per cent in 1965 up to 4.65 per cent in 1979.

A Salomon Brothers & Hutzler syndicate bid 98.0737 for the certificates, also as 4½s.

United Utilities

United Utilities, Inc., has set the subscription price for its offering of stock to shareholders at 39½, Kidder, Peabody & Co., managing underwriters, announced yesterday.

The offering is to be made on the basis of one new share for each 10 held of record of March 10. A total of 527,571 shares is included in the offering, and rights expire March 24.

Scurry-Rainbow

Scurry-Rainbow Oi
arranged for a $15-m
in Canadian funds,
Talin, chairman,
yesterday.

The 10-year loan
inated the need to
Mr. Talin said, ad
would provide fund
Scurry-Rainbow's
development prog
pay short-term lo
from one to four y

Anheuser

A $40-million
heuser-Busch, In
debentures, due
on the market
each, appeared
4.47 per cent y

The offerin
through an u
dicate led by
Co., Inc.

Proceeds fr
be added to
of the brewi
used for ca

M. A

The
sold
Steel
day -
throu
heade

The
each
quick
derwr
aftern
$52.50
Excha

M.
vestm
the s
ficati

Ho
Bear,
under
300,000 shares of Kinney Service Corporation common stock at $18 a share. The shares are being sold for certain stockholders.

Midland-Guardian

Kidder, Peabody & Co., Inc., managing underwriter, announced yesterday the public offering of 250,000 shares of Midland-Guardian Company common stock at $17.50 a share.

Also offered were three debt issues: $4 million of 5¼ per cent subordinated notes; $1 million of 5½ per cent junior subordinated notes, and $1 million of 5¾ per cent capital notes. All were priced at 100 and mature in 1984.

Inter-American Bank To Offer $5 Million Bonds Later in March

By a WALL STREET JOURNAL *Staff Reporter*

NEW YORK—The Inter-American Development Bank, Washington, is planning a $50 million public offering of 20-year bonds later this month, it was announced. The bonds will be underwritten and distributed by a group of securities firms headed by Lehman Brothers, Blyth & Co. and Lazard Freres & Co.

The bank is an inter-governmental lending institution formed in 1960 to promote economic development in the Western hemisphere. Its most recent public borrowing was a sale of $75 million of 4¼% 20-year bonds in December 1962 through a syndicate headed by the same three investment banking houses.

The new proposed bonds, whose ...
mains to be announced ...
1984 ...

International Interest Rates

A drop in the net yield on domestic Treasury bills and a rise of nearly 8 basis points in the return on U. K. bills shifted the yield spread in favor of British short-term securities to 14 basis points last week. Meanwhile, Canadian bills continue to hold a favorable spread of 20 basis points over U. S. Treasury issues, according to data compiled by the overseas banking division of American Express Co., Inc.

(Per cent per annum)

	U. S.	Canada	France	Germany	Gt. Brit.	Belgium	Netherlands	Switz.	Japan
Central Bank discount Rate	3.50	4.00	4.00	3.00	5.00	4.25	4.00	2.00	5.84
Prime Rate Loans	4.50	5.75	6.00	6.00	6.00	6.75	5.50	4.50	8.4[illegible]
Demand Deposit	....	....	*0.50	*⅜-¾	..	0.50	0.50	1.00	....
Time Dep.: 90 Days	3.375	4.00	*1¾-2⅛	*2.25	4.875	3.00	2.00	2.00	4.00
Treas. Bills: 90 Days	3.53	3.90	....	*2.625	4.30	‡4.70	2.375	....	....
Swap from Dollar	....	—0.07	—0.69	+0.79	—0.63	‡—0.53	+0.74	+0.86	—0.11
Net Yield	3.53	3.83	....	*3.415	3.67	‡4.17	3.115	....	....

*Not applicable to non-residents, ‡120 days. The interest rates quoted are exclusive of bank charges which are customary to many countries. Rates are for Friday, Mar. 6. The sole purpose of this table is to indicate the range and trends in various money markets.

at least in "emergency" periods. This occasions a deep and abiding interest in the capital market among deposit banks, which hold prodigious totals of Treasury securities, often of long term.

States and their subdivisions, and corporate borrowers of high reputation, also have access to the market on relatively cheap terms. State and local governments, indeed, can frequently borrow at even lower rates than the federal Treasury can command, owing to the fact that interest on their bonds is immune to federal income taxation. The tax status of new issues also plays a part in determining the value of some corporate securities, where state laws require certain payments.

The securities of enterprises which are less well established require a "risk premium," which raises the cost of borrowing or floating equities. The more risky the enterprise, the higher the cost. Bonds, debentures, and notes, which are evidences of indebtedness, are the less risky securities. New ventures often do not command sufficient investment faith to make debt issues possible, and in such instances they have to confine themselves to stock flotations.

But in the infinite variety of the capital market, stocks of some companies may well be more highly regarded than the bonds of others. A sensible handling of corporate finance suggests a reasonable division of the capital structure between debt and equities. This usually calls for the issuance of preferred and common stocks by the largest corporations. They could borrow capital more cheaply through a new bond issue, but to do so might increase their debt load to an unwarranted extent. The stock issues do not constitute debt.

In the bargaining of the capital market the terms of new issues are determined. Some borrowers, like the United States Treasury, can stipulate the maturities and interest rates on their obligations, and even the prices, within limits. Stock issues frequently tend to be priced more in line with what investors regard as a proper figure.

The investment banker or underwriter, as the intermediary, requires considerable capital of his own and the ability to appraise all aspects of the market—for the initial risk is his. His compensation varies accordingly, and may be only a fraction of 1 per cent on a large and sound bond issue, or may amount to a sizable part of the sum raised on a risky stock offering. In the prospectus all such details are set forth.

The financial markets in the United States are the largest in the world. They are international in that foreign banks, governments, and corporations come to America to raise new money or to place investments in securities that are already outstanding. There is also a reverse flow of foreign funds to this country, especially with respect to securities of foreign affiliates of established American enterprises.

Shares of our corporations, such as those listed on the New York Stock Exchange and American Stock Exchange, are held by investors in virtually every country in the world, and foreign investors have even a greater participation in our money market, which is the market for Treasury bills and other short-term securities, used by world investors as depositories of interest-bearing cash.

While the United States has had its share of experiences with inflation, that curse has been less noticeable here than in most countries. Consequently there is a faith in the American dollar, and because of this the American capital market attracts large sums for long-term loans, such as mortgages and outright purchases of productive real estate.

Our currency has lost much of its purchasing power over the last twenty to thirty years, but the loss has been small compared with what has happened to currencies of less fortunate nations. Consequently, an investor, or group of investors, seeking to preserve the real value of their funds for an extended period, looks to that market where past history indicates relative stability. The borrower with a good credit rating knows that funds are available here, at relatively low interest rates and lower flotation costs, and that the market will be receptive should he later decided to liquidate.

A calculation by the Federal Reserve Board indicates that net funds raised by nonfinancial sectors of our economy in 1963 were a record-breaking $59.1 billion, of which $41.8 billion was in long-term securities and mortgages. The public's savings, channeled mostly through financial institutions, made $28.1 billion available for an increase in mortgage indebtedness and supplied around 60 per cent of $46.6 billion expended on private construction in that year. Public utilities and other corporations raised $3.4 billion through sales of stocks and bonds, while state and local governments obtained a net amount of $6.7 billion through the issuance of new securities. Foreigners in that year raised a net of about $1.1 billion.

These amounts do not include the vast amount of refinancing transactions which our capital market handles, and obviously they do not include trading between investors in outstanding securities.

This gives an idea of the immensity of our capital market flotations, which are handled through underwriters, brokers, and dealers, who bring together buyers and sellers of securities, and are paid by commission.

4

~~~~~~

TRADING IN SECURITIES

A NEWSPAPER IS SOMETIMES REFERRED TO AS A DE-partment store of information. No one reads everything that is offered; he selects only what he wants. The financial section is similarly classified. A survey made a few years ago of the reading habits of the public showed that the feature that commanded the greatest numerical following was the table of transactions in stocks on the New York Stock Exchange. Second was the daily descriptive story of the market, which details the over-all trend, the action of certain selected stocks, and the reasons for their price changes. It was found that readership of these two features was greatest during periods of rising prices.

A survey of all daily newspapers published in the United States, conducted by the New York Stock Exchange, frequently referred to as the Big Board, showed that 562 dailies carry either complete or partial tables of stocks and that of this number 136 run the complete list.

The table, revised and published daily, concerns transactions of the previous day. A few newspapers, in addition, publish a weekly table for both the New York Stock Exchange and the American

Stock Exchange. This represents a recapitulation of the previous week's transactions. In addition some newspapers publish an annual recapitulation near the first of each new year.

THE DAILY TABLE

The daily table is the one most frequently consulted by the reader. Examine the accompanying reproduction of a small portion of a stock market table. The two columns on the left show the highest price and the lowest price at which each stock has sold thus far during the current year. There follows the name of the stock and its indicated dividend rate.

Many footnotes are necessary in the case of the dividend rates. This is because not all corporations maintain a regular rate. The amount they pay their stockholders is subject to change at any meeting of the board of directors. Directors may increase it, decrease it, eliminate it completely, or declare an extra payment. The amount is dependent first on the money the corporation has earned, and second on the proportion of current or former earnings which directors decide should be disbursed.

If, at a meeting, directors declare a dividend of $1 a share and designate it as a regular quarterly payment, the newspaper will print a 4 beside the name, indicating that this is the current annual rate, which presumably will be maintained until there is a change for the better or worse in the affairs of the corporation. No footnote is carried in such cases.

In other instances the footnotes explain such things as: that the corporation has declared or paid so much in the current year or previous year but has not announced a regular rate; that it has declared one or more extra dividends; or that it has declared a dividend payable in shares of stock instead of in cash.

It will be seen from the accompanying table that Republic Steel sold as high as 44 during the year in question and as low as 34¾. Its regular annual dividend rate was $2, or 50 cents a quarter. After the name of the stock is the symbol x, which means any purchase or

99½	56	RCA 1.40b	1510	89¾	94⅛	89	93¾	+8¾
40	31⅜	RalstonPur 1	40	34	34	33½	33⅝	— ⅛
18½	15⅛	Ranco .80	x14	16¼	16½	16¼	16½	+ ¼
13½	9¼	Rand House	17	9⅜	9½	9⅜	9⅜	— ⅛
44⅞	38	Raybestos 2	3	39¾	40¼	39¾	40	+ ¼
. ..	.	RayD fn 1.73g	11	47¾	47¾	47⅜	47⅜	....
13⅝	8⅝	RaymIntl .60	31	11¾	12⅜	11¾	12⅜	+ ⅝
33⅞	21½	Rayonier 1	148	27½	28⅛	27¼	27¾	+ ½
34	19¼	Raythn .87f	216	22¾	23	22⅛	22⅛	+1⅝
14¼	7½	Reading Co	9	10½	10¾	10½	10¾	+ ½
21	14⅜	Reading 1pf	10	15⅛	15⅞	14⅞	15⅞	+1⅛
16¼	10½	Reading 2pf	6	12⅞	13⅜	12½	13⅜	+ ⅞
29⅝	22⅝	Red Owl .90	9	22⅞	23	22¼	22½	— ⅛
17⅜	13⅜	Reed RollBit	8	13⅜	13⅝	13¼	13⅜	.....
17½	12	ReevBro .50	17	14⅛	14¾	14⅛	14¾	+1¼
14	9⅜	ReichCh .10d	78	9⅝	9⅞	9½	9⅝	+ ¼
23⅞	18⅜	ReliabSt 1.20	1	22⅛	22⅛	22⅛	22⅛	— ¼
47¾	38⅛	RelianEl 1.80	2	38⅞	39¾	38⅞	39¾	+1½
20½	9⅞	Relian Mf	17	10⅜	10¾	10⅛	10¾	+ ⅞
18½	14	RepubAv 1	61	14⅜	14¾	14¼	14⅝	+ ⅜
10¼	6¾	RepubCp .60	27	8⅝	8¾	8⅝	8¾	— ⅛
16¾	14	RepCorp pf1	2	15	15	15	15	— ¼
44	34¾	Repub Stl 2	x242	38½	40⅜	38½	40	+2¼
53	36⅛	RevereCop 2	7	46½	46½	46	46¼	—1¼
48½	37	Revlon 1.10b	100	38½	39⅜	38½	39⅛	+2⅛
42⅜	29	Rexall .50b	50	37¼	37¾	36¾	37¾	+1½
37¼	23⅝	ReynMet .50	272	29½	30⅞	29⅜	30⅞	+2¾
110	102⅛	ReyM pf4.50	6	104¼	104¼	102½	102½	— ½
47⅜	36¾	ReyTob 1.80	194	39	39¾	39	39⅝	+1⅛
17¼	10⅜	Rheem Mfg	54	14⅞	15¾	14⅞	15⅝	+ ¾
6¼	4¼	Rhodesn .19g	47	6	6⅛	6	6⅛	+ ¼
65¾	51	Rich Merr 1	360	51	53	51	53	+ ⅜
50¼	39	RichfOil 1.80	41	42¼	42¼	41¾	42	+1¼
36⅜	28¼	RiegelP 1.20	x15	32	32⅞	31¾	32⅞	+ ¾
31½	19⅞	RitterCo .80b	11	28¼	29½	28¼	29	+1½
30⅜	23	RobertCont 1	13	26	26⅛	26	26⅛	+ ¼
38¾	27	RochGE 1b	22	33	34¼	33	33½	+ ½
45¼	37¾	RochTel 1.30	3	43⅞	43⅞	43⅞	43⅞	— ⅛
44⅜	34⅛	RockwStd 2b	153	39	39½	39	39⅜	+4¾
145	104	Rohm&H 1a	9	130	130	129½	129½	+2
17⅞	15	Rohr Corp 1	26	15⅞	16⅜	15⅞	16¼	+ ¼
34⅛	21	Ronson .60b	50	30⅛	30¾	30	30⅜	+ ⅞
47⅜	18⅝	RoperGD 1	9	42½	43¼	42½	43¼	+2¼
44⅝	33⅝	RorerWm .60	53	34⅛	34½	33⅝	34⅛	+ ½

sale of the stock the previous day was without the 50 cent quarterly dividend payment recently declared by directors.

This is followed by the number 242, which indicates the volume of the previous day's trading. As it is the practice to give such figures in round lots of 100 shares each, the volume in Republic Steel the previous day was 24,200 shares.

The next four figures show that the first trade the previous day was at 38½, its highest price for the day was 40⅜, its lowest 38½, and the final price for the day was 40. Then there is the notation that this closing price was 2¼ points higher than the close of the day before.

EX-DIVIDEND

Actually Republic closed the previous day at 38¼, apparently up only 1¾, but as it was quoted the next day without the quarterly dividend of 50 cents; the practice is to adjust for this on the day it became ex-dividend. The buyer on the day before it went ex, will get that dividend, even though he sold the following morning. The stock therefore advanced 1¾ in actual market price and also made up the additional half point, which represents the dividend.

The date a stock shall be quoted ex-dividend is announced in advance by the stock exchange on which the shares are listed. It precedes by a few days the date the corporation actually closes its books and determines which individuals are entitled to the dividend. This is because shares sold in the regular manner are not deliverable until the fourth business day following the transaction, excluding days the market is closed.

When the corporation's directors declared the dividend they said they would pay on a certain date, say July 15, to stockholders of record June 17. The lapse is to give the corporation time to determine which individuals are on its transfer books as stockholders. The stock exchange will then specify a date a few days prior to June 17, to allow time for the securities to be delivered and transferred, and will announce that on, say June 13, or possibly June 12, the stock in question will be quoted without the dividend. In like manner a stock may be quoted ex some other benefit, such as warrants or rights.

CASH SALES

Another notation in the table of transactions which appears from time to time concerns sales made for cash and immediate delivery. The four-day delivery rule is set aside in such cases, and the seller must deliver the stock the day it is sold. He also receives his money that day.

In such instances the price at which the trade is made appears on the ticker with the letter *C* beside it. In the newspapers the word "cash" appears in the net change column. No net change is shown, as the transaction was not made in the regular manner. Presumably, if the seller wanted his cash immediately, he would have to give a small concession in the price. If, on the other hand, the buyer wanted his stock immediately, for some particular reason of his own, he would bid up moderately.

On the last four business days of any calendar year there are many such cash sales. That is because of a tax ruling. The Tax Court of the United States has ruled that, for tax purposes, profits are taxable when "realized," and that losses are allowable when "sustained." Profits are not considered "realized" for tax purposes until the securities are delivered to the buyer. Securities sold on the New York Stock Exchange in the regular way on the third business day prior to the end of the year or thereafter are not delivered until January.

This means that on the various securities exchanges which have the delayed delivery rule, the investor who has a paper profit in a security, and wishes to turn it into a cash profit and have such profit taxed for the year about to end, must sell in time to make delivery before midnight, December 31. If his sale to establish the profit is made in less than four business days from the close of the year, he must sell for next day (nd) delivery on the first of these three days and for cash, and make delivery on the final business day of the year. Otherwise the profit will be reported on his income tax statement for the new year.

Losses, on the other hand, are said to be "sustained" when the sale is made on the floor of the exchange, regardless of the time of delivery of the certificate. Hence losses may be taken for tax purposes by regular sales right up to the close of the old year.

The rule as now stated on profits applies only to taxpayers reporting on a cash basis. Taxpayers on an accrual basis can establish profits by sales up to the last minute. Most individuals are on a cash basis; most partnerships and companies are on an accrual basis.

SELLER'S OPTION

The opposite of selling for cash and immediate delivery, or selling in the regular manner, is to sell with a more distant date specified as the day for delivery. This happens on rare occasions.

The seller may have his certificate of stock deposited for safekeeping at some distant point. He wants to sell but realizes he will be unable to deliver on time. He notifies his broker to sell, but to specify that delivery will be made in seven days, or even later. This is termed a Sellers 7 sale, and on the tape it is so designated. It is recorded in the newspapers, but no net change is shown, as it was not made in the regular manner. In such cases the seller normally would have to offer a slight price concession to attract buyers.

TEN-SHARE LOTS

In a few cases the reader may see a footnote indicating that a stock was traded in lots of less than the regular round lot of 100 shares. These are usually inactive issues which rarely appear on the ticker. The stock exchange may designate such issues and declare that for them the round lot is ten shares.

In such cases the reader of the daily table of transactions will see the volume quoted in a slightly different manner, which is explained by a footnote. Thus if a stock is traded in the normal manner, the figure 20 would mean that 2,000 shares changed hands. But if an inactive issue has ten shares designated as its unit for trading, the figure 20 would mean that exactly 20 shares changed hands.

UNDER THE RULE

If a sale is consummated and for any reason the seller is unable to make delivery, he either "fails to deliver," by agreement with the other party to the contract, or is bought in under the rule.

Delivery must be made at the time specified by the stock exchange, and if the customer is short, the broker must borrow the necessary stock with which to make delivery. If he does not do so, the ruling of the exchange is that the stock may be bought at the market for immediate delivery to the purchaser. The seller is said to have been bought in under the rule. An official of the exchange goes to the floor and completes the transaction.

STREET NAMES

Not all dividend checks go directly to the owners of the shares. This is because many of the certificates are held in what is known as a "Street name"—a name other than that of the actual owner. The purchaser of 100 shares of American Telephone & Telegraph may not have ordered his broker to deliver the certificate, preferring to leave it with the firm. On the books of the company, the brokerage firm would appear as the registered owner, since its name is on the certificate. Thus, when the payable date comes, the company sends the dividend check to the firm, which in turn credits the account of the customer who is the real owner.

When margin trading is high, there is relatively more stock kept in Street names, as the investor is not entitled to his certificate as long as he owes the broker part of the purchase price. Some years ago the Federal Reserve Board placed all listed stock trading on a full cash basis, eliminating margin trading. At that time more investors were inclined to take delivery of their certificates in their own names and place them in strong boxes, rather than leave them on deposit to their accounts at the brokerage offices.

STOCK SPLITS

Stock splits and large stock dividends are frequently regarded as synonymous. For instance, a 300 per cent stock dividend is frequently referred to as a four-for-one split. There is a technical difference, however. In the case of a stock dividend, the company's earned surplus account is debited for the amount, and the capital stock is increased by the amount. Another way of expressing it is that a part of the surplus has been capitalized. The stock dividend means that the company has earned the amount it charges the surplus account and, rather than distribute it in the form of cash dividends, it decides to retain the money in the business.

From a tax aspect, a stockholder, especially one in the upper brackets, may prefer stock dividends, either large ones or regular small ones, to cash dividends. For instance, a stockholder in the 50 per cent bracket, who had already taken his $50 personal deduction granted on dividends received, and who might receive a $10 dividend on each of 100 shares of stock—or $1,000—would be taxed 50 per cent, or $500. If he received a 10 per cent stock dividend, he would now have 110 shares, and this is not taxed. If he holds the shares for six months and then sells, he pays a maximum of 25 per cent on any profit. The cost price of his stock is computed by taking the original cost price of the 100 shares and dividing by 110 to get the price per share.

From the corporate point of view there is an advantage in declaring a dividend in stock rather than in cash. It conserves the cash in the company's treasury, where it can be used in the business. The added number of shares also contributes to a wider distribution of the stock. A third point is that earnings are divided among a greater number of shares; consequently, lower per share earnings can be reported. This may be an offset to union or political demands.

Similar advantages are obtained by a stock split, but in the case of the split the number of shares is merely increased. There is no change in the surplus account.

SHORT SELLING

In security trading, as well as in commodity trading, it is not necessary to own something in order to sell it. In the former case, the securities involved may be borrowed in order to make delivery.

In the case of commodity futures, the seller binds himself by a contract to make delivery at a specified future date. The practice frequently is criticized, sometimes on moral grounds, although there are fewer of these attacks when markets are rising than when they are falling. Usually the opposition develops because the service performed by short selling is misunderstood, even in the market place itself.

The practice is recognized by all markets as a thoroughly legitimate method of trading. Nevertheless, various rules and regulations have been thrown around it to avoid abuses. Most of these are of academic interest to the ordinary trader, who can sell short almost as easily as he can buy long. There is more bookkeeping for his broker, however, and such sales receive somewhat different tax treatment.

Probably the most impressive defense against attacks on short selling as a way of doing business is that markets are better balanced when it is permitted. Several European exchanges tried barring it years ago. As a result they got into trouble and abandoned the restriction. It was found that without the restraining influence of short sales, prices frequently did not reflect a true picture of values. If a stock continued to run up beyond its conceivable true value, it was necessary to search for sellers who would liquidate, and thus keep the quotation more in line with the facts. That was not always easy.

The short seller fills this void; he is more inclined to be a speculator than is the purchaser of long stock. He is willing to take a chance, and sell something he does not own, if he feels it is overpriced. Eventually he will be on the buying side, because the time will come when he must even up his account. In the meantime he renders a service to the market, at his own risk.

Profits or losses on short sales of securities are ordinarily short term, no matter how much time elapses before the short position is covered. That is because what counts is the length of time the stock used to cover the short position is owned. In the usual case, when a short position is covered, stock is bought and immediately used to make good on the short sale. There is hence a fleeting period of ownership of the covering stock instead of the six months required for a long-term gain or loss.

The situation in commodities is somewhat different. An individual speculator or investor can establish a short commodity position and more than six months later sell his position as distinguished from covering the short sale. His profit or loss on the sale of his position will be long term.

There are rules that apply to both security and commodity short sales. If to the particular taxpayer, securities are ordinary assets, as in the case of dealers, or commodities are ordinary assets, as in the case of farmers, the short sales will be considered as merchandising transactions resulting in ordinary gain or loss. If to the particular taxpayer securities or commodities are a capital asset, as in the case of speculators or investors, the short sale results will be capital gain or capital loss.

For several years both the New York Stock Exchange and the American Stock Exchange have required their member firms to submit reports as to the amount of short interest in their offices. These figures are received from the brokers and the total is made public once a month. It specifies the number of shares short in each particular stock.

Of course the number of shares reported as short does not include private borrowings between individuals, of which there would be no record in the brokerage offices.

In virtually all cases your broker will set up a separate account in your name when you sell short. This is so it will not become confused with your long account. This short account shows a credit balance of so many dollars in your favor, but obviously it is not your money, to be withdrawn as you see fit. In fact your broker does not retain that particular block of money either. He deposits it with the lender of the shares, as a safeguard.

You may sell short on margin, just as you can buy long on margin. Be assured, however, that your broker is going to watch your account carefully, to make certain the maintenance requirements of the stock exchange are observed. The federal regulation at this time of writing is that the margin must be 70 per cent. (This is Regulation T, and can be changed by the Federal Reserve Board without notice.) In addition, the stock exchange has its own maintenance rate of 30 per cent or $5 per share, whichever is greater, for short sales. Aside from the federal regulation, individual exchanges, and their member firms, usually impose their own stringent regulations.

Let us see what would happen to the margin in the event a speculator made an unwise short sale. We will assume he sold 100 shares of stock short at $25 a share. Rules vary slightly among the various exchanges. For the purposes of this illustration we will assume it was a sale on the New York Stock Exchange.

His short account shows a credit of $2,500, representing the proceeds of the sale, plus $1,750 which he must deposit. The latter represents 70 per cent of the amount of the sale. Thus his short account shows a balance of $4,250.

The so-called maintenance required by the exchange is 30 per cent of the $2,500, or $750. The difference between the margin requirement of $1,750 and the exchange's maintenance requirement of $750 is $1,000. Thus far our speculator has a leeway of safety.

Instead of going down, as he had hoped, we will assume the stock advances a point, to $26 a share. Now his maintenance must be 30 per cent of $2,600 instead of 30 per cent of $2,500. It moves up $30 to $780. At the same time his equity is reduced by $100, which represents the loss he has sustained when the 100 shares of stock moved against him one point.

Now the difference between the margin requirement and the maintenance requirement has been reduced to $870 from the $1,000. (Former equity of $1,750 reduced by $100 to $1,650.) The previous margin of $1,750 has also been reduced by this $100, to $1,650. This amount minus the new maintenance of $780 leaves a difference of $870, against the previous difference of $1,000. Now our speculator is not quite as happy.

Assume a further rise, to $28 a share. Using the same formula the maintenance increases to $840 and the equity drops to $1,450, a difference of $610. Then, we will assume, the stock jumps to 32⅝.

Now the New York Stock Exchange requirement is $979, and the equity has dropped to $987, a difference of a mere $8.

The following table illustrates the point:

SHORT SALE OF 100 SHARES AT $25 PER SHARE

Market Price per Share	Equity	N.Y. Stock Exchange Requirement	Difference
$25	$1,750	$750	$1,000
26	1,650	780	870
28	1,450	840	610
30	1,250	900	350
32⅝	987	979	8

In other words, any rise of roughly 30 per cent reduces a margin account virtually to the minimum requirements, and unless the short seller is able and willing to deposit additional cash or collateral, he will be bought in. In actual practice firms usually have their own house rules, which are higher, in order to provide a cushion should the market move against their short customer. If he gets at or near the minimum, he is required to settle promptly.

There are several rules in effect which are designed to keep the practice of short selling free of abuse. Probably the most important one is that short sales cannot be used to depress the market in any security. By this it is meant that a short sale is never the cause of depressing a price, even by an eighth. To go short, the sale must be up from its previous *different* price. It need not necessarily be up over the last sale.

On the floor this is a "zero plus tick," in contrast to a "zero minus tick," when it is at the same price as the previous sale but below its previous different price. Indicators at the individual posts, where stocks are traded in, are changed by floor reporters to indicate whether the tick is plus or minus. The short seller may do business at the same price as the previous price if it is marked plus, but not if it is marked minus. If minus, he may sell short only at a higher price. This effectively stops the practice, common back in the 1920s, of raids by short sellers to depress a price suddenly, so as to shake out weakly margined speculators and provide the short selling speculators with an opportunity to cover their commitments at a profit.

There is another ruling, enforced by the Securities and Exchange Commission. This is that a broker cannot accept an order from a customer unless he finds out whether it is long stock or short stock that is being sold. He must so designate it. When the sale is completed it is printed on the ticker in the usual manner.

There are other rules applying to short selling but they are technical in nature and apply only to a few special situations. They are rarely of interest to the ordinary investor, even though his broker must keep them in mind.

PREMIUM RATES

As has been noted, when a customer is short a block of stock, his broker must borrow the shares in order to make delivery. He deposits with the lender a sufficient amount of money to protect the lender. The shares may be borrowed from another broker.

In times of excessively high interest rates, such as prevailed in the hectic days of the late 1920s, the lender, who now holds money as security, may pay the borrower of the stock a small percentage of interest. This is unusual. If no interest is paid, the stock is said to be lending flat. That condition prevails in virtually all stocks in which there is a short interest.

On the other hand, if it becomes difficult to borrow shares, the lender charges a fee, which he receives in addition to the use of the money during the period of the loan. This fee is called a premium. It starts at $1 a day for 100 shares and is increased if the supply and demand situation warrants. This is extremely rare.

Premium rates may reflect a small floating supply of shares or at least a small number available for lending in the financial district; or they could mean that the floating supply is becoming concentrated in the hands of one group.

In recent years there have been only a few cases in which the borrowers faced any great difficulties in borrowing shares to meet their short commitments. One notable exception was in the case of E. L. Bruce & Co., on the American Stock Exchange. There were a number of such cases in the 1920s, and one time the premium was set at $700 for the loan of 100 shares for twenty-four hours. At such times a corner is said to exist.

ODD LOTS

In most cases, shares are traded in on the exchange in lots of 100 shares, known as round lots. Many customers, however, become interested in a wide selection of stocks, and if their buying power does not permit them to invest in round lots, they buy or sell blocks of less than 100 shares. These are known as odd lots. The odd-lot volume normally runs around 22 per cent of the round lot volume.

Such a customer gives his order to his broker in the regular manner. The broker sends it to the trading floor, where it is handled by one of the firms specializing in such transactions. They are dealers, not brokers, in that they take a position in the market themselves. They assume a personal risk, because of the price action of the market; of necessity they find themselves long or short of various assortments of stocks as they buy round lots and break them up into odd lots, or vice versa. They are obligated to fill the order. They deal in round lots during the day to keep positions as they want them.

For their service they charge a differential. This must be paid by the customer, who also pays his own broker the regular commission. It is important to keep this differential in mind. For instance, if you order your broker to sell fifteen shares of American Can at the market, and after your order arrives at the post a transaction occurs, at 44¾, your selling price is 44½. If you ordered him to buy at the market for your account, and the next transaction was at 44¾, your price would be 45. The extra quarter point, either way, is the differential, which goes to the odd-lot dealer.

If you limited your order and instructed your broker not to sell at less than 44¾, the price in the round-lot market would have to touch 45 before the dealer would be obligated to take your stock. If you limited a buy order to a price not more than 44¾, the stock would have to sell thereafter at 44½ before he would be obligated to meet your demand. On stocks selling below $40, the differential is ⅛.

Figures on odd-lot trading are issued daily by the New York Stock Exchange and are published in the financial section of daily newspapers. They show the number of shares involved in odd-lot purchases and odd-lot sales, and the number sold short through odd-lot trading. The Securities and Exchange Commission also reports on this kind of trading weekly, giving the number of individual transactions as well as the number of shares involved. It reports for both the New York Stock Exchange and the American Stock Exchange.

These figures are watched closely by a number of market traders, especially those of a technical turn of mind. Man is forever trying to discover methods for predicting the future course of stock market prices. One formula involves a consideration of odd-lot figures, based on an evaluation of the excess of odd-lot buying over odd-lot selling, or vice versa.

Normally, small investors who customarily buy or sell less than a hundred shares are on the buying side of the market. They accumulate shares far more often than they liquidate them. At times the public becomes too enthusiastic, and there is a bulge in the volume of odd-lot buying. At the same time the volume of short selling through odd lots declines. The belief of some students of the market is that such a combination indicates an overbought condition, and that the technical condition of the list has been weakened. In such cases it is not unusual to have the list turn downward. The break is referred to in Wall Street and in news stories as a technical correction. It need not necessarily indicate any change in the market's longer-term trend.

Conversely, on the few occasions when odd-lot selling exceeds odd-lot buying, it is taken to indicate that the public has oversold. The same conclusion may also be justified if the margin of buy orders over sell orders narrows sharply. If a technical student of the market becomes convinced that the list is in an oversold condition, he becomes bullish, figuring that at least a short-term rally is in the making, and that possibly a major turn is developing.

The theory rests on the assumption the public is inclined to be carried away either by excessive optimism or excessive pessimism, and that in either case it is wrong for the short term and possibly for the long term.

GUARANTEED STOCKS

A stock is said to be a "guaranteed stock" when a fixed amount of income on the shares is guaranteed by another corporation. In the vast majority of cases these shares are securities of a railroad company which owns strategically located real estate and/or rights of way needed by a larger operating railroad. There are a few guaranteed telegraph stocks, arising from companies leased by the Western Union Telegraph Company.

There are approximately a hundred guaranteed and leased line railroad stock issues. The number has dwindled over the last few decades as some were exchanged for bonds of the operating system which guaranteed their dividends, and others disappeared as the operating system bought in the shares and amalgamated the property with its own.

In most cases the credit rating of a guaranteed stock is high, as the property covered is vital. The capitalization of a leased line company is small in comparison with the value of the property concerned. Even during the depression years of the 1930s, when more than a third of the railroad mileage in the United States was being operated in bankruptcy, there was only a handful of defaults on guaranteed stocks. They came through the depression, and the later years of vast economic upheaval, with a record better than that of first-mortgage railroad bonds.

During this period and also when bankruptcies became less numerous, the operating company would pay the rental for the vital property concerned even if it had to delay paying other debts, because if it defaulted it would thereby break the lease and the original company could proceed to dispose of its real property. This could mean the loss of a terminal or the loss of a connecting link of track and right of way between two parts of its system, without which it would not only be bankrupt but could well be faced with liquidation.

In one respect a guaranteed stock is similar to a railroad bond, in that such a share pays a regular and fixed dividend the same as a bond, which pays a regular and fixed amount of interest. A major difference is that a guaranteed stock represents the ownership of an equity whereas a bond is evidence of a debt. The stockholder is in the position of a landlord, owning a piece of property, which usually cannot be mortgaged, instead of being a creditor.

Another difference between a bond and a guaranteed stock is that bonds are redeemable, and therefore the debt can be renegotiated by the debtor railroad every few years. In virtually all cases guaranteed stocks cannot be called. Still another difference is that bonds usually are of the coupon variety and can be transferred through delivery, whereas guaranteed stocks, like other equities, are not negotiable without the signature of the owner.

CONVERTIBLES

Convertibles, usually preferred shares or bonds, are securities which the owner may exchange for a company's common shares, at a specified ratio, if he so desires. Their attractiveness arises from the fact that while any preferred has a prior claim on dividends ahead of common stock, and the bond has a claim for interest prior to both classes of stock, the convertible preferred shares, or bonds, also have a chance eventually to participate in the future welfare of the company, assuming it does well and the price of the common advances in the market. While the investor in a convertible is waiting for the company to become more prosperous, he has his preferred dividend, or his bond interest, and when he decides it would be better to own the common, he has the privilege of doing so.

The convertible feature therefore sweetens his investment. Many new bond issues carry the right to convert. In the case of convertible preferreds, they are usually issued at times when one company takes over another, through an exchange of securities, or when there is a reorganization and investors need a little extra enticement.

There has been a sharp increase in the number of convertible bonds and preferred stocks in the last few years. The straight preferred, which offers nothing more than a set dividend rate and has no additional feature such as the right to vote at annual meetings, a regular rate of redemption, or a participation in earnings after they reach a certain amount, is occupying a steadily diminishing role in the investment field.

If this straight preferred is the issue of a company with a high investment rating, in which risk is minimal, then the market value of these shares will tend to fluctuate conversely with changes in the prevailing rate for other types of money. A dividend return of 5 per cent of par, for instance, which a top-grade straight preferred may be paying, looks attractive to investors when short-term and long-term money rates are low, or when little return can be obtained from government or municipal bonds. In such cases this preferred may be bid to well above par, where its actual return becomes less than 5 per cent. But if these competing havens for the investors' money trend higher, then the straight preferred shares of this nature, on which there is a minimum of risk, become relatively less attractive, and the price sinks to below par, where the actual yield on a new purchase of such shares rises to above 5 per cent.

Should a straight preferred be an issue of a company that has come upon more difficult times, and thus have had its credit standing lowered, then the market price would fluctuate not only in accordance with changes in the money market but would also reflect the added risk.

In this case the holder of a convertible preferred would have the satisfaction of knowing that as long as the company is able to pay the dividend, he at least will rank ahead of the holder of common shares; and when a better day comes he will have the right to shift into the more volatile common stock, which represents equity capital. It is considerations such as these that have tended to increase the popularity of convertibles with institutional buyers, who usually invest for a long term. They are less likely to invest in a straight preferred.

LISTED SECURITIES

All exchanges have certain rules governing the admission of securities to their trading list. In most cases these rules are very strict, and they have been tightened considerably in recent years. When new listings are approved, the news is usually carried in the leading newspapers, frequently with a picture and a discussion of the information contained in the company's application to the exchange. From time to time there are stories of securities being stricken from the list.

The New York Stock Exchange has certain standards for listing securities. A discussion of all agreements entered into by the company with the exchange would entail considerable space, but the general basic requirements provide that the company be a going concern, having substantial assets or a record of substantial earnings over a period of years, and that the issue be of a size to warrant listing and sufficiently distributed to permit the maintenance of a free and open market. The company must agree with the exchange to publish regularly complete corporate statements pertaining to its financial condition for the benefit of shareholders. Before listing, companies must also comply with the requirements of the Securities and Exchange Commission for the registration of the issue.

MARKET AND LIMITED ORDERS

In reading that part of the financial section devoted to markets, whether in securities or commodities, the reader will frequently encounter terms which, although well understood in the financial community, are not as familiar elsewhere. In security trading there are references to bid-and-asked quotations, market orders, limited orders, stop orders, the work of the specialist, and a host of other things.

It is well to remember that while the newspapers, in the case of listed securities, publish the actual prices at which stocks change hands, each trade has developed after a bid and offered price had been made. Just as in a real estate transaction, or any other sale, the prospective buyer makes a bid. He is willing to pay that price. A prospective seller makes an offer. That is the price at which he will do business.

Bid and offered quotations result. That is the market. If you call your broker and ask him for the market in, say, United States Steel, he will quote the best prevailing bid and offer, with possibly the last price at which a sale took place. For instance he might reply, "Steel, 68½ to ¾, last ⅝," meaning someone is ready to pay $68.50 a share, some one else has already entered an order to sell at $68.75, and that the last actual trade was $68.62½ a share.

If you order your broker to "buy at the market" (a *market order*), your order is executed without delay. If the best offer is at 68¾, that is what you will pay. If you order him to "sell at the market," your order will get the best bid of 68½. Your broker will, of course, try to obtain better than the quoted price.

If you give him a *limited order* to buy at 65⅝, your order will go to the floor, but you have no guarantee you will get the stock unless a willing seller at that price enters the market. The difference between the bid and offer is called the *spread*. It is usually narrow in the case of active and widely distributed shares, such as Steel. Normally it is wider in the case of higher priced issues, such as International Business Machines, or relatively inactive ones. When the bid and offer meet each other, a sale takes place, and thereupon a new bid and offered market is established.

A limited order, good for that day only is called a *day order*. If not completed by closing time, it is destroyed. If you wish it to remain in the market, for possible completion the following day or even at a later date, you must so instruct your broker. Then it becomes known as a *G.T.C. order*, meaning good 'til canceled or good 'til countermanded. It is also known as an *open order*. It is essential to remember the open orders you have placed with your broker, as he will complete them, when possible, unless you have canceled them.

Under stock exchange rules, all open buy orders and open sell orders must be reduced by the amount of the dividend on an ex date. Thus, if you had an open order to buy 100 Telephone at 72, it would be changed to read 71½ on the day Telephone was quoted ex its quarterly dividend of 50 cents (½ point).

THE SPECIALIST

In numerous cases your order will be handled by a *specialist*, not by your own broker. This is almost certain to be the case if you entered a G.T.C. order or a limited order, and in some instances it is the case if you gave a market order.

On the floor of the New York Stock Exchange there are some 350 of these individuals. They ordinarily do not do business directly with the public, so you are not apt to meet them personally. They deal only with other members of the exchange, executing orders for the commission brokers who deal directly with the public. It is estimated that normally half the day's volume goes through the hands of these specialists, for which their portion of the commission averages about 10 per cent.

The specialist is charged with the responsibility of maintaining a good market in the particular stock or stocks assigned to him, by dealing for his own account. He applies to the exchange to be appointed as a specialist in the stock of his choice, and if he wins the appointment he assumes definite obligations. There can be more than one specialist in some stocks.

He expedites the transaction. If your broker has an order to buy 100 shares of stock at, say, 98 and it is currently selling for 100, he cannot spend his time waiting around the post just on the chance the price will drop sufficiently to meet your bid. He may have orders in five different stocks at different trading posts all at the same time, and he cannot be everywhere. He might turn each limited order over to a specialist and execute market orders himself.

The specialist keeps a book of buy and sell orders. If your order comes in to buy 100 at 98, it is entered in his book. If your order is the first in line, you get the first hundred shares he is able to purchase at that price. It is the same on the sell side. Your buy order takes precedence over any buying the specialist may wish to do for his own account at the price of your order, or at any price if yours is a market order to buy. The same principle applies with respect to selling orders when the specialist sells for his own account.

A *floor trader*, since Aug. 1964 known as a *registered trader*, is also a member of the stock exchange, and is likewise prohibited from taking precedence over the public with his orders to buy or sell. The public order must be executed first.

The Special Study of Securities Markets, made for the SEC in

1963, was critical of the role of the floor trader. He dealt only for his own account, and the contention was that while he supplied liquid capital to the stock market at times, which the stock exchange maintained, there were other instances when this group accentuated a move, up or down, to the detriment of the individual investor. The contention of the SEC was that the floor trader failed to justify his existence, because he added to the flames of speculation in times of stress instead of countering such swings.

In compliance with the wishes of the SEC the New York Stock Exchange and the American Stock Exchange, in August, 1964, about a year after the completion of the Special Study, adopted stringent new regulations with respect to the trading of these members. The two exchanges acted before Congress had completed legislating the various recommendations made by the SEC.

Those members who had been floor traders got another title, that of "registered trader," once they had passed a comprehensive examination and registered with their respective exchanges. Also exacted was a new regulation calling for minimum capital requirements. A major new rule was that registered traders make at least 75 per cent of their transactions "stabilizing" in nature. The purpose of this was to require them to buy stock in a declining market and supply stock in a rising market if they wished to trade. An exception to this move permits them to make liquidations at a loss without penalizing their over-all record.

There were some 35 floor trader members of the New York Stock Exchange who were full-time professionals, trading for their own account, and perhaps another three to four hundred of the 850 members normally on the floor who engaged in floor trading for their own account with varying frequency.

On the American Stock Exchange there were 24 floor traders who dealt exclusively for their own account and another 50 who dealt in this manner on occasion. The number of registered traders, at the time the new regulation went into effect, was expected to remain approximately the same.

The specialist is expected to deal for his own account, as he has the responsibility of maintaining a fair and orderly market. That means he must frequently go long or short of a stock in order to maintain a balance, and keep fluctuations within reason. Although he is in a favored position, in that he gets a good idea of the prospective buying or selling in the particular stock, he must frequently take a position on the side that is contrary to his judgment, and he never knows, any more than anyone else, what the next movement may bring in the way of supply or demand.

This happens quite often. There may be a news development overnight that causes a sudden wave of buying or selling. The specialist must either supply stock or take it, as the case requires.

You will occasionally note in the newspapers a statement to the effect that such and such a stock could not be opened until after a delay. At times these delays can run into hours. That means the specialist was overburdened with orders, the bulk of which were on one side of the market. He may have orders to buy 10,000 shares at the market and several thousand more shares at various limited prices. To offset these, he finds he has sell orders that are picayune. At what price is he going to open the market?

Under the supervision of a floor official, the buy and sell orders are matched up. Most orders received overnight by brokers are sent to the specialist. He attempts to open the stock as near as possible to the previous day's price by using these orders and also by dealing for his own account.

He does this as soon as possible. Occasionally there are special cases in which there is a preponderance of buy orders or a preponderance of sell orders, due to news developments. In such a case, a governor of the stock exchange is called in to supervise the opening, and all orders are handed to the specialist.

During the delay, information with respect to the preponderance of buyers or sellers is disseminated to member firms. This usually results in a certain number of cancellations and also new orders on the other side (opposite of the preponderant).

The specialist and the governor reappraise the situation and arrive at what they consider to be a suitable bid and offer quotation. This is printed on the tape and may result in additional orders. At that point, the two discuss the matter again, and the stock is opened at a price which the governor feels is fair to both buyers and sellers in light of the circumstances.

STOP ORDERS

In addition to keeping a book in which he records prospective orders to buy or sell in the regular way, the specialist also has to contend with *stop orders*. These are orders placed in the market by customers, with instructions that they be completed when, as, and if a certain stock reaches a particular point. When this happens, the stop order automatically becomes a market order, to be completed at the most advantageous price possible.

Stop orders are used both to protect profits and to limit losses. Suppose an investor bought a certain stock at 20. He sees it go to 25, which means he has a handsome profit. But he hesitates to liquidate because he thinks it is acting so well. Then it goes to 30. He is nervous, but still hesitant to sell. He instructs his broker to put in a stop order, to sell at 28. If it eases to 28, this order will be executed at the market. But assume that it goes to 35. Now he is happier, but more nervous. He cancels the stop order at 28 and enters another at 32.

In this manner he follows up the rise in his stock. Somewhere along the line the forward move will stop, and when it sinks to the level of his stop order, he will be sold out. But not necessarily at exactly his price. If it hits 32, the stock will be sold at the best bid, which may be somewhat less.

Conversely, stop orders are used to limit losses. Perhaps our investor guessed poorly and the shares for which he paid 20 are now selling at 17. He gives his broker a stop order at 15. If it hits that price, he wants to sell rather than to risk incurring an even larger loss. A short seller may use a stop order to limit a loss. If he sold short at 35 he might enter a buy stop order at 38, hoping to limit his loss to 3 points in the event the stock rises rather than declines in price.

MARGIN TRADING AND BROKERS' LOANS

Trading on margin consists of borrowing a part of the purchase price from your broker who, in turn, can use your securities as collateral for a loan at the bank. These are known as brokers' loans, and the total is announced monthly by both the New York Stock Exchange and the American Stock Exchange, each report covering "member borrowings" by the exchange's own member firms. In addition the Federal Reserve releases a weekly total which includes borrowings by dealers as well as brokers.

Among the reforms of the early 1930s was one which gave the Federal Reserve the authority and responsibility to regulate the terms of credit extended to brokers. Prior to that time there had been abuses, which consisted of firms granting credit to customers with insufficient collateral. Accounts became thinly margined, and traders were sold out on intermittent dips in the market.

The Federal Reserve changes the margin requirement at will, and without previous notice. It has done so many times and from January 21, 1946, to February 1, 1947, it forbade margin trading entirely, making the requirement the full 100 per cent of the sum involved. In addition each exchange and each firm can set its own more stringent margin requirements.

In late 1964 the requirement was 70 per cent. This means that to invest in securities, the customer must deposit with his broker a minimum of 70 per cent of the total purchase price. To buy $10,000 worth of stock, he must deposit at least $7,000. The remaining $3,000 could be borrowed. The broker makes a monthly interest charge on the customer's debit balance.

If the stock in question declines in value and the account thus becomes undermargined, no further trading is permitted until the customer has either liquidated a part of his holdings, or deposited sufficient money or additional collateral to bring the percentage of borrowing within the maintenance margin limit established by the stock exchange. The Federal Reserve does not have a maintenance-of-margin requirement.

The account is not liquidated without consultation with the customer, as was the case before this reform was established. The customer is notified, and his account is restricted. But his holdings are not thrown indiscriminately on the market until all avenues of adjustment have been explored.

Margin trading is not as prevalent as it was during the years when "trading on a shoestring" was common. The bulk of investing is on a cash basis. While numerous individual accounts may be restricted, and countless others have debit balances up to the full permissible limit, the total of member borrowings is insignificant if measured against the total value of listed shares. Normally it runs around 1 per cent. News stories on brokers' loans are not featured in the newspapers as much as formerly.

Those who feel the Federal Reserve has been too strict with its margin requirements contend that if consumer goods—such as venetian blinds, furniture, carpets, and automobiles—can be bought with a deposit of little more than a promise and a smile, it is unrealistic to require the purchaser of top grade securities to deposit a large part of the purchase price.

The other side of the agrument is that consumer goods are used and therefore are presumed to improve society's standard of living, whereas securities are passed from hand to hand and are not consumed. On this basis the authorities have exerted their influence to limit the portion of the total amount of credit which flows into Wall Street.

SECONDARY DISTRIBUTIONS

In recent years a method of distributing large blocks of stock off the market has been perfected by what is known as "secondary distributions." This method was used early in World War II to liquidate blocks of British holdings of American securities, and it is used now frequently in the liquidation of estates or other large holdings.

These sales are made off the floor of the exchange and usually after trading hours, with a price concession to dealers to encourage them to put more effort behind the selling job. Member firms of the exchange may participate in such transactions only with the approval of the exchange, but nonmembers naturally do not have to receive permission.

Should a large investor wish to liquidate a sizable block of a relatively inactive stock, he would realize that to offer this stock on the exchange might cause a sharp price reaction. Thereupon he makes an arrangement with a broker or an investment banking firm which announces it will make a secondary distribution of the shares at the closing price that day, with a dealer discount.

The dealer discount usually is more per share than the brokers would obtain in commissions by selling the stock in the regular way. The offering firm may get other firms to participate with it, and this may include exchange firms if the stock exchange has approved. Should the exchange think its own facilities capable of absorbing the offering, it might refuse to permit its members to participate.

The exchange has provided other special marketing methods to facilitate the purchase or sale of large blocks within a reasonable time and at a reasonable price. Three were instituted late in 1956—the special bid, the exchange acquisition, and the specialist block sale. These three are designed to aid in the purchase of major blocks, whereas previous methods were concerned with the sale of such blocks. All of these special procedures require prior approval by the exchange. The specialist block purchase and the specialist block sale provide that the broker may negotiate a direct purchase or sale of stock with the stock exchange specialist in that stock. The transaction takes place outside the regular auction market.

The exchange distribution and the exchange acquisition provide that the member firm may accumulate the necessary orders and then cross them with the original block order on the floor of the auction market at prices between the current bid and offer.

The special offering and the special bid provide that when the size of the block order or current market conditions make it necessary to enlist the marketing services of the entire exchange community, the broker announces a fixed offering price or bid price over the ticker, opening the transaction to all members and their customers. The fixed price transactions are made on the exchange floor but not as part of the auction market.

5

~~~~~~

VARIOUS SECURITIES MARKETS

THE NATION'S SECOND LARGEST SECURITIES MARKET IS the American Stock Exchange, at 86 Trinity Place in the heart of New York City's financial district. More than 1,000 securities of nearly 950 domestic and foreign companies are publicly traded on the American Exchange. These securities total more than 1.8 billion shares with an aggregate market value of over $25 billion.

The American Exchange list includes virtually every industrial, commercial, and service function. Many are leading corporate names. The exchange's special economic contribution, however, is its role as a primary market for the most promising of the nation's corporate youth.

Trading is active on the American Exchange, and transactions are reported promptly over a nationwide network of some 2,000 stock tickers in approximately 400 cities in the United States and Canada. The exchange has nearly 1,000 regular and associate members. The approximately 650 member organizations maintain more than 3,000 main and branch offices in nearly 800 cities in 50 states and the District of Columbia. There are also about 140 member offices in 19 foreign countries.

[47]

For a company to qualify for listing on this exchange today, it must have net tangible assets of at least $1 million, 750 or more shareholders, and 200,000 or more shares in the hands of the public. Net earnings for the year preceding listing are required to be at least $150,000, with average earnings of $100,000 a year for the past three fiscal years. The company also must agree to solicit proxies and to publish quarterly earnings reports.

Issues which fail to meet standards for continued dealings—such as earnings, share distribution, and financial and ownership criteria —are subject to removal.

A 32-member board of governors is responsible for exchange policy. This board is elected by the regular members, except for the president, who is the exchange's principal officer and chief executive, and three representatives of the public who are not in the securities business. These three are appointed by the president. The board's presiding officer, the chairman, is elected by the regular members.

Most authorities trace the beginnings of the American Exchange to the 1849 discovery of gold in California. In those early days—and for many years afterward—dealings were conducted outdoors, principally along the curbstones of Broad Street.

Outdoor trading was an informal affair until 1911, when the New York Curb Market Association was formed by a number of progressive curb brokers and certain rules were established. At an open meeting of this association in 1919, a decision was made that trading had expanded to the point where it should be conducted indoors under formal procedures.

This was accomplished on June 27, 1921, when the New York Curb Market moved into the original exchange structure on the present site, a constitution was formulated, and a ticker system established.

The New York Curb Market became, in 1929, the New York Curb Exchange, which joined the original building to the present fourteen-story facility in 1931. The exchange adopted its present name in 1953, to reflect the scope of its influence in North and South America.

The organization of the American Stock Exchange, frequently referred to as the Amex, is quite similar to that of the New York Stock Exchange. When an Amex issue is listed on the so-called Big Board, it is automatically delisted from the Amex. Thus the two exchanges never trade in the same security at the same time, although a company with more than one class of stocks, or bonds, outstanding, may have some on one board and some on the other.

MARKETS IN OTHER CITIES

In all there are eighteen stock exchanges in the United States, and they all come under the regulations of the Securities and Exchange Commission. Their combined total of trading in one recent year amounted to 1.7 billion shares, worth $54.7 billion. This is in addition to the over-the-counter market, where business is transacted outside of the organized exchanges.

In addition to the New York Stock Exchange and the American Stock Exchange, New York has one other regulated exchange, the National Stock Exchange. It was organized early in 1962, but to date its volume of business has been small.

The Pacific Coast Stock Exchange and the Midwest Stock Exchange account for a large volume of trading. The former is located in San Francisco and was formed through a merger of the former San Francisco and Los Angeles exchanges. In general, it and the Midwest Exchange specialize in the securities in their respective areas, but the Pacific Coast board also gets a large amount of business in stocks listed in New York. The time differential permits trading there after the New York markets are closed, and the Pacific Coast board may be especially busy if there is an important news development after 3:30 P.M. Eastern time.

The Midwest Exchange was formed through a merger of four former exchanges in that part of the country. It is located in Chicago and has branches in Cleveland and St. Louis, which are linked with Chicago by teletype.

Another major market is the Philadelphia-Baltimore-Washington Stock Exchange, which is a combination of three earlier markets in those cities. The Detroit Stock Exchange was formed primarily to deal in shares connected with the automobile industry.

Toronto and Montreal have active markets, the former specializing in mining shares, many of which are quoted in pennies and are highly speculative. In numerical volume of shares that change hands on any trading day, Toronto usually has a far larger figure than the New York Stock Exchange, but the dollar value of transactions is quite a different story.

The London Stock Exchange is the best known of the many overseas boards. Others, which are quoted in several of our leading newspapers, include Paris, Frankfurt, Brussels, Milan, Zurich, Amsterdam, Tokyo, and Johannesburg. The Tokyo market, like that in Toronto, deals in a number of lower-priced issues, so its daily share volume reaches a fantastically high figure.

The London Stock Exchange was able to continue trading throughout World War II, carrying on business in the building it had occupied for 144 years, despite bombs and the later nationalization of a significant portion of England's basic industries.

During the war, members of the London Exchange traded for cash, as in the United States, instead of having two settlement dates a month, as before the war. This method of settlement, known as "fortnightly settlements," was subsequently re-established. It facilitates trading on credit for a limited period.

Securities traded on the London board are largely home industries, as regulations hamper the trading in American or other foreign securities. There is an active market there for South African mining issues. The floor of the London Exchange is divided into various markets. The more important ones are known as "gilt-edged" securities. There is active trading in home railways, South African mining (Kaffirs), breweries, groceries, and industrials. One section, known as the "dirt track," is the scene of trading in greyhound-racing shares.

THE OTC MARKET

Trading in securities over the counter antedates all security exchanges. There was an active market for securities in England a hundred years before the New York Stock Exchange was formed, in 1817. Buyers and sellers, or their agents, met at various times in various places, usually at a particular securities counter in a bank, counting house, or the market place, and transacted business.

When one considers the thousands of corporations in existence and the large number of security issues they have outstanding, it is obvious that only a small percentage of the total is [to be found] listed on the registered stock exchanges. All securities, whether listed or not, can be traded in the over-the-counter market, generally known as the OTC market.

To the investor, transacting business over the counter is similar to trading on a registered exchange. He calls his broker to determine the market, makes a bid if he wishes to buy or an offer if he wishes to sell, or he can buy or sell at the market. He can also trade on margin in a vast number of unlisted securities. A difference is that the specialists in unlisted securities usually act as dealers rather than brokers. They may have a position in the security themselves, and thus sell to or buy from the customer instead of completing his order as an agent and for a commission.

On an exchange, the collective buying and selling inquiries in a particular stock are sent to one focal point, and the orders are executed at a fixed commission rate. In the OTC market the purchaser or seller, or his representative, retains the power of negotiation and trades with the dealers, who buy and sell for their own accounts at fixed net prices; that is, the dealer attempts to make a profit instead of a commission as on an exchange.

This market place has no building as its headquarters. Business is transacted by telephone, which means it takes place in every city big enough to have a broker-dealer. There are some 4,700 of these broker-dealers in the United States, and it is estimated they trade in some 8,000 individual issues a day, some 3,000 of which are active daily, not to mention an additional 30,000 extremely inactive issues in which they are prepared to find and quote a market. These figures compare with some 3,000 individual issues that are traded in on listed markets. In dollar volume it is presumed the total of trading off the board far exceeds that of the more familiar listed boards, but exact figures cannot be compiled. There is no way to measure the volume.

The trading, on a bid and asked basis, is conducted by a variety of firms, including those that limit themselves to the OTC market, and by departments of registered brokerage houses. They, along with an estimated 100,000 employed salesmen, are subject to regulations of the National Association of Securities Dealers, Incorporated (NASD), the self-policing organization, chartered by Congress, to which over-the-counter firms belong. Strictly speaking, an independent OTC broker-dealer cannot be forced to join the NASD, but if he does not join he cannot trade with a member who does belong except on the same basis as would any individual investor among the general public.

This association is empowered to inspect the books of any member, to discipline member firms or individuals, and to take steps which could lead to the revocation of broker-dealer licenses. When formed, its objectives were stated as: "to adopt, administer and enforce rules of fair practice, and rules to prevent fraud and manipulative acts and practices, and in general to promote just and equitable principles of trade for the protection of investors." Inspections are made at frequent intervals. The association also interprets the rulings of the Securities and Exchange Commission.

These objectives became scheduled for broadening following the Special Study of the Securities Markets, which was submitted to Congress in April 1963. The commission told Congress the securities markets were free of fraudulent practices, but that "all important problems exist, grave abuses occur, and additional controls and improvements are much needed."

In order to raise the standards of the OTC industry and enlarge the supervision of this sprawling market, the report to Congress made several recommendations for new legislation.

Chiefly these recommendations were:

1. Broaden the scope of financial reporting, proxy, and insider trading regulations, which heretofore had applied only to companies

with shares listed on national securities exchanges, to include those in the over-the-counter market, especially those with three hundred or more stockholders

2. Limit entry into the securities business new broker-dealers and salesmen by establishing minimum capital requirements (for the companies) and establishing certain standards of character and competence for the individual salesmen

3. Broaden the disciplinary powers of the SEC and the industry's self-policing agencies, notably the NASD, by requiring that all securities concerns join self-policing organizations and by bestowing on the SEC greater disciplinary powers which it might use on broker-dealers and salesmen

4. Require securities price quotations systems, such as the National Quotations Bureau, to register with the commission and submit to its supervision

5. Permit the SEC, in handling the "hot issue" problem, to order a broker selling a new stock to deliver a prospectus, covering the issuing company's financial condition, to each prospective buyer for a period running ninety days after the offering starts. Previously this period was only forty days. The hope was that this might help prevent an uninformed group of speculators from running up the price of a new issue without regard to its merit.

While these were the chief recommendations for new legislation, the report to Congress covered a wide range, including: the qualifications of individuals in the securities business; the activities and responsibilities of brokers and investment advisers; primary and secondary offerings of securities, including the hot issues; offerings of real estate securities; disclosure requirements for the OTC market; and corporate publicity and public relations.

The commission listed a number of specific charges against certain elements in the OTC market, and cited specific examples. Briefly it charged that in some cases: brokers had not always tried to get the best prices for customers, did not provide sufficient data on the activity of a stock and price markups, collaborated to supply misleading data to compilers of official price lists, and also gave misleading quotations to newspapers. It also said some dealers "back away" from prices they have quoted on unlisted stocks, that some dealers feel no responsibility to maintain a market in a stock they had previously sponsored, that there were cases in which they had concealed the true supply and demand of a stock, that profit markups varied widely, that bid and asked prices supplied to newspapers did not always reflect the true market, and that price quotations given newspapers at times had reflected nothing more than suggestions made by one broker to another.

Reputable broker-dealers in OTC securities assert that none of these practices is widespread, and they urge the public to investigate their broker-dealers before doing business with them. As an example of the determination of the NASD and the OTC industry to deal with would-be violators before there could be further violations as outlined in the commission's report, the NASD joined with the New York Stock Exchange and the American Stock Exchange in adopting a plan of procedure for administering registered representatives' examinations in sixty-three centrally located NASD test centers throughout the United States. This went into effect July 1, 1963. It culminated three years of intraindustry effort to revise and coordinate examination systems, and instituted a single basic securities industry test, with special NASD, New York Stock Exchange, and American Stock Exchange sections.

In view of the criticisms in the Special Study and also others made by investors, there has been a feeling at times that because a stock is not listed, it necessarily may be lacking in quality. This is far from being the case, as the OTC market contains securities of good, bad, and indifferent quality, as do all markets. It contains securities of some of our best-known financial and business institutions, many of them with long records of unbroken dividend payments.

For instance, all bank and virtually all insurance stocks, and all mutual fund shares, are traded over the counter, and the unlisted market also conducts the bulk of the trading in government and other high-grade bonds. In general, two types of securities more readily lend themselves to transactions in the OTC market than on the exchanges.

1. Securities that are closely held, lack distribution, or are high priced.

2. High-grade, generally extremely liquid securities where the buying or selling is generally "en bloc" by institutions, etc., and where the buyers or sellers prefer to accept or reject a bid or offering "en bloc" without treating with small amounts in the course of fulfilling a sizable order—for example, government bonds, municipal bonds, and high-grade railroad preferred stocks.

In August, 1964 a major change in the method of quoting the bid and asked quotations of OTC securities became law. Prior thereto the NASD, through the National Quotations Bureau, had what amounted to a two-price system. One was printed in the newspapers, furnished for the benefit of the retail trade. As such the spreads between the respective bid and asked prices were wide. There was, in addition, the wholesale market. It had a narrower spread and was the market on which the dealers operated.

In an amendment to the Securities Act of 1933, which became law, there was a section that:

"The rules of the association (the NASD) shall include provisions governing the form and content of quotations relating to securities sold otherwise than on a national securities exchange which may be disseminated by any member or any person associated with a member, and the persons to whom such quotations may be supplied. Such rules relating to quotations shall be designed to produce fair and informative quotations, both at wholesale and retail level, to prevent fictitious or misleading quotations, and to promote orderly procedures for collecting and publishing quotations."

Legally this didn't rule out a two-price system but it imposed on the NASD an obligation to provide newspapers and others with "fair and informative" quotations. This it does, and the bid and asked quotations seen by the investor in the daily newspapers represent the area in which business can be done.

6

~~~~~~

MARKET AVERAGES

A NUMBER OF PUBLICATIONS COMPILE AVERAGES OF stock market prices and of individual groups of stocks within the market in an effort better to judge trends and keep a record of the over-all ups and downs over a long period. With figures made available by such compilations it is possible to draw charts that give a pictorial view of the past, for they show graphically what the average itself, or an index, shows numerically.

An average differs from an index only in that the latter is based on a theoretical value of 100, at some specified date. Each occupies a position similar to that of a sampling, such as a miller would take from a carload of wheat in order to determine the relative quality of the entire quantity he bought.

In preparing these compilations an effort is made to select stocks that are representative of the list as a whole, but no matter how painstaking the effort, the ravages of time make it necessary occasionally to substitute one stock for another, to change a divisor, add or subtract a weight, or otherwise depart slightly from the original base. This is true of any average or index, not merely those that tell the statistical story of the stock market.

There are several reasons why statisticians must make arbitrary changes in their basic data. The most frequent ones, in the case of stock market averages, include mergers which result in the creation of one company where two existed before; large stock dividends or splits, which drastically lower the value of a single share of stock; the disappearance, or near disappearance, of an old industry, such as trolley cars; the emergence of a new industry, through the world's spectacular progress in the field of the sciences; or the growth within one industry of a company to a point where it becomes more representative of the general market than does a competitor whose volume of business and service is no longer considered typical of the group.

A bond average would have to be changed in the event of a maturity. Various publications adopt different methods of adjusting for such changes.

DOW-JONES AVERAGES

Best known of the market averages are those compiled by Dow Jones & Co. They date back to 1897, when only twelve stocks were used, and when there was no serious problem of compilation. Prices of the twelve were added, and then the total was divided by twelve. In 1916 the number of stocks was raised to twenty, whereupon the total was divided by twenty, and there were still no complications.

At present the number of stocks in the Dow Jones calculation is 65, divided into 30 industrial common stocks, 20 railroad common stocks, and 15 public utility common stocks. But because of numerous stock splits, especially in the blue chip industrials, it would no longer give an accurate picture to divide by 65. One of the stocks, selling for 200, might split four for one, at which time the one new share would have an indicated value of 50 instead of the 200 previously used. This would subtract 150 points from the total value of the entire group.

At first the necessary adjustment was made by multiplying the price of 50 by four, as four shares became outstanding for each one share prior to the split. In 1928, however, the method now in use was adopted. It consists in changing the divisor. Instead of dividing the total value of each of the 30 industrials, or the 65 stocks, by 30, or 65, the divisor was lowered to adjust for the reduced price of the split shares.

The new divisor is then used until another split, or major stock dividend, is declared in one of the components used in the compilation. Each day's changes in the four averages compiled by Dow Jones are published daily on its news ticker and in the *Wall Street Journal,* in points and also in percentages. The ticker also prints the averages at various times throughout the day, as of 10 and 11 A.M., noon, 1 and 2 P.M., and then at the close. These averages thus receive nationwide and international distribution during trading hours. The stocks used, and the amount of the divisor, may be seen in the *Wall Street Journal* and many other newspapers.

STANDARD & POOR'S INDEXES

Standard & Poor's Corporation, a statistical organization, has compiled market averages for a number of years. In 1957 it started publication of its present stock price indexes. These are based on 500 listed stocks which, it is estimated, represent 85 per cent of the market value of all common stocks listed on the New York Stock Exchange. The "portfolio" consists of all of the shares of the 500 issues, and as the multiplier is the number of shares outstanding, the final figures are not affected by stock dividends or splits. Changes in market value reflect price fluctuations of the group.

The market value of the portfolio is expressed as an index number, with 1941–1943 equal to 10. The 500 stock issues are divided into 93 individual groups, which comprise four main groups, namely, the industrial composite, rails, utilities, and the 500 composite. Figures on the main groups appear hourly on the tickers of the American Stock Exchange, the Commodity News Service, the Cotton Exchange ticker, and the United Press International financial news wires. The Associated Press and United Press International send the closing indexes over their financial news wires daily, for publication by member newspapers.

AVERAGES ARE NOT UNIFORM

There are various other market averages, including those compiled by the Associated Press, the *New York Times*, and the *New York Herald Tribune*. Each has its following, but as methods and components differ, so do the results.

Thus we have days when one average may make a new high while others will fail to do so. Frequently on days when the over-all change in the market is small, one or more average will show a slight advance and others will post declines. For the student, however, they tend to average out, and each will give a picture of the past performance of a block of wealth that has a going value of some $440 billion.

The *New York Times* average is based on 50 stocks, 25 rails and 25 industrials. It dates back to 1911 and is published after each stock market day, with a Sunday compilation which shows the averages for the preceding week. It adjusts its components for stock splits by changing the multiplier of the split issue. Thus, if an issue were split three for one, it will multiply the price of the new shares by three. In some cases a component will split several times over the years, and each time the multiplier is raised proportionately.

The *New York Herald Tribune*'s average is based on 100 stocks divided into 70 industrials and 30 rails. It also has an average of ten aircraft issues, but this group is not included in the 100-stock average.

To adjust for splits the *Herald Tribune* substitutes another stock for the split issue, or else adds a weight to the group containing the split issue. This weight tends to balance the change in the market price caused by the split. An effort is made to keep weights as low as possible, and when a group's total weight can be lowered through a suitable substitution, this is done.

The *Herald Tribune*, for many years, has also published an average of Amex stocks.

7

~~~~~~

THE OPTION MARKET—
(PUTS AND CALLS)

PUTS AND CALLS, AND COMBINATIONS OF THE TWO
known as *straddles* and *spreads*, are options. The option market is as
old as security trading itself, possibly older, as options are used in
real estate transactions and in any other form of business where one
party purchases from another the privilege of acquiring a certain
asset at a price within a specified length of time.

There is an active securities option market in Wall Street, where
the business is supervised by the Put and Call Brokers and Dealers
Association, Incorporated, an organization formed in 1932 to foster
the maintenance of high standards of integrity. There is no case on
record of a member of the association failing to carry out his side of
a contract. Despite this enviable record, the business has been avoided
by a large group of investors, doubtless because it is misunderstood.
There is an assumption that trading in options is purely speculative,
little removed from direct gambling.

A large number of options are bought on a speculative basis.
Under certain conditions the risk of a relatively small amount of
money can result in a major profit. The bulk of the business in options, however, results from a desire to limit risks, and is thus the

opposite of speculation. There are also conditions under which options can be used to advantage taxwise.

It is not a mysterious or complex method of trading, but at the same time it does not enjoy the daily publicity accorded listed and unlisted markets, and therefore is not well known outside of financial circles. Quotations, or comments on the put and call market, are mentioned frequently, but not regularly, in the daily financial press.

An option is a contract. A purchaser acquires the right to require the seller of the option to perform his part of the agreement. The holder of the option is under no compunction to exercise his privilege, and if at the expiration of the specified life of the option he sees he would reap no advantage by doing so, he merely lets the option lapse. The price he paid to acquire the privilege becomes a capital loss, which he can write off on his next income tax statement.

These options are written for various periods of time, usually thirty days, sixty days, ninety days, and "over six months." Under New York Stock Exchange rulings, no member of that body is permitted to endorse an option of less than 21 days' duration. The longer-term options have been growing in popularity during the last few years. A profit on an asset held for more than six months and a day becomes a long-term capital gain and thus is granted kinder tax treatment than a short-term gain.

There are four types of these options and in each case the purchaser pays a fee, the bulk of which goes to the writer of the contract as compensation for extending the privilege; and a smaller amount goes to the dealer for bringing the two parties together. The four types are:

A PUT—This is a contract that entitles the holder to sell to, or put to, the writer of the option a definite amount of a specified stock at the agreed upon price within the period of the life of the agreement.

A CALL—This entitles the holder to buy from, or call on, the seller of the option, requiring the seller to deliver a definite amount of a specific stock at the agreed upon price within the life of the agreement.

A STRADDLE—This is merely a combination of a put and a call, written on the same stock at the same time and at the same price, with the number of shares and the time limit identical. The exercise of one side of the straddle does not invalidate the other.

A SPREAD—This is quite similar to a straddle but it is two separate contracts, a put and a call, written on the same stock and running for the same length of time. The put, however, specifies a price below the current market for the stock, and the call specifies a price above the market.

Thus, if an investor bought a spread on 100 shares of a certain stock which was currently selling at $50 a share, the put side would entitle him to sell 100 shares of the stock to the writer of the spread at a price of, say, 48, whereas the call side would entitle him to buy from, or call on, the writer for 100 shares at, say, 53. As the terms of the spread are not as advantageous to him as a straddle would be— in that the two sides of a straddle would both read $50 a share in this case—he could doubtless buy a spread at a lower price.

In all four types of stock options, the cost of the option is the full amount of the risk assumed by the purchaser. He has the privilege of exercising his right, or he can ignore the whole thing and write off the cost.

Under the rules of the Put and Call Brokers and Dealers Association, each option carries the notation that it has been sold by a member of the association. Each is endorsed by a member firm of the New York Stock Exchange. In the case of calls, the option must also carry federal and state tax stamps.

Fees charged for options vary according to the terms of the contract. There is no table of rates and charges, as each is subject to negotiation. In actual practice, however, dealers who are active in this business charge about the same, as competition keeps their schedules more or less together. A number of dealers advertise in the financial sections of newspapers, giving representative prices at which they will write options.

Many years ago the short-term contract, or thirty-day option, was popular, but there has been a swing to longer-term agreements which obviously cost more, since they grant more. Starting with the simplest of them, the thirty-day agreement is written a few points away from the market, and for the low charge of $137.50 in the case of a put and $137.50, plus taxes, for a call.

In this case the buyer of the option is paying such a low price that the writer of the option, or seller, would quote the price "away from the market." If the market price of the stock in question were $50, he would specify a price of possibly 53 on a call, or around 48 on a put. The seller would thus obligate himself to deliver to the buyer 100 shares of this stock, at $53 a share, on demand any time within thirty days. Or if it were a put, he would obligate himself to take delivery of 100 shares from the holder of the put, at $48 a share, any time within thirty days.

As the terms change, either with regard to the life of the contract or the price at which it may be exercised, obviously the writer of the option will demand more compensation. Thus if instead of the specified price being "away from the market" it is "at the market" ($50 a share in this case), or if the agreement runs for 60, 90, or 180 days plus, then the cost will be upped to $275, $350, $500, or somewhere in that area. As mentioned previously, the bulk of the business in puts and calls is now written in these longer periods, and usually at the market at the time of the agreement, instead of points away from the market.

In the exercise of options, it is important to keep in mind the treatment of dividends, or any other benefits that might accrue to a stock during the life of the contract. These benefits go with the stock. Thus if the holder of our hypothetical stock held a call and during the life of the call the stock went ex-dividend, say $1 a share, he gets the benefit. The way it works out is that if the call specified a price of 50, it is written down automatically to 49, as he is entitled to the dividend but would not receive it directly from the corporation.

On the other hand if he has a put on the stock at 50, the market price will presumably fall a dollar when the shares go ex-dividend, and he is not entitled to this extra advantage, even if he chooses to exercise his option. He can put the stock at 49, but not at 50. The same applies in cases when a stock is ex any other privilege, such as rights or warrants.

Writers of options are usually individuals or corporations that already have a large position in the shares on which they issue puts and calls. They are willing to sell or buy more stock of their favorites, at a price. For this they receive the bulk of the fee, and in the event the option is never exercised, they are in a position to write down their original cost.

Suppose our individual holds 1,000 shares of a stock which originally cost him $50 a share. He regards this as a fair price. He could sell at that level if he chose. Instead he instructs a dealer to sell options on his holdings, on either side. The dealer sells a put on 100 shares at 50, for ninety days, for which our investor receives possibly $250. If the put is exercised, he finds he has another 100 shares, worth in his estimation $50 a share; but he got them for $250 less than $5,000. If the put is not exercised, he has a $250 profit.

If the dealer sells a call on 100 shares and it is exercised, our individual has to sell for $5,000, which presumably is less than the then current market; but again he has picked up $250, and the advance in the market is no worry to him, since he has a paper profit on the balance of his original holdings.

The buyer of an option usually is an individual who is seeking a speculative profit or seeking to insure the retention of a major portion of a paper profit already at hand, or to insure himself against a possible major loss. Here is the way the option market may be used by this individual.

Suppose he likes our hypothetical $50 stock, but hesitates to tie up an investment of $5,000 for 100 shares. He finds he can buy a call on it, good for ninety days, for possibly $350. That may be more in line with the amount of risk he wishes to assume. If at no time during the ninety days the stock advances sufficiently to show him a profit, at least he has limited his loss to $350. If he is a philosopher he will doubtless congratulate himself on having escaped investing $5,000 in a stock that was a disappointment. He has only a minor loss and can charge part of it to Uncle Sam.

If, on the other hand, the stock advances—say to $60—he can call for 100 shares for $5,000, and sell at $6,000. After deducting commissions and the option cost of $350, he has a major percentage profit.

It is much the same in the case of a put. Let us assume he has a $5,000 investment in 100 shares. He thinks the stock is going to advance, but he wants insurance. So for $350 he buys a put, at 50 for ninety days. If he is wrong and the stock sinks to, say, 40, he puts the stock to the writer of the put at $5,000, and his loss, which would have been $1,000, is only $350 plus commissions. He feels he is well out of a situation that did not go the way he had expected.

Instead of sinking, suppose the stock moves up to 60. Now he has a profit of $1,000, minus the $350 and commissions. Either way, he had insurance. Those who are short of the market likewise can use puts and calls as an insurance against a major loss.

Readers may wonder why prices for calls usually are higher than prices for puts. The answer appears to be that most of us are optimists. It is more normal to want to buy than to want to sell short. The human tendency is to think things are going up, not down. Consequently it is characteristic of us that we will pay more for the privilege of acquiring an asset at a favorable price than for the privilege of getting rid of it. Those who write options, and the dealers who act as go-betweens, can sell calls at a higher price than they can sell puts.

It is not necessary to go to a dealer to get an option. Your regular broker has contacts, and can do business for you on your instructions. Usually options are written on stocks which are the most active in the market, but they are obtainable, through negotiation, on inactive issues and on OTC shares as well.

8

~~~~~~

MUTUAL FUNDS AND
CLOSED-END
INVESTMENT COMPANIES

THE READER OF A MODERN FINANCIAL SECTION CANNOT
pick up his newspaper without seeing references, quotations, or news
stories concerning mutual funds and other investment companies.
This has become increasingly true in recent years as the popularity
of this type of investing has grown steadily. In the past fifteen years,
investment company shareholder accounts have grown from 1 million to over 6.4 million. Assets of investment companies have increased from $2.3 billion to $27.31 billion in the same period. In
1963 alone, $2.5 billion of new money was invested by individuals
and institutions in open-end investment company shares.

Our greater knowledge of business and financial affairs, and of the
importance of equity investments in individual financial plans, has
led to a steady increase in the number of individuals owning shares
in American corporations directly, and also has fostered the spread
of indirect ownership, through open-end (mutual funds) and closed-
end investment companies.

An investment company, stated simply, is a pooling of investment
monies by a large number of investors so that the combined fund
is (1) large enough to diversify through investment in a number of

different corporate securities, thus reducing the risk of loss, and (2) large enough so that professional investment management may be economically employed to select and supervise the company's securities. Purchase of investment company shares helps provide these two safeguards, regardless of the amount of money available to the individual: diversification and professional management.

STOCK IN SYNTEX SOLD BY LEHMAN

30,000 Shares Marketed at $4.2 Million Profit

The Lehman Corporation sold 30,000 common shares of the Syntex Corporation this year at a profit of about $4.2 million, it was disclosed yesterday at the annual meeting of the closed-end investment company.

In answer to a stockholder's question, Robert Lehman, chairman, said the stock was sold at an average price of $152 a share, with the best price one-half point below Syntex's record of 190½. The investment company, he said, retains the remainder of its original 60,000-share Syntex holding, which cost $725,126.

The drug company's stock, listed on the American Stock Exchange, moved in price—adjusted for a stock split — from a 1963 low of 11⅝ to a 1963-64 high of 190½, and closed yesterday at 87¾. Syntex, which makes a key ingredient for oral contraceptives, has drawn much attention, particularly from speculative investors.

The investment company has as its objective the profitable investment of money entrusted to it by investors. Not all investment companies, however, seek the same investment objective or place the same degree of emphasis on a particular objective. Some companies, for example, stress growth of capital and income over the years, others concentrate on producing current income, and still others attempt to secure stability in capital and income.

To reach these long-term objectives, differing policies and types of securities are used. Some companies invest only in common stock, and in a number of cases, only in the common stocks of one or a few industries or the issues of companies in a specific geographical area. Specialized in a different way are a few investment companies providing an important degree of tax shelter.

There are two types of management investment companies—the closed-end company and the open-end (mutual fund) company. Their differences lie largely in the way they raise their capital. Both offer professional management and widely diversified investment portfolios.

CLOSED-END INVESTMENT COMPANIES

The closed-end form of company has been used for more than 100 years, the first ones having been started in Europe and Great Britain in the early and mid-1800s. The first American companies started in the late 1800s. The closed-end company raises its capital, as do most industrial corporations, in a single initial public offering of its shares. Thus, a closed-end company has a fixed number of its shares outstanding, and an investor wishing to buy or sell its shares has to find another investor willing to buy from or sell to him. As a number of closed-end company issues are listed on the New York Stock Exchange, the purchase or sale may be made there. Other closed-end issues are found on the American Stock Exchange and in the over-the-counter markets.

Behind each share is the *asset value*, determined by dividing the total assets of the company available to the common stock on a given day by the number of shares outstanding. The price the investor pays or receives in the market, however, is not the asset value but the market price. This *market price* may be more or less than the asset value—at a premium or discount—depending on many factors of supply and demand for the fixed number of shares of the closed-end company outstanding.

The closed-end companies in some cases have senior securities outstanding besides the common stock. This permits the investor to purchase investment company securities that have the characteristics of corporate bonds and also of preferred stock.

The existence of senior issues, or in the case of some closed-end companies, borrowed money such as bank loans, can generate a feature called *leverage*. Leverage means the use of borrowed money in a company's capital. (See page 216.)

There are comparatively few closed-end investment companies at the moment that are still in the leverage category. In cases where it has been retained, through the retention of a preferred stock issue or through borrowing by means of an issue of bonds or from the banks, the result is to make the shares of the closed-end company more volatile. In a rising market, its shares normally would tend to advance more rapidly, and in a declining market, they would sell off faster.

For example, if a company has investments worth $10 million and has a million shares of common stock outstanding, each common share is worth $10. If the portfolio increases in value by 10 per cent to $11 million, the value of each of the investment company's common shares is worth $11. This company has no leverage.

Now let us assume an investment company has portfolio securities worth $10 million, and capital composed of a bank loan for $5 million and 500,000 common stock shares. Each common stock share is worth $10, allowing for the $5 million of borrowed money.

If the value of the portfolio securities should go from $10 million to $11 million, however, the common stock shares would be worth not $11, as in the case without leverage, but would be worth $12

($11 million minus $5 million owed leaves $6 million for the 500,000 shares of common stock). Leverage also works in reverse, of course, in market breaks.

OPEN-END (MUTUAL FUND) COMPANIES

Open-end investment companies are relatively new to the financial scene. The first of this type was formed in 1924. The open-end investment company has only one class of securities, common stocks, but they have an unlimited capitalization. This basic feature of continuous offering of shares is one of the salient factors in the steady growth of open-end companies.

Investors buying or selling shares go, in effect, to the company sponsor, which will sell shares to them or buy shares back at prices directly reflecting the asset value of the securities held in the portfolio. To the asset value, for most open-end companies, a charge of 7.5 to 8.5 per cent of the total offering price is added, to cover all costs of distribution. On redemption, the company pays investors the asset value of each share.

Prices of mutual funds are usually computed twice daily and published in the financial sections of most newspapers. And at any time, of course, prices are available from securities dealers or from the mutual funds themselves. Prospectuses and supplementary literature describing individual mutual funds are readily available from distributors.

INVESTMENT COMPANY DISTRIBUTION

Investment companies may make two types of payments to the shareholder. One is called an *investment income dividend* which is derived from the dividends earned on the corporate securities the investment company owns. Usually investment income dividends are paid four times a year.

The other type of payment is called a *capital gains distribution*. Such payments are net profits on the sale of portfolio securities by the investment companies and are distributed to shareholders. The two sources of payments to shareholders are clearly delineated and it is important that they are. For federal tax purposes, of course, investment income dividends are taxed at regular income rates and capital gains at the capital gains rate. But more important is the fact that one source—investment income—represents what investors' capital has earned, while the other—capital gains distribution—is a return of part of capital and, in effect, represents a reduction in the amount of capital invested.

Additional investor services are available in connection with both closed-end and open-end investment companies. For example, closed-end investment company shares are one of the most popular types of security in the New York Stock Exchange's Monthly Investment Plan, which permits an individual to purchase as little as $40 worth of listed stock each month or quarter.

Open-end companies have special services such as accumulation plans, under which individuals may invest $25, $50, or more on a regular monthly or quarterly basis. Investors may also avail themselves of automatic dividend reinvestment plans, which provide that all distributions by the investment company are automatically reinvested in additional shares.

Many open-end companies provide an automatic withdrawal plan whereby a shareholder may withdraw a specified dollar amount at monthly or quarterly intervals. Exchange privileges between companies under the same sponsorship are often available without recurrence of a sales charge. Services to the self-employed person who wishes to take advantage of the tax-saving features of the Self-Employed Individuals Tax Retirement Act of 1962 are also provided by many open-end companies.

In summary, investment companies are built upon the cardinal principles of broad diversification and full-time professional management and the convenience of a ready market for open-end share purchases and redemptions.

9

~~~~~~

THE BOND MARKET

BONDS ARE LISTED AND TRADED ON THE VARIOUS SE-
curity exchanges and are also active in the unlisted, or over-the-
counter (OTC), market.

Bonds are receipts for loans made to corporations or governments.
They are obligations of the debtor and differ from stocks in that the
latter represent ownership of the issuing corporation. Bondholders
have no voice in the management of enterprises to which they loaned
money, as long as the loan service and other provisions of the mortgage or bond indenture are met; but if any infraction occurs, the
senior nature of bonds becomes apparent in the right of the holders
to take possession of the property securing the loan.

Investors who desire safety and a definite return on their capital
look to the bond market rather than to preferred or common stocks.
This does not mean that all bonds are sounder than any stocks, for
the financial pages record many instances of bankruptcy and heavy
losses for bondholders, while defaults by government units also are
frequent. As a rule, however, bonds are sounder and have a more
stable market.

As bonds represent a debt of the issuer, usually a corporation, and do not represent equity ownership of the corporation, they are considered a poorer hedge against inflation than stocks, real estate, or other equity property. The face value of a bond is a definite stated amount of dollars. That is what is due the lender or bondholder at maturity. The interest is also a definite and stated amount. Neither is a share in the profits. There are various types of bonds:

Municipals —Declines For Month

The municipal-bond market has had a month-long decline in prices but there is still little evidence that a bottom has been reached.

As in any free market, the encouraging factor in the market for tax-exempts is the price decline itself. Over the last four weeks, as measured by the Bond Buyer's 20-bond index, yields have risen 14 basic points to 3.27 per cent, the highest since early last December, and only a few points below the highest yield available in 1963.

On the other hand, investors have not been overly eager to snap up offerings, except for the so-called specialty issues. A case in point is the attractive yields of 4 and 4.10 per cent on last week's issue of $135 million Jacksonville Expressway revenue bonds.

Underlying some hesitancy on the part of institutional portfolio managers is the fundamental question of the trend of interest rates. There is general agreement, although not unanimous, that rates later this year will be higher.

In the meantime, it appears institutional investors will continue to be selective, sighting their demands on particular forthcoming issues.

Today's sale of $50 million Tacoma, Wash., light and power revenue and refunding bonds, for example, is a yield situation.

Also, there are the $141.36 million of Public Housing Authority bonds due the first of April, followed a week later by an offering of $93 million New York State Housing Finance Authority revenue bonds.

Not that high-rated general obligations are out of favor. Rather, they entail a longer process of marketing. Last week's $50 million State of Connecticut triple-A rated highway bonds got off slowly on initial sales, but continue to move steadily. The balance is $23,985,000, down 300 bonds yesterday.

MUNICIPAL BONDS—The term involves far more than bonds that are issued by municipalities. It applies in a broad sense to obligations of cities, townships, villages, states, local government agencies, port authorities, toll pike authorities, and various local government agencies that may be responsible for the building and maintaining of such widely differing public services as schools, highways, bridges and tunnels, power plants, water plants, sewerage disposal, in fact anything that is considered by voters to be an essential service which they feel can be better administered by a public body than by a corporation of individual stockholders.

Interest paid to holders of municipal bonds is exempt from federal income taxes. In many cases interest is exempt from state taxes as well, if the bond is held by a resident of the community benefited by the bond issue. Thus, municipals have a high rating among investors. The investor can afford to accept the low yield usually available on municipals because the tax exemption makes such a bond worth more net to him than an industrial bond, with its higher—but fully taxable—coupon. This appeals especially to an investor in a high income tax bracket.

The fact that a specific municipal bond is tax exempt is not a guarantee that the bond is a sound investment. Payment of interest, and of principal on maturity, depends upon the faith of the issuer, which in turn is dependent upon tax collections, highway tolls, assessments on the use of a sewer system, or charges for power from a municipally owned power plant or other public facility.

In most cases municipal bonds have a maturity date some twenty to twenty-five years from the date of their offering to the public. In size they usually range all the way from a million dollars or two up to several hundred million dollars, which is typical of big state issues. There is an active bid and asked market in these securities, even though original investors are far more likely to stay with their investment to maturity than are original investors in industrial bonds.

COUPON AND REGISTERED BONDS—A coupon bond is payable to the bearer. Attached to it are coupons stating the amount of interest due at the various specific interest dates. These may be clipped from the bond on the dates specified and the coupon presented to one's bank for collection from the debtor.

Coupon bonds are widely used by both corporate issuers and also by federal, state, and local governments. At the end of 1962 about 90 per cent of the estimated $400 billion in bonds of corporations and government units outstanding was estimated to be in bearer (coupon) form.

A registered bond has the owner's name printed on its face, and it cannot be negotiated except by transfer and endorsement on the books of the issuer. There are no coupons attached, except in a few rare cases where a bond is registered with respect to the principal only. If registered with respect to both interest and principal, which is the usual form of a registered bond, the issuer must care for the disbursements of interest checks at periodic intervals and also for the check due on the maturity of the bond.

Thus it is less expensive for the issuer to have his outstanding bonds in bearer (coupon) form. He does not, indeed could not, keep a record of the names and addresses of those holding his bonds. The banks take care of the tedious task of disbursing the interest, and they usually do it free, as a service to their depositors.

The bulk of the federal debt is in coupon form, the chief exception being some $50 billion in U.S. savings bonds. Consequently the Treasury is among those favoring a continuation of the present preference for coupon bonds over registered bonds. Most underwriters agree with the Treasury, both feeling that a major swing to registered bonds would increase costs to the issuer and hence necessitate the sale of the bonds to the investor at a slightly higher price.

There is a strong movement, however, to have fixed-interest securities of corporations and governments replaced increasingly by registered bonds. The drive is being led by a group within the American Bankers Association. This influential association of commercial and savings bankers contends that it costs institutional holders of bonds at least $2 million a year to clip and care for a year's crop of coupons.

They also contend that as the investor's name and address would be on the books of the issuing corporation, the bondholder would automatically receive notices that might be of vital interest to him with respect to his investment.

A third point is that the Internal Revenue Service would have less trouble tracing interest payments made by checks from a governmental unit or corporation than is now experienced in tracing payments made by banks on the presentation of coupons. The American Bankers Association estimates there are 283 million so presented at banks annually.

Irrespective of the difference between coupon and registered bonds, there are other differences that revolve chiefly around the security that is behind a particular bond. Brief descriptions of various types of debt obligations follow:

ADJUSTMENT BOND—Similar in many respects to income bonds, these are usually issued in a reorganization to bring several bond issues of a corporation into one class, at a uniform rate. They have been used frequently by reorganized railroads. They have a stated par value and maturity date, but differ from income bonds in that they are usually secured by a mortgage. Interest on such bonds is payable only when earned and declared by directors, the same as with income bonds. Thus they rate low in the matter of security and whether they can be refunded at maturity depends upon the financial health of the corporation.

CERTIFICATES OF INDEBTEDNESS—These are unsecured short-term notes with a maturity no longer than a year. They are issued mainly by the governments.

COLLATERAL TRUST BOND—This is secured by collateral such as other bonds, notes, or stocks.

CONVERTIBLE BOND—This bond carries the privilege of transferring the debt into an equity at stated relative values within specified periods of time, at the will of the holder.

DEBENTURE BOND—Ordinarily this represents an unsecured corporate obligation. It is backed by the general assets and credit of the issuer and not by a specific mortgage.

DISCOUNT BILLS—Also unsecured, these are short-term obligations sold by the government at competitive bidding. Currently they are ninety-one-day paper, and are sold by the United States Treasury every Monday. Newspapers carry a story each Tuesday morning about such sales, as the rate is a sensitive one and is used as an indicator of conditions in the money market. These bills do not carry a regular interest rate but they are sold at a discount below par. The amount of this discount thus represents the return that will accrue to the holder at maturity.

EQUIPMENT TRUST CERTIFICATES—These represent loans made to a railroad for specific rolling stock or other equipment. The trustee for the equipment trust, normally an investment banking firm, owns the rolling stock but leases it back to the railroad at a stipulated rental. Usually such issues run ten to fifteen years, and title to the equipment does not pass to the railroad until the trust certificates have been fully liquidated. Normally equipment trust certificates run serially so that small amounts are retired each year as the equipment becomes more obsolete and thus represents less security for the loan.

INCOME BOND—Usually these are issued in reorganizations when there has been a default on mortgage bonds. The company may or may not have gone bankrupt, but it has changed its capital structure. These bonds are issued to holders of the defaulted mortgage bonds. Interest on them is contingent upon earnings, and they are not secured by a mortgage. Failure to pay interest, assuming it is not earned, does not entitle the holder of an income bond to sue the corporation. This interest may be cumulative or noncumulative.

MORTGAGE BOND—This is a bond secured by a mortgage on a specific property. Bondholders may sell this property to satisfy the debt if interest or principal is defaulted.

NOTE—This is similar to a bond except that it covers a loan for a relatively short term, less than five years. It is usually unsecured.

SERIAL BOND—This is payable in installments. For instance, there might be a $10 million bond issue, one-tenth of which matures every year.

TAX EXEMPT BOND—This is exempt from federal and/or state

taxes, either in whole or in part. Such bonds consist largely of issues of state and local governments and various authorities, such as bridge, tunnel, and turnpike authorities.

TRADING IN BONDS

All bonds carry a definite interest rate, and with the exception of some state and municipal warrants, they also have a specified maturity. They are issued mostly in denominations of $1,000 par value, but could be available in "pieces" of $500, $100, and even $50. In many instances bonds may be available in $5,000 and $10,000 pieces, while some forms of United States government obligations are obtainable in $100,000 and $1,000,000 pieces.

For purposes of valuation in newspapers they are quoted in percentages of par value, and not in the amount of dollars per unit, as in the case of stocks. Thus a $1,000 United States government bond quoted at 99 sells for $990, while a $1,000 Greek government bond quoted at 38 sells for $380.

When an investor buys an interest-paying bond he pays the price agreed upon, plus accumulated interest from the last coupon payment date. When the loan is in default, or some doubt exists as to payment of the next coupon due, the bond is traded in "flat," or without adjustment for accumulated interest. As it is important for the investor to know on what basis he is buying a bond, newspapers designate whether an issue is dealt in "flat," and also when such bonds are quoted ex-interest.

In quoting bonds the issues are divided into United States government obligations, those of foreign governments and corporations, and those of domestic corporations. Virtually all the trading in United States government issues is done over the counter.

BOND QUOTATIONS

United States government bonds are quoted in a slightly different manner from other bonds, because fluctuations are narrower. Whereas movements in other bonds are measured in eighths of a point, United States Treasury obligations vary by thirty-seconds of a point. Thus, a Federal Land Bank bond quoted at 97.22 is selling at $97^{22}/_{32}$ per cent of par, or $976.87½.

Investors who are interested mainly in the highest grades of bonds care more about yields than about dollar prices. In the tables of over-the-counter market quotations, New York State bonds are quoted on the basis of yields.

DETERMINING BOND YIELDS

The yield on a bond is the net result of a tedious computation taking into account the maturity date at which the obligation is repayable at par value, the immediate market price, the coupon or interest rate, the proportion of future interest payments allocable to any deviation from par at the moment, and the reinvestment value of coupons remaining on the bond at the date of purchase. In American practice the reinvestment value of coupons is computed on an annual basis, although payments of interest almost always are made semiannually. In European practice the precise semiannual basis is used. Ponderous "tables of bond values," requiring years of calculation on the part of the compilers, are used to arrive at the final results quickly.

Interest rates on senior securities necessarily are set when the loan is made, but subsequent money market and other developments may change materially the actual rate of return available on previously issued bonds. The coupon rate cannot be changed to conform to the new conditions, and the market therefore reflects the alterations by price changes. It is at this point that "yield" enters.

To illustrate, a corporate 4 per cent bond due in one year may be so valued in the market as to afford the purchaser of the moment a yield of only 3 per cent, and the price accordingly is 101. Contrary tendencies, indicating a yield of 5 per cent on the same bond, would be expressed in a price of 99. These are rough figures, accurate only under American practice for the short maturity mentioned. On longer-term loans the factors relating to reinvested interest and other values become increasingly important, and they cause even greater variations from the "farmer's method" results of the rough illustration. In American practice, again, sinking fund drawings are not included in the tabulations, although they may result in redemption of a good part of an issue prior to maturity.

MONEY MARKET OBLIGATIONS

Highest-grade bonds, in which the element of risk is small or nonexistent, vary in dollar prices chiefly in accordance with money market changes. They frequently are referred to as money market obligations, or as selling on a money basis. If the cost of money is cheap and the United States government, for instance, is able to borrow on long term at 2.5 per cent, then previously issued 4 per cent bonds of the Treasury also will tend to sell at a yield close to 2.5 per cent, or at a dollar price considerably above par value.

Conversely, a period of high money costs is likely to result in relatively low quotations for previously issued low-coupon bonds, other things being equal. The element of risk enters into bond values in varying degrees, and as a risk increases the values are apt to represent to an even greater degree a speculative judgment of capacity or willingness to pay. The yield, in such instances, is of relatively modest importance.

Much information is printed day by day regarding new bond issues and bonds called or drawn for redemption and retirement. Instances of default also are recorded. The investor who follows the news carefully thus has at hand a fairly complete survey of developments of the most importance to him.

The financial section does not stop with a mere tabulation of transactions and a brief discussion of fluctuations. In the field of bond investments an effort is made to bring to investors and to the many individuals dealing in these securities the latest information regarding their holdings. Special articles are published frequently, discussing in detail various phases of bond financing. While such articles are written more for the technician than the casual reader, they are couched in terms which make it possible for the student of finance to follow accurately the major developments in financing operations throughout the country.

Government, Agency, World Bank Bonds

Bonds and Notes

Rate	Maturity	Bid	Asked	Net chge	Yield
1½	4- 1-'64-N	99.27	99.31	—	2.94
4¾	5-15-'64-N	100.7	100.9	—	2.98
3¾	5-15-'64-N	100.2	100.4	—	2.99
5	8-15-'64-N	100.17	100.19	—	3.57
3¾	8-15-'64-N	100.1	100.3	—	3.52
1½	10- 1-'64-N	99.1	99.3	—	3.17
4⅞	11-15-'64-N	100.24	100.26	—	3.64
3¾	11-15-'64-N	100.	100.2	—	3.66
2⅝	2-15-'65	99.2	99.4	—	3.58
1½	4- 1-'65-N	98.2	98.6	—	3.27
4⅝	5-15-'65-N	100.24	100.26	—	3.91
3⅞	5-15-'65-N	99.28	99.30	—.1	3.93
3⅞	8-13-'65-N	99.27	99.29	—.1	3.94
1½	10- 1-'65-N	97.2	97.10	—.1	3.29
3½	11-15-'65-N	99.5	99.7	—.1	3.99
3⅝	2-15-'66-N	99.6	99.8	—.1	4.03
1½	4- 1-'66-N	95.3	95.6	—.3	3.44
3¾	5-15-'66	99.14	99.16	—	3.99
3	8-15-'66	97.27	97.31	—.1	3.88
4	[illegible]-N	99.28	99.30	—.1	4.03
1½	10- 1-'66-N	95.	95.8	—.2	3.46
3⅜	11-15-'66	98.14	98.16	—.1	3.97
3⅝	2-15-'67-N	98.22	98.24	—.1	4.08
1½	4- 1-'67-N	93.28	94.	—.4	3.55
2½	6-15-'62-'67	95.26	95.29	—.3	3.85
3¾	8-15-'67-N	98.26	98.30	—.1	4.09
1½	10- 1-'67-N	92.26	93.2	—.2	3.60
3⅝	11-15-'67	98.12	98.14	—.1	4.09
1½	4- 1-'68-N	91.26	92.	—.2	3.62
3⅞	5-15-'68	99.4	99.8	—.2	4.07
3¾	8-15-'68	98.12	98.16	—.1	4.12
1½	10- 1-'68-N	90.27	91.3	—.1	3.64
3⅞	11-15-'68	98.26	98.28	—.1	4.14
2½	12-15-'63-'68	93.19	93.25	—.3	3.95
4	2-15-'69	99.17	99.21	—.3	4.08
2½	6-15-'64-'69	92.19	92.25	—.1	4.04
4	10- 1-'69	99.18	99.22	—.3	4.07
2½	12-15-'64-'69	91.31	92.5	—.2	4.04
2½	3-15-'65-'70	91.18	91.22	—.2	4.08
4	8-15-'70	99.	99.4	—.2	4.16
2½	3-15-'66-'71	90.17	90.21	—.2	4.05
4	8-15-'71	98.26	98.30	—.3	4.17
3⅞	11-15-'71	97.26	97.30	—.3	4.19

2,500	4-15-'64	3.51	3.47	+.01	3.53
2,100	4-16-'64	3.51	3.48	+.01	3.54
2,100	4-23-'64	3.51	3.48	+.01	3.54
2,100	4-30-'64	3.49	3.45	—.01	3.51
2,100	5- 7-'64	3.52	3.49	+.01	3.56
2,100	5-14-'64	3.52	3.49	—	3.56
2,000	5-21-'64	3.52	3.49	—	3.56
2,000	5-28-'64	3.54	3.50	+.01	3.58
2,100	6- 4-'64	3.55	3.52	+.01	3.60
2,100	6-11-'64	3.56	3.53	+.01	3.61
800	6-18-'64	3.53	3.48	—	3.56
2,500	6-22-'64-TA	3.50	3.47	+.01	3.55
800	6-25-'64	3.52	3.48	—	3.56
800	7- 2-'64	3.58	3.53	+.01	3.62
800	7- 9-'64	3.60	3.55	+.01	3.64
2,000	7-15-'64	3.64	3.60	+.01	3.70
800	7-16-'64	3.65	3.61	—	3.71
800	7-23-'64	3.67	3.63	+.01	3.73
800	7-30-'64	3.68	3.64	—	3.74
900	8- 6-'64	3.71	3.67	—	3.78
900	8-13-'64	3.71	3.67	+.01	3.78
900	8-20-'64	3.71	3.67	+.01	3.78
900	8-27-'64	3.72	3.68	+.01	3.80
1,000	8-31-'64	3.71	3.67	—	3.79
900	9- 3-'64	3.72	3.70	+.01	3.82
900	9-10-'64	3.74	3.71	+.01	3.83
1,000	9-30-'64	3.70	3.66	—	3.78
1,000	10-31-'64	3.71	3.68	—	3.81
1,000	11-30-'64	3.73	3.70	—	3.83
1,000	12-31-'64	3.73	3.69	+.01	3.83
1,000	1-31-'65	3.76	3.74	—	3.89
1,000	2-28-'65	3.78	3.76	—	3.92

Certificates of Indebtedness

Rate	Maturity	Bid	Asked	Net Chge	Yield
3¼	5-15-'64	99.31	100.1	—	2.95

Fed. Intermed. Cred. Bk. Debs.

Oustanding (Mils)	Rate	Maturity	Bid	Asked	Yield
232	3.45	4- 1-'64	99.31	100.	3.37
223	3.65	5- 4-'64	99.31	100.	3.57
197	3¾	6- 1-'64	99.30	99.31	3.75
188	3⅞	7- 1-'64	99.31	100.	3.81
178	3⅞	8- 3-'64	99.30	99.31	3.86
203	3.95	9- 1-'64	99.31	100.	3.88

108	3¾	3-10-'66	99.10	99.14	4.05
93	4⅛	12-12-'66	99.30	100.6	4.05
87	3⅝	3-11-'68	97.24	98.8	4.10
88	4⅝	4-10-'69	100.24	101.8	4.18
146	4⅝	4-10-'70	101.28	102.12	4.17
119	4⅛	9-10-'70	99.4	99.20	4.19
63	4⅛	8-10-'71	99.	99.16	4.20
98	4½	9-10-'71	101.12	101.28	4.20
100	5⅛	2-10-'72	105.16	106.	4.22
100	4⅝	6-12-'72	100.16	101.	4.23
146	4¼	6-12-'73	99.16	100.	4.25
198	4½	2-10-'77	101.16	102.	4.30

Bank for Cooperatives

Outstanding (Mils)	Rate	Maturity	Bid	Asked	Yield
192	3.80	4- 1-'64	99.31	100.	3.43
196	3⅞	6- 1-'64	100.	100.1	3.69
200	3.90	8- 3-'64	99.31	100.	3.88

Federal Land Bank Bonds

Outstanding (Mils)	Rate	Maturity	Bid	Asked	Yield
147	4½	4-20-'64	100.2	100.4	3.22
215	3⅞	8-20-'64	99.30	99.31	3.90
142	4	10-20-'64	100.	100.2	3.89
160	4	10-20-'65	99.30	100.2	3.96
115	4	12-20-'65	99.30	100.2	3.96
150	3⅝	2-21-'66	98.30	99.6	4.06
108	3¼	5- 2-'66	98.6	98.14	4.02
193	4¼	7-20-'66	100.4	100.12	4.08
180	4	5-22-'67	99.14	99.22	4.10
174	4⅛	10-23-'67	99.28	100.	4.12
86	4¼	3-20-'68	100.2	100.10	4.16
186	4	6-20-'68	99.10	99.18	4.11
100	4⅜	3-20-'69	100.20	101.4	4.13
60	4⅝	7-15-'69	101.24	102.8	4.15
82	5⅛	2-20-'70	104.16	105.	4.17
83	3½	4- 1-'70	95.28	96.12	4.38
85	5⅛	7-20-'70	104.16	105.	4.22
75	4½	10- 1-'70-'67	100.24	101.8	4.12
60	3½	5- 1-'71	95.	95.16	4.24
72	4⅛	2-15-'72-'67	99.20	100.4	4.08
110	3⅞	9-15-'72	97.	97.16	4.23
155	4½	2-20-'74	101.16	102.	4.25
148	4⅛	2-20-'78-'73	98.16	99.	4.22

Tennessee Valley Authority

Outstanding

Bond Sales on New York Stock Exchange

New York City Bonds

1963-'64 High	1963-'64 Low	Bonds	Sales in $1,000s	High	Low	Close	Net chg
99.28	97.9	3s 80	13	98.10	98.2	98.10+	.8

Figures after decimal are 32nds of a point.

Domestic Bonds

1963-'64 High	1963-'64 Low	Bonds	Sales in $1,000s	High	Low	Close	Net chg
110⅞	101½	Air Red cv3⅞s87	10	108¾	108¾	108¾	+ ¾
140½	111	Aldens cv 5s80	25	132	132	132	+ ½
95	91½	Allied Ch 3½s78	5	91⅞	91⅞	91⅞	.....
106⅞	101	Allied St cv4½s81	35	107	106¾	107	+ ⅛
101⅞	98½	Alcoa 4¼s 82	11	99⅞	99⅞	99⅞	.....
90	86⅝	Alcoa 3s 79	50	87½	87⅜	87⅜	.....
100	99	Alum Can 3⅞s70	1	99¼	99¼	99¼	.....
106	103½	Am Can 4¾s90	2	103¾	103¾	103¾	.....
78	65	Am FP 5s2030	12	73½	73	73⅜	.....
75¾	63	Am FP 4.80s87	12	72½	72⅛	72⅛	+ ⅛
98	88¾	AmMchF cv4¼s81	102	89¾	88¾	89¼	— ¾
142	121½	Am Opt cv4.40s80	1	128	128	128	.....
108	104½	Am Sug 5.30s93	2	105⅝	105⅝	105⅝	.....
103⅞	99⅛	Am T&T 4⅜s85	103	100⅝	100¼	100⅜	— ½
403	313	Am T&T cv4¼s73	3	386	384	386	+2
96	91	Am T&T 3⅞s90	16	92¼	91¾	92¼	+ ¾
95⅝	91	Am T&T 3⅜s73	6	92¼	92⅛	92⅛	.....
87½	83⅜	Am T&T 3¼s84	15	84¼	84⅛	84⅛	.....
91¾	89¾	Am T&T 2¾s71	1	90¼	90¼	90¼	.....
88¼	83¼	Am T&T 2¾s75	3	85	84¾	84¾	.....
83	79⅝	Am T&T 2¾s80	9	80¼	80	80⅛	— ½
98½	96	Am To b3s69	22	97¾	97½	97¾	+ ¼
70¾	63¼	Ann Arb 4s95	1	68	68	68	+1
99¾	91½	Armour 5s 84f	34	99	98¾	98¾	— ½
117¾	103	Armour cv 4½s83	72	117	116	116⅞	— ⅛
120	101⅝	Ashl Oil cv3⅞s93	450	121½	118½	121½	+3½
96⅞	92¼	Atchison 4s 95	5	92¾	92¾	92¾	.....
102[illegible]	99½	Atl CsL 4½s64	6	100¼	100¼	100¼	— 1/32
118⅞	109¼	Atl Ref cv4½s87	39	112	111¼	111¼	— ¼
[illegible]	95	AutoCan cv4¾s81	10	98	98	98	.....

Wednesday, March 11, 1964

	Wednesday	Tuesday	Year ago	Jan 1 to date 1964	Jan 1 to date 1963	Jan 1 to date 1962
U. S. Gov't bonds	—	—	—	—	—	—
Railroad bonds	$1,530,000	$1,430,000	$1,320,000	$80,375,000	$89,150 000	$68,280,000
Other bonds	8,220,000	8,270,000	3,061,000	514,663,400	175,691,200	220,928,000
All bonds	9,750,000	9,700,000	4,381,000	595,038,400	264,841,200	289 208,000

1963-'64 High	1963-'64 Low	Bonds	Sales in $1,000s	High	Low	Close	Net chg
114	93¼	Fansteel cv4¾s76	3	97	96¼	96¼	— ¾
92½	90	Firestone 3¼s 77	1	90½	90½	90½	— ½
108½	102	Flintkt cv 4½s80	1	107½	107½	107½	—1
59½	30⅝	FlaEC cv5½s2011f	25	57⅞	57	57⅞	+ ¾
79	70⅛	Fla ECst 5s2011	4	76	76	76	+ ⅜
101	92½	Food Fair cv4s79	17	93½	92¾	92¾	.....
184¾	128	GardDen cv4¼s76	2	185	185	185	+ ¼
105⅛	101	Gen Cig 5½s87	1	103	103	103	— ½
96	92	Gen Elec 3½s76	7	93⅝	93⅜	93⅝	+ ½
107	104½	GMot Acc 5s77	7	105	104½	105	.....
107	102⅞	GMot Acc 5s80	22	104	103½	104	+ ⅜
107¼	104⅛	GMot Acc 5s81	8	104	104	104	— ¾
104⅝	100⅜	GMot Acc 4⅝s82	10	102⅜	102⅛	102⅜	— ¼
104½	100⅝	GMot Acc 4⅝s83	1	102⅛	102⅛	102⅛	— ⅜
101⅝	99	GMot Acc 4½s85	137	100⅜	100⅛	100⅛	— ⅛
98⅞	93	GMot Acc 4s79	56	95⅜	94⅞	95⅛	.....
95¾	91¾	GMot Acc 3⅝s75	14	92⅝	92⅛	92⅝	.....
96	92½	GMot Acc 3½s72	10	93⅜	93⅜	93⅜	.....
96⅝	92	GMot Acc 3s69	33	93¾	93½	93¾	— ⅛
101¾	98½	GMot Acc 2¾s64					
			2645	100⅜	100 5-32	100 3-16	—7-32
208¾	148¼	Gen Tel cv4½s77	36	200¼	198	200	+2
203½	144	Gen Tel cv4s71	81	196	195	196	+1
100½	87	G Time cv4¾s79	3	94	94	94	—1
105¼	102⅛	Goodrich 4⅝s 85	6	103¼	103¼	103¼	— ¾
100½	97½	Goodrich 2¾s 65	8	98¾	98⅝	98⅝	— ⅜
220⅛	153½	Grace cv 3½s75	11	213	212	212	+ ¼
106	95	GrandUn cv4⅛s78	21	102⅞	102½	102½	+1½
107½	104¾	Gt NorRy 5s73	1	105¼	105¼	105¼	+ ¼
103⅝	99⅞	Gt NoRy 4½s76	10	100	99⅞	99⅞	— ⅛
182½	131½	Gt WFin cv5s74	175	151½	150	150⅛	+1⅛

1963-'64 High	1963-'64 Low	Bonds	Sales in $1,000s	High	Low	Close	Net chg
89¼	85½	Pen Pw&Lt 3s75	1	87⅛	87⅛	87⅛	+ ⅛
101⅞	100	Pen RR 4½s65	27	100¾	100½	100½	.....
90	74½	Pen RR 4¼s81	1	89	89	89	....
89	74	Pen RR 4¼s84	7	87	87	87	.....
69½	59	Pen RR 3⅛s85	4	68	67⅞	68	—1
103⅛	99	Phila BW 5s74	1	101½	101½	101½	+1½
104¼	101	Phila El 4⅝s87	2	102½	102½	102½	.....
90¾	88½	Phila El 2¾s71	3	88⅞	88⅞	88⅞	+ ¼
119½	110	PhillipsP cv4¼s87	65	113	112¼	112¾	— ¼
101½	94	PCC & SL 5s70	3	101¼	101¼	101¼	— ⅛
100⅝	91⅛	PCC & SL 5s75	3	99½	99½	99½	.....
58⅝	45	Readg 3⅛s 95	10	58½	58½	58½	— ⅛
143	122	Richfld cv 4⅜s83	25	136½	135½	135½	— ½
113	104	Rohr A cv5¼s77	12	109⅞	109⅞	109⅞	— ⅛
107½	102	RoyMcB cv6¼s77	5	106¾	106¾	106¾	+ ¼
146½	108½	Ryder S cv5¼s83	26	145	142½	143	.....
86	69¼	StL SF 5s2006f	29	86⅛	85¼	85⅛	+ ⅜
93½	74	StLSF cv4½s2022f	21	93½	92¾	92¾	— ¼
84	76½	StL SF 4s 97	6	83⅝	83⅝	83⅝	.....
105¾	103⅜	Sears R 4¾s83	10	104⅛	104	104	+ ½
90½	88⅝	Shell Un 2½s71	50	89¼	89¼	89¼	+ ¼
103	101¾	Sinclair 4.60s 88	2	101⅝	101⅝	101⅝	— ¼
105⅜	100½	Sinclair cv 4⅜s86	23	102⅞	102½	102¾	....
123½	96	Smith C cv5¼s79	38	121	118½	118½	—2
85½	82⅝	Socony 2½s 76	2	83¾	83¾	83¾	.....
86¾	82	SoBell TT 3s79	10	83⅞	83⅞	83⅞	+ ⅝
79½	77½	SoBell TT 2⅞s87	5	77¾	77¾	77¾	.....
107	103½	So Pac 5¼s83	5	105¼	105¼	105¼	+ ⅝
100	95	So Pac 4½s81	5	96	95¾	95¾	— 1
101½	98¼	So Pac Or 4½s77	13	99¾	99	99	...
108	104½	South Ry 5s94	9	105½	105¼	105¼	—

The subjects treated cover a wide range and include legislative measures in any country that may affect the issuance of new securities or the values of those currently outstanding. Measures of our federal administration may prove of peculiar significance to investors and careful attention is paid to such developments. Tax collections in our cities bear closely on values of municipal securities, and they are reported and analyzed. Defaults and the prospects of resumption of payment in the case of government issues, or reorganization in the case of corporate loans, comprise another large division of bond reporting.

10

GOVERNMENT FINANCES

FOR THE STUDENT OF ECONOMIC AFFAIRS, A CONTINU-
ing attention to the federal budget and the federal debt is indispen-
sable. The figures are sufficiently impressive by themselves. They
gain added significance as measures of the rapidly rising importance
of United States government activities in virtually all spheres and of
the impingement of such activities upon all private business and
financial doings.

The economic area in which the federal government operates has
expanded sharply in recent decades, and taxes, of course, also have
increased. Activities that formerly were conducted on a private basis
have been invaded progressively by government. Social services have
increased in extent and ramifications, and the permanent army of
civil servants has mounted. All this has a profound impact on ordinary business affairs.

Owing to the depression of the 1930s, a vastly important change
developed in the handling of the federal budget and debt. In re-
sponse to the theories of the British economist Lord Keynes, who
held that oversavings are an important factor in the business cycle,
the notion of a "compensating budget" took hold, for good or ill.
This theory, which has not worked well in practice in other countries,
calls for enlarged spending and deficit financing by the central gov-

ernment in times of depression, and debt retirement in times of prosperity. The enlarged spending has so far been found easy; the retrenchment another matter. It has met with more success in the United States so far and has been defended by presidents Eisenhower and Kennedy and their Councils of Economic Advisers as a built-in stabilizer.

Overshadowing all other aspects of government finance, however, have been the world wars. These conflicts, like three preceding great wars in which this country engaged, occasioned vast advances in budgets and debts, and brought widespread inflation in their trains. Effects of the three preceding wars left few economic traces, but those of the world wars promise to be with us for many years to come.

In the years immediately before our involvement in World War I, the federal budget ranged around the annual level of $750 million and was, by and large, in balance. The federal debt was about $1.2 billion and was kept in existence mainly as an instrument fostering the circulating medium.

War is an expensive activity; in the years 1917–1919 the federal outlay mounted rapidly. It reached $18.5 billion in 1919, and only a relatively small part was covered by taxation. The federal debt rose to a peak of $26,956 million in August 1919, but was whittled down steadily in the subsequent eleven years, during which outlays were reduced to the $3 billion level for other purposes although income ranged around the $4 billion figure. The lowest debt figure between the two wars was $16,026 million, recorded on December 31, 1930.

From that point on, deficit financing as a means of combating depression influences took place on an enormous scale. Federal outlays mounted to the $9 billion annual level in the years preceding the second world war. Our defense preparations added to the deficit, and on June 30, 1941, the federal debt totaled $48,961 million.

In World War II the federal budget expanded until expenditures topped the $100 billion level in 1945. Total outlays of the government in the five fiscal years from July 1, 1941, to June 30, 1946, were $370 billion. From current tax receipts the government met $169 billion, or 46 per cent. The balance of $201 billion was met by borrowing. The borrowing was effected in eight huge war loan drives, during which securities were offered that were suitable for every type of investor. As a direct stimulus to our expanding wartime economy, $5 billion of Treasury securities were sold directly to commercial banks in each of the first two drives.

Some borrowing in excess of requirements was done during the war years, and this surplus was utilized in 1946 and 1947 for reduction of the debt. An excess of cash receipts over expenditures also developed after the war, and the excess likewise was applied to debt retirement. Thus, the federal debt attained a peak of $279,764 million on February 28, 1946, and in the subsequent eighteen months it fell to about $259 billion. That financial heritage of the wars and the interim deficit financing are of vast importance.

One respect in which the debt is of lasting consequence concerns the manner in which the sum was raised. Actual Treasury borrowings in the five-year period were $214 billion, of which $128 billion was placed with institutional, corporate, and private investors. Commercial banks absorbed $64 billion, and the Federal Reserve banks bought $22 billion. The placements within the banking system were inflationary.

A second important effect of the debt was the estimated $7.3 billion of annual interest requirements, which constituted a first charge in the postwar budgets. In the realization that the war would prove costly, the Treasury and the Federal Reserve banks made it clear in 1942 that Treasury borrowing would be done on a scale from ⅜ per cent for three-month bills to 2½ per cent for long-term marketable bonds. These were then the current market rates, which were historically low because of the depression of the thirties and the massive flight of capital from Europe to the United States during those prewar years. Some borrowing also was done through Series E savings bonds, which are not marketable, at a cost of 2.90 per cent if the bonds were held for their full ten-year term. The rate was raised to 3¼ per cent in 1957, and to 3¾ per cent in June 1959 while the maturity period was shortened to 7 years and 9 months.

Sales of Savings Bonds Rise 9.8%

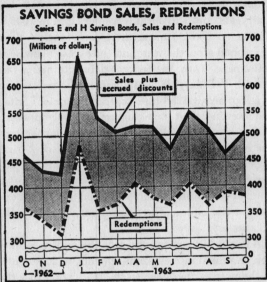

SAVINGS BOND SALES, REDEMPTIONS

Series E and H Savings Bonds, Sales and Redemptions

(Millions of dollars)

Sales plus accrued discounts

Redemptions

—1962— 1963

The New York Times   Nov. 6, 1963

October E and H bond sales plus accrued interest were $503,000,000. Redemptions advanced to $382,000,000.

Sales of United States savings bonds rose 9.8 per cent in October from the 1962 level, the Treasury Department reported yesterday.

Cash sales of Series E and and H bonds came to $395,000,000 last month, up from $360,000,000 in the 1962 period. Such sales totaled $347,000,000 in September of this year.

In addition, accrued interest on outstanding E bonds in October came to $109,000,000, compared with $107,000,000 in the 1962 month andc $114,000,000 in September of this year.

The Treasury also noted that redemptions of E and H savings bonds last month totaled $382,000,000, of which

accrued interest on redeemed E bonds was $59,000,000. In October, 1962, these figures were $306,000,000 and $61,000,000. Total redemptions for September, 1963, totaled $387,000,000.

Total E and H bonds outstanding rose by $122,000,000 from September to last month, when they stood at $46,843,000,000. At the end of October, 1962, there were $45,284,000,000 of the bonds outstanding.

Series E bonds are sold at less than face value and yield 3.75 per cent interest when held to maturity in seven and nine months. The H bonds are sold at face amount and pay the same interest in semiannual checks.

The marketable war issues set the tone of the entire money market in the United States, not only during the war but also after it ended. Any marked increase of the rates, it was evident, would affect prices of outstanding market issues and possibly bring the banking system into danger. This factor, combined with the desire of the Treasury to keep its borrowing costs low for an almost limitless series of re-fundings, tended to keep the rates close to the wartime levels. Only modest increases in short-term rates were considered feasible in the period immediately after the recent war.

Thus, an unprecedentedly low scale of interest rates was foisted upon our economy, with a consequent inflationary stimulus after the war ended. Liquid assets held by the people—currency, demand deposits, and other liquid holdings—trebled during the war. Ordinary central-banking theory would call for sharply restrictive measures in such a situation, and particularly for such quantitative controls as a rise of the discount rate. The Federal Reserve banks, however, had to content themselves with relatively feeble qualitative controls.

A change in the easy money policy came in March 1951, when the Treasury consented to the issuance of a long-term nonmarketable government bond bearing 2¾ per cent interest. This was the first change in the long-term rate since 1942, although the short-term rate had previously been permitted to rise gradually. Consent to the new issue climaxed a long disagreement between the Federal Reserve System and the Treasury Department, the former seeking higher rates as a method of curbing inflation and the latter adhering to its easy money policy in an effort to keep down the interest charges on the mounting government debt. Since March 1951, the Federal Reserve has been free to conduct its credit policy with primary regard for economic conditions, and the Treasury has sold its securities in a free market.

Although the federal budget came into balance right after World War II, the "compensating budget" remained a factor of importance in all calculations. Moreover, the annual outlays were reduced in the immediate postwar period to the level of $37.5 billion, and only modest provision was made for debt retirement. After the first world war the budget was reduced swiftly to about one-sixth of the war-time peak, but after World War II it remained at more than one-third of the peak outlay of that conflict. In 1950, the outbreak of the Korean War once again caused a sharp rise in the federal budget, largely because of mounting defense expenditures. This suggests the mounting economic influence of federal budgets and debts.

11

FEDERAL RESERVE
SYSTEM

HISTORICAL BACKGROUND

THE PRINCIPAL INTENT OF CONGRESS WHEN IT ESTAB-
lished the Federal Reserve System was to provide an elastic currency
and a more flexible monetary system. Prior to the founding of the
system, currency was based largely on gold and consisted mainly of
gold certificates, gold coin plus limited amounts of silver certificates
and coin, United States notes (greenbacks), and bond-secured national bank notes. Bank reserves (the margin of safety set aside from
bank assets to meet heavy calls for funds) were represented partly
by cash and partly by deposits in other banks. Most of the reserves
of small banks were on deposit with banks in the great money centers, such as New York and Chicago, which were designated as
central reserve cities at that time. They are now classified as reserve
cities along with other leading commercial cities.

It was imperative, in times of stress, that the supply of currency be
readily expansible. Under the old system this could not be done
unless a considerable amount of gold became available, and such
additions were not likely to occur when most needed. Practices followed prior to setting up of the Reserve banks worked very well so
long as business and finance operated at a stable pace, but the whole

structure was extremely vulnerable in the event of a widespread and heavy drain on the funds of banks, as in a boom. Even more important: As the country grew, the money supply should have grown too.

When a large call on bank funds occurred, the central reserve city banks often would be forced to sell securities and call loans in order to acquire cash to protect their reserve positions and to meet their own obligations and the obligations of those banks for whom they acted as reserve depositories. Because of these moves, sharp declines occurred in security prices, interest rates rose rapidly, funds for lending to business tended to disappear, and many businesses found themselves in difficulties as a result of banks calling in their loans. A situation of this sort is called a money panic, and it was due to a very severe one in 1907 that Congress decided to seek ways of preventing a recurrence.

A National Monetary Commission was named to make a study of both our monetary and banking systems and to recommend improvements for them. These recommendations and those of other authorities were embodied in the Federal Reserve Act passed by Congress on December 23, 1913.

MAJOR PROVISIONS OF THE FEDERAL RESERVE ACT

The Federal Reserve Act provided for establishment of the twelve Federal Reserve banks, and made them the legal depositories for the reserves of member banks. The reserve authorities were given the right to rediscount commercial paper and to engage in "open-market operations" for the purchase and sale of United States government securities and bankers' acceptances. Using the amount of commercial paper held by the Reserve banks as a base, the system was given the power to issue Federal Reserve notes as a form of currency, which is still the principal medium of circulation today.

Thus a central banking system was set up to oversee the activities and hold the reserves of the member banks. The amount of currency was related to the volume of business and the demand for credit, instead of to the availability of gold; and the supply of money and credit could be expanded or contracted along with the needs of business.

MANAGEMENT OF THE FEDERAL RESERVE SYSTEM

The broad policies of the system are set by the Board of Governors of the Federal Reserve System and the Federal Open Market Committee, which are responsible for the maintenance of "sound banking conditions and an adequate supply of credit at reasonable cost for the use of commerce, industry, and agriculture, and for supervision over the operations of the twelve Federal Reserve banks." Usually this board is referred to in financial circles and in the newspapers as the Federal Reserve Board or the "Fed."

The Board of Governors is composed of seven members appointed by the President of the United States with the advice and consent of the Senate. Each governor is appointed for a term of fourteen years.

The twelve Federal Reserve banks are separate corporations whose stock is owned by the various member banks in the district which they serve. A board of nine directors form the top management of each bank. Six of them are elected by the member banks in the district, while the remaining three are appointed by the Reserve Board. Presidents, first vice presidents, and all other officers of the various Reserve banks are chosen by the directorates, but the first two appointees must be approved by the Reserve Board.

CHANGES AFFECTING THE RESERVE SYSTEM

If the American economy had remained static, the system as originally conceived would have been adequate to assure the financial well-being of the country. However, two world wars, the "boom and bust" of the 1920s, the great depression of the 1930s, and the consequent expansion of the public debt as a result of these influences had a profound effect on both the Reserve banks and the member banks of the system.

The most important of these changes was an evolution of the member banks from being primarily short-term credit institutions to holders of other forms of indebtedness, notably United States government securities. It was not until 1952 that total loans of all member banks once again exceeded holdings of government securities.

Three long-range trends that had already started when the system was founded, and that have continued to exert an influence up to the present time, are among the underlying causes in the change in the character of bank assets. They are:

1. The trend toward larger and larger business organizations that are able to finance a major part of their operations from earnings, or else can finance both their capital and working capital requirements through the issuance of marketable securities. The effect of this has been to reduce the dependence of business on the banks as a source of funds.

2. Development of large retail organizations possessing the buying power to purchase inventories direct from the manufacturer, thereby bypassing the traditional middleman known as the wholesaler. Since wholesalers are large users of bank credits, a reduction in their importance caused a commensurate decline in the amount of such credit used.

3. The building of more efficient means of transport and communication on a nationwide scale, which has enabled sellers to operate their businesses on smaller inventories, thus lowering the need for bank loans to finance inventory needs.

GOVERNMENT DEBT

Expansion of the public debt to a figure in excess of $300 billion, however, has been the prime factor in accelerating the trend toward security investments by the commercial banks in the United States. The debt was reduced to approximately $250 billion after the close of World War II and then went back to $300 to $308 billion.

While the public debt is still a principal factor, largely because it provides most of the banks' liquid "secondary," or money market, reserve, loans are several times as large; and in many banks municipal holdings are as large as Treasury holdings.

The Reserve System made funds available all during World War II by standing ready to purchase in the market short-term government securities in the form of ninety-one-day Treasury bills and twelve-month Treasury certificates of indebtedness. This assured a ready market to the banks whenever they needed to sell securities in order to acquire reserves or funds to increase their loans and investments as a means of assisting the war effort and meeting public demands for currency.

It is important to remember that Reserve banks *create* reserves whenever they buy government securities, and that the created reserves are immediately deposited in banks by the sellers of the securities.

The "cheap money policy" of the Treasury, which was designed to relieve taxpayers as far as possible from the interest burden inherent in such a huge debt, was maintained by these policies of the Reserve banks during the war. This was because additional bank reserves and funds could be obtained at so low a cost to the member banks that they in turn could loan money to others at extremely low rates. During the war rates rose slightly from 1940–1941 levels; they declined modestly in 1946, despite heavy demand for money. The Reserve System's policy of standing ready at all times to purchase short-term government securities constituted a serious obstacle to its efforts to restrain inflationary tendencies in the postwar period.

EFFECTS OF CHANGES ON THE SYSTEM

Since the founding of the Federal Reserve System the changes wrought in our economy by troubled and warlike times have had a profound effect not only on the country but also on its financial structure, including the Federal Reserve.

The Reserve System controlled the flow of consumers' credit. This power was terminated on November 30, 1947, revived briefly in 1948 and 1949, and reinstated in 1950 to help in restraining inflationary pressures growing out of the war in Korea and the expanded national defense program. In May 1952, Federal Reserve control of consumer credit was terminated and has not been reinstated since. Congressional action would be required to revive consumer credit control.

Regulation W of the Federal Reserve Board controlled the amount of consumers' credit that was permitted for the purchase of war-scarce civilian goods. It primarily affected installment loans. The regulation stemmed from the war powers of the President of the United States.

The Federal Reserve still sets margin requirements for the purchase of securities listed on a national securities exchange. Both of these powers were a part of the evolution of the system caused by changing conditions. The system has seen the relative importance of commercial loans diminish, and largely as a result of the last war has watched the amount of money in circulation rise to more than $35 billion and bank deposits expand from $15 billion in 1913 to seventeen times this amount at the time of writing. In addition, the authority of the Reserve System over its member banks has been substantially increased.

While the Reserve banks have always acted as fiscal agents for the Treasury, due to the rise in public debt, they have continued to move toward a closer and closer relationship with the government. Also the powers of the Reserve Board have of necessity been expanded, while the authority of the individual Reserve banks has declined.

LEGISLATION AFFECTING THE SYSTEM

A substantial amount of legislation was required to give the Reserve System the powers and flexibility needed to meet changing circumstances in our financial and economic structure during the last forty or more years. Some of the more important legislative acts in this respect are:

AMENDMENT OF 1917 TO THE FEDERAL RESERVE ACT—This amendment permitted the Reserve banks to accept government obligations as security for loans to member banks. A further step was the Glass-Steagall Act of 1932, which for a limited period allowed the Reserve banks to pledge government securities for the issuance of Federal Reserve notes. This latter power was placed on a permanent basis at a later date.

The evolution of these powers marks the slow abandonment of the original theory of the system, which was that adequate control over the money and credit of the country could be maintained through the discounting of commercial paper.

THE BANKING ACT OF 1933—This act gave legal status and recognition to the value of the Open Market Committee of the Federal Reserve as a means of controlling the flow of funds and the supply of credit. Originally the Open Market Committee for the purchase and sale of government securities was created on an informal basis in 1922. Formerly the committee members were appointed by the twelve Reserve banks, but this procedure was changed in 1933 when the power to make appointments was taken over by the Federal Reserve Board.

By the Banking Act of 1935, further changes in the Open Market Committee were effected. It substituted a committee composed of the seven members of the Reserve Board and five members representing the Reserve banks for the original group which represented the Reserve banks only. Thus the power of the Reserve banks was sharply reduced and control of the all-important committee passed more largely into the hands of the board.

THE SECURITIES EXCHANGE ACT OF 1934—This gave the Board of Governors of the Federal Reserve the power to control the amount of credit to be made available for speculation in securities. This act was the outgrowth of the stock market slump of 1929 and the following depression, which was blamed largely on overexpansion and subsequent liquidations of credit for the purchase of securities. It represented the first specific or selective credit control accorded the Federal Reserve to be used as an adjunct to its general credit control powers and activities.

Regulation T of the Federal Reserve Board, by which the amount of margin required for the purchase of listed securities is governed, and Regulation U, limiting the amount of bank loans for margin trading, are offshoots of this law.

In 1945 gold reserve requirements of the banks were reduced to 25 per cent of notes and deposits. It had been 40 per cent of notes and 35 per cent of deposits.

STATISTICAL AND INFORMATION SERVICES

Publication of weekly and monthly banking and business statistics, and of bulletins and reviews on the same subjects, is one of the most important activities of the Federal Reserve Board and of the individual Reserve banks. So important are these publications that no banker or businessman can afford to miss them if he wishes to keep informed on current trends and changes in economic and financial conditions that may have a vital bearing on banking and other forms of business.

THE SHORT STATEMENT

This combines certain accounts from the condition statement of the twelve Federal Reserve banks with items in the circulation statement of the Treasury, and is probably the most important of all the statistical releases of the Reserve Board so far as bankers are concerned, since all of the accounts included in the short statement have a direct effect on the supply of and the demand for reserve funds. It is released every Thursday night and is dated as of the close of business on Wednesday. On Friday morning it appears in the newspapers along with an exhaustive commentary on the changes therein and of conditions in the banking industry that caused them. The statement shows the amount held in each of the accounts in millions of dollars and gives the increase or decrease since the previous week and year.

BANK RESERVES

To understand the meaning of the short statement, one must understand the meaning of bank reserves and how their rise and fall affect the amount of bank credit and funds available to borrowers. The primary function of reserves historically was to provide a cushion which the banks could fall back on when in urgent need of money to pay their obligations to depositors.

However, legal reserve requirements are now thought of chiefly as a means of controlling the banks' ability to make loans and invest-

Figures of Federal Reserve Districts for March 4

(Figures in millions of dollars; six ciphers omitted.)

ASSETS	Boston	New York	Phila-delphia	Cleve-land/e	Rich-mond	At-lanta	Chi-cago	St. Louis	Minne-apolis	Kansas City	Dallas	San/e Fran-cisco
Total loans and Investments	5,332	41,678	5,027	10,979	4,934	5,393	19,087	3,847	2,012	4,683	6,213	29,931
Loans and investments adjusted/e	5,291	41,029	4,970	10,878	4,897	5,294	18,870	3,772	2,007	4,638	6,151	29,754
Loans adjusted/a	3,626	26,810	3,416	6,265	3,192	3,370	11,555	3,414	1,313	3,056	4,069	20,837
Commercial and industrial loans	1,689	13,529	1,353	2,267	1,117	1,372	4,770	908	546	1,238	2,004	6,794
Agricultural loans	6	50	8	2	12	44	67	34	39	261	47	940
Loans to brokers and dealers for purchasing or carrying:												
United States Govt. securities	12	238		20	3	5	97	3	3	2	20	72
Other securities	53	1,997	88	214	77	67	465	92	18	31	55	209
Other loans for purchasing or carrying:												
United States Govt. securities		26	7	8	12	6	22	2		3	3	7
Other securities	8	620	66	186	27	40	313	40	32	59	262	115
Loans to nonbank financial institutions:												
Sales finance, personal fin., etc.	155	1,473	193	255	138	152	776	114	114	127	100	485
Other	34	885	108	138	170	196	422	122	47	146	257	812
Loans to foreign banks		574	23	29	1	2	84	1			3	245
Real estate loans	632	3,499	539	1,598	594	399	2,164	126	253	463	342	7,256
Other loans	973	4,650	1,145	1,674	1,105	1,155	2,688	714	283	774	1,053	4,264
Loans to domestic commercial banks	41	649	57	101	37	99	217	75	5	45		177
United States Govt. securities—total/d	932	7,448	1,020	2,447	1,161	1,344	4,342	881	470	1,096	1,402	5,517
Treasury bills	256	1,713	236	445	138	131	594	164	39	203	121	763
Treasury certificates of indebtedness	4	24	3	20	2	8	15	17	3	4	7	4
Treasury notes and U. S. bonds maturing:												
Within one year	59	639	142	162	141	235	464	119	72	134	135	604
One to five years	476	3,603	489	1,469	655	723	2,275	458	240	594	733	2,648
After five years	137	1,469	150	351	225	247	994	123	116	161	406	1,498
Other securities	733	6,771	534	2,166	543	580	2,973	477	224	486	680	3,400
Reserves with Federal Reserve banks	457	3,809	474	864	478	490	1,790	382	192	459	604	2,703
Currency and coin	91	390	93	159	113	81	198	46	17	51	56	331
Balances with domestic banks	124	299	165	194	114	405	343	173	73	341	505	344
Other assets—net	123	2,789	160	202	147	157	475	74	75	143	234	1,159
Total assets/liabilities	6,674	54,049	6,426	13,076	6,286	7,208	23,568	4,943	2,677	6,275	8,237	36,774
LIABILITIES:												
Demand deposits adjusted/b	3,208	19,317	2,689									
Demand deposits—total/c	4,127	28,883	3,842									
Individuals, partnerships, and corporations	3,246	19,510	2,946									
States and political subdivisions	257	1,192	127									
United States Government	163	1,133	178									
Domestic interbank:												
Commercial	258	3,349	468									
Mutual savings	117	354	44									
Foreign:												
Governments, official institutions, etc.	4	492	10									
Commercial banks	30	846	29									
Time and savings deposits—total/d	1,577	16,270	1,767									
Individuals, partnerships, and corporations:												
Savings deposits	984	7,407	1,101									
Other time deposits	394	5,307	510									
States and political subdivisions	112	852	62									
Domestic interbank	8	192	11									
Foreign:												
Governments, official institutions, etc.	69	2,339	72									
Commercial banks	4	93	10									
Memo: Negotiable Time CD's included above												
From Federal Reserve banks	434	4,393	311									
From others		3	1									
Other liabilities	79	846	67									
Capital accounts	234	3,208	166									
	657	4,639	583									

aExclusive of loans to domestic commercial banks and after deduction of valuation reserves.
bIncludes all demand deposits except those of United States Gove... collection.
cIncludes certified and officers' checks not shown separately.
dIncludes time deposits of United States Government and postal savings.
ePreliminary (Cleveland and San Francisco districts).

Assets, Liabilities of Member Banks

WASHINGTON, Mar. 11.—The Federal Reserve Board's condition statement for member banks in 107 cities Wednesday, March 4, together with the increase or decrease from the previous week and from the corresponding week a year ago (000,000 omitted):

ASSETS	Current week		Previous week		Year ago
Total loans and investments	$139,116	+	$575	+	89,258
*Loans and investments adjusted	137,551	+	704	+	9,393
*Loans adjusted	89,924	+	49	+	8,933
Commercial & industrial loans	37,587	—	3	+	2,948
Agriculture loans	1,510	—	3		....
Loans to brokers and dealers for purchasing or carrying:					
U. S. government securities	475	—	108	+	1,891
Other securities	3,366	+	87	+	782
Other loans for purchasing or carrying:					
U. S. government securities	96	—	1	—	6
Other securities	1,768	+	32	+	366
Loans to non-bank financial institutions:					
Sales finance, personal finance, etc.	4,082	+	49	+	382
Other	3,451	+	27	+	746
Loans to foreign banks	996	—	4	+	333
Real estate loans	18,165	+	4	+	2,381
Other loans	20,478	+	21	+	2,192
Loans to domestic commercial banks	1,565	—	129	—	135
U. S. government securities	28,060	+	469	—	2,880
Other securities	19,567	+	186	+	3,340
Reserves with Federal Reserve Banks	12,702	—	209	+	636
Currency and coin	1,626	+	167	+	92
Balances with domestic banks	3,080	+	174	+	18
Other assets-net	5,787	+	82	+	631
Total assets/liabilities	176,193	+	892	+	11,180
LIABILITIES					
Demand deposits adjusted	62,293	—	272	+	892
Demand deposits-total	91,840	+	1,265	+	1,758
Time and savings deposits-total	61,115	+	185	+	8,553
Borrowings:					
From Federal Reserve Banks	12	—	516	—	118
From others	2,247	—	192	—	356
Other liabilities	6,262	—	131	+	376

*Exclusive of loans to domestic commercial banks and after deduction of valuation reserves; individual loan items are shown gross.

ments, and hence they are viewed as a means of checking inflationary expansion or deflationary contraction of the money supply.

The amount of such reserves, which under the law must be deposited with the twelve banks or held as vault cash, is set by the Federal Reserve Board, and within the limits of the law the board may raise or lower them as it sees fit. At this writing, for instance, reserve requirements for banks in what are called reserve cities are 16.5 per cent of net demand deposits, while for country banks reserves are set at 12 per cent. On time deposits held by member banks, requirements are 4 per cent, as of November 1963. Thus a very substantial part of a bank's funds is not available for lending purposes.

Aside from the fact that reserves are important to member banks because they supply a reservoir of funds for periods when heavy withdrawals materialize, they are also important in that the necessity for the banks to keep these balances up to the required percentages has a direct influence on their willingness and ability to make loans to business or to increase their investments in securities.

This is because when a reserve city bank loans money, the borrower usually "deposits" the proceeds in the lender bank, thereby increasing reserve requirements of the bank by an amount equal to 16.5 per cent of the loan without any increase in the amount of funds available to the bank for deposit in its reserve account. For example, when a bank lends a corporation $1 million, it does so by "crediting" that amount to the corporation's account at the bank. This increases the bank's deposit liabilities by $1 million, against which it must have approximately $165,000 or $120,000 in cash reserve (depending on the class of the bank) in cash or on deposit at its Federal Reserve bank. In order to get these funds it may have to sell securities, borrow them from the Federal Reserve bank in its district, or borrow them from another member bank that has an excess of reserve funds; and it can make a big difference to the bank as to how the needed funds are acquired.

The Reserve banks themselves point out that the importance of the factors governing the supply and use of member bank reserves "lies in the fact that the ability of the member banks to make loans or investments, and their attitude in the matter are influenced by the availability of reserves and by the method through which these reserves are obtained," as the different ways differ in cost to the banks.

DESCRIPTION OF THE SHORT STATEMENT

The importance of the short statement published every Friday morning is that it shows the different factors that affect the supply and use of bank reserves. The statement can be divided into two parts. The Federal Reserve considers what all other factors are doing to bank reserves, and then undertakes open market operations to achieve the desired net effect. Under the first grouping come the following accounts:

1. Total Reserve bank credit, including (a) U.S. government and other obligations owned by the Reserve banks; (b) loans, discounts, and advances made by the Reserve banks; and (c) float, or the excess of uncollected cash items over deferred availability cash items.

2. Gold stock.

3. Treasury currency outstanding.

Under the second groupings are the uses of bank reserve funds:

1. Currency in circulation

2. Treasury cash holdings

3. Treasury deposits with Federal Reserve banks

4. Foreign deposits with Federal Reserve banks

5. Other deposits with Federal Reserve banks

6. Other Federal Reserve accounts (net)

After the two groupings there are shown actual member bank reserve balances with the twelve Reserve banks or in the form of vault cash, required reserves, and excess reserves. It is well to keep in mind that a plus in any account supplying reserves means an addition to reserve balances, while the reverse is true when a minus is shown. When a plus appears in accounts using reserves, it means that bank reserves have been drawn upon.

SIGNIFICANCE OF SHORT STATEMENT ACCOUNTS

TOTAL RESERVE BANK CREDIT.

This account is the sum of all the credit items held by the Federal Reserve banks in their portfolios, plus the Reserve bank float. Thus on September 18, 1963, the date of the short statement used here, the figures were as follows (these figures represent an average of the daily figures for the week in question and are in millions of dollars):

Reserve bank credit:	
U.S. Government securities:	
Bought outright—System account	$32,209
Held under repurchase agreement	—
Acceptances—bought outright	36
Discounts and advances:	
Member bank borrowings	193
Other	32
Float	1,995
Total Reserve bank credit	$34,465

When total Reserve bank credit increases, it means that the Reserve banks have been making funds available to the member banks so that they may have additional funds to meet demands for currency or other drains on their reserves, or for lending or investment. This is because:

1. When the Reserve banks purchase government securities in the open market, they pay for them by check, which, on presentation for payment, is credited to the reserve balance of the member bank requesting payment on the check. If, however, the Reserve banks sell securities, they in turn are paid by check, the amount of which is debited to the account of the member bank on which the check is drawn; and thus reserve balances are reduced.

2. An increase in discounts and advances usually means that some member banks have unexpectedly lost reserve balances or have had to meet an unexpected increase in reserve requirements because of a rise in their loans to business. Thus they have to borrow from the

Reserve banks in order to make up a deficiency in reserves. A decline in loans, discounts, and advances at the Reserve banks may indicate that the member banks have obtained additional funds from some other source or that reserve requirements have been reduced as a result of a drop in deposits which has enabled the member banks to pay off their indebtedness to the Reserve banks.

3. The third item of Reserve bank credit is *float*. It arises from the fact that the Reserve banks give the member banks credit for checks deposited for collection according to a time schedule, which provides for payment on collection items in one or two days, depending on the locations of the banks on which the items are drawn. Actually it may take a day or two longer than the time schedule to make the collection in the case of some checks. Thus the banks depositing checks for collection are getting paid by the Reserve banks prior to the date on which the banks on which some checks are drawn are charged for them. The difference between payment to the reserve balances of banks depositing checks for collection and the amount of such collection actually made, is the "float." An increase in the float increases all bank reserves on a temporary basis until the charge is made to the banks on which the checks are drawn.

GOLD STOCK.

Gold stock is one of the most important sources of bank reserves. This is because when a foreign country or other holder of gold sells it to the Treasury for dollars, the dollar proceeds are credited to the reserve balances of the recipients' banks. Since the gold is from outside the United States or from a mine here, there is no commensurate charge to the reserve balances of any other bank. Of course, when gold stocks decline, the banks lose correspondingly, as the full withdrawal of gold is debited to reserve balances when the foreign buyer of gold withdraws dollars from his bank in order to pay the Treasury. Title to all gold stocks is held by the United States Treasury, which issues gold certificates for it to the Federal Reserve banks in exchange for deposits to the credit of the Treasury in these banks.

TREASURY CURRENCY.

This consists of coins, silver certificates, United States notes, Treasury notes of 1890, Federal Reserve bank notes, and national bank notes, all of which are types of currency for which the Treasury is directly responsible, either because it was the original issuer, or because the issuers have paid the Treasury to take over the liability. Aside from coin, most of this currency is made up of small bills in denominations under $10. Most of the larger denominations of bills are issued by the Reserve System and are called Federal Reserve notes.

When the Treasury has new currency made up, it is usually deposited with the Reserve banks in the Treasury's deposit accounts, and when these proceeds are disbursed the funds usually flow into the banking system and thus increase bank reserves. However, when the Treasury redeems currency, it draws down its balances with the Reserve banks; this decline may be offset by withdrawals from Treasury accounts with commercial banks; thus reserves are reduced.

CURRENCY IN CIRCULATION.

Reserves of member banks are very sensitive to changes in the demand for money. When a bank has a demand for currency, it requests additional money from its Reserve bank. On receipt of the currency the reserve balance of the member bank is debited for an amount equal to the money it received. If a bank finds it holds an excess of currency and turns it in to its Reserve bank, its reserve balance is increased by an amount equal to the money turned in. Thus a rise in circulation means a loss to reserves, while a decline increases reserves of member banks.

TREASURY CASH.

This represents the cash assets of the Treasury, including some gold bullion against which no gold certificates have been issued, silver coins, and Treasury currency not in circulation. This account was increased by $2.8 billion as a result of profit accruing to the

Treasury on reduction of the gold content of the dollar in 1934, almost all of which was used for various purposes, including payment of the United States subscription to the International Monetary Fund and the World Bank.

TREASURY DEPOSITS.

This is the general account of the Treasury with the twelve Federal Reserve banks. Main sources of these deposits are tax collections and other receipts of the department. When this account increases it means that the Treasury is collecting more money than it is paying out. When it declines it indicates that the Treasury is paying out more funds than it is receiving.

If the Treasury pays out money from the account, it does so by check, and as the checks are returned to the Reserve bank for payment, the reserve accounts of the member banks are credited for their amount. Member banks lose reserves when the Treasury shifts funds to its Federal Reserve deposits from the tax and loan accounts it maintains at about 12,000 commercial banks, only about half of which are members. These accounts serve as depositories for Treasury receipts from taxes or securities sales. At times tax and loan receipts are credited directly to the Treasury's account at the Federal Reserve banks. This too would reduce member bank reserves, because the taxpayer or security buyer pays his bill by check, the amount of which is charged to the reserve balance of the member bank on which it is drawn.

The Treasury tries to maintain its deposits at Federal Reserve banks at about $800 to $1,000 million.

FOREIGN DEPOSITS.

This account comprises the deposits of foreign central banks and governments. An increase in foreign deposits causes a reduction in member bank balances, as normally they are built up out of funds transferred from reserve accounts of member banks. When this account declines, it indicates disbursements of funds which find their way into the member banks and cause additions to reserve balances.

OTHER DEPOSITS.

This account comprises the deposits of nonmember banks that use the check-clearing facilities of the system and also deposits of the United States Exchange Stabilization Fund and of the International Monetary Fund and the World Bank. Changes in this account affect member bank reserves in the same manner as changes in foreign deposits.

These are the total net balances of the member banks on deposit with the Federal Reserve banks, plus currency and coin held as vault cash. These constitute the only legal reserves of the members of the system.

Required reserves are deposits which member banks are required to maintain as reserves against their deposit liabilities. They must amount to from 7 to 22 per cent of net demand deposits, depending upon the class of bank, and 3 to 6 per cent of time deposits. The Board of Governors sets the exact requirements within this range.

Excess reserves are the net differences between actual reserve balances and the required reserves of member banks. They represent idle funds of the banks that can be used to expand loans and investments.

12

<hr/>

BALANCE OF PAYMENTS

READERS OF THE FINANCIAL SECTION OF A NEWSPAPER, and of page one, see frequent references to the balance of payments of the United States or some other country. It became an increasingly important subject in recent years because the United States was on the losing end in its balances with other nations.

If an individual buys from others more in services and goods than he supplies to them, he incurs a deficit balance. If he reverses this procedure, his balance shows a credit. It is the same between nations, although here the problem takes on complications far greater than making one's salary pay the butcher, the baker, and candlestick maker.

Both a nation and a householder have the problem of settling differences eventually. If the householder has a few dollars tucked under the mattress he can stave off the bill collectors for a while. If a nation has an excess supply of gold, or dollars, which represent the strongest currency in the world, it too can compensate for any deficit in its balance of payments for a long time. It can sell gold, which is either shipped bodily or credited to a foreign central bank for the latter's account, or it can use some of its dollars to credit these foreign accounts.

The United States, in order to satisfy the deficit in its balance of payments, lost gold to foreign governments between 1950 and 1964 with the single exception of one year, 1957, when the Suez crisis caused a temporary change in the trend. Losses were severe. In 1948 the Treasury's gold holdings were at a peak of $24.7 billion. They were under $16 billion early in 1963, and at that time there was no indication that the flow had changed its course.

There was a time within the last two decades when guesses were made that eventually the United States would have all the world's monetary gold stock. That fear is not heard now. While our gold stock is still a most substantial figure, it must be remembered that Federal Reserve banks must hold a reserve in the form of gold certificates of 25 per cent of the outstanding Federal Reserve notes and of 25 per cent of their deposit liabilities.

Taking this into consideration, the free gold stock that is available to settle continuing adverse balance of payments does not appear too healthy. That is why the nation's balance of payments problem is ever present and in recent years crops up in your newspaper reading. These articles are concerned with causes and suggested cures.

If all that had to be considered were the exports from the United States of its goods and services, balanced against the import of goods and services we receive from other countries, the problem would be simple. There would not be a problem, for in this field the balance of payments consistently flows in this direction. We supply the foreign butcher, baker, and candlestick maker with more than he supplies us.

The modern world brings about a more complicated situation however, and myriad other elements enter into the establishing of balances between nations. In our own case major ones include capital investments made abroad and military and civil aid. To this must be added the desire of many foreign governments to increase their deposits of gold and dollars; for this purpose they make every effort to limit their imports.

These items, along with others, tend to create a balance of international payments that at times has been adverse to the United

States. We spent more abroad than we took in. A balance in favor of foreigners may be invested here in long-term investments but more often it is in short-term obligations. Then there comes a time when a foreign central bank may decide to convert some of its balance into gold bars and, as we are on a gold bullion standard, they buy gold from us at $35 an ounce. They could take it back home if they wished, but usually they leave it on deposit with the Federal Reserve, duly earmarked for their account.

Suggested cures are many. They range all the way from such picayune things as limiting the amount of imported goods which tourists may bring in duty free and limiting the number of dependents a man in the armed services may have with him while abroad, to the sounder banking approach of permitting interest rates to rise and a determined effort by legislators and the public to see to it that our federal budget is kept in true balance. With the latter would doubtless go a reduction in foreign aid. There is also the periodical suggestion that we raise the price of gold and charge more than the statutory rate of $35 an ounce. To take such a step would bring about a devaluation of the dollar, which would further weaken confidence in the currency that, for many years, has been the world's accepted standard of value.

13

~~~~~~

REGULATION AND
CONTROL

CONTROL AND REGULATION OF THE INDIVIDUAL IS AS
old as government itself. The impact of government on trade and
industry, however, while doubtless present in ancient history, has
increased by such leaps and bounds in the last hundred years to the
point where no business can be successfully handled without taking
cognizance of the regulations imposed by government—federal,
state, and local.

In reading the financial news in a newspaper, one is constantly
made aware of the strong arm of government, and news columns
regularly carry stories of changes in laws and legal interpretations,
and occasionally of the formation of some new agency that is created
to enforce additional statutes.

In the United States the regulation of business may be said to have
started with the railroads, a few years after the first tracks were laid.
It started in various states, where abuses by the carriers included an
almost complete disregard for the public welfare and led to demands
for reforms. In 1887 the federal government created the Interstate
Commerce Commission, the first of our many so-called independent
regulatory agencies. Others followed in due course and in the depression days of the 1930s the number of independent agencies, as

well as countless bureaus, authorities, commissions, and federal corporations, multiplied rapidly. There were so many they were dubbed
the "alphabetical agencies," and there was a complaint that in some
cases they were formed for punitive reasons rather than to regulate
and to reform business practices.

No one can be expected to have a personal knowledge of any-
where near all the federal agencies and commissions. There are nine,
however, that are most frequently referred to in the press and which
have almost a daily impact on some phase of business and finance.
These are the so-called independent agencies. There are twenty or
more semi-independent ones that are frequently referred to in the
financial sections of newspapers; if we include all agencies the number would run into the hundreds.

The nine that are called independent derive that distinction because they were created by Congress as quasi-governmental agencies, with broad powers, to carry out the desires of Congress but as
part of the executive branch. Congress sought to give them an inde-
pendence from the executive. They are commissions, appointed by
the President, but once appointed, a commissioner cannot be removed except for malfeasance in office. Each commissioner serves a
stated term in office. Only when that term expires is the President
able to make a change.

There was one important exception, when President Franklin D.
Roosevelt summarily removed William E. Humphrey from the Federal Trade Commission in 1933, on the ground that Mr. Humphrey's
mind and the President's mind did not "go along together on either
the policies or the administering of the Federal Trade Commission."
It is interesting that in this single case the Supreme Court unani-
mously repudiated this doctrine. It ordered the salary of Mr.
Humphrey paid to his family for the time for which he had been
appointed to the time of his death, and held that commissioners
could not be removed except for such causes as specified in the law
by Congress.

That decision did much to assure that individual commissioners
of independent agencies can indeed be independent, once they are

appointed. Obviously it has no bearing on what particular individuals a President may choose to appoint, and while appointments must receive the endorsement of the Senate, and Congress requires that individuals of different political faiths be seated, a chief executive may be expected to name new commissioners who, as far as he knows, holds views in keeping with his own.

This may contribute to the belief in some quarters that the prestige of independent agencies is not as high as when the various commissions were first formed. Each independent agency has duties and powers that may be said to be quasi-judicial, just as they are quasi-legislative and quasi-executive. Yet questions as to whether a few individual commissioners are always as independent of outside influences as has come to be expected of the federal judiciary, led in 1958 to a House committee study of the regulatory agencies.

The Hoover Commission also had a complaint about the independent agencies, charging that too often an agency becomes bogged down in case-by-case activities instead of devoting its talents to the broad regulation and furthering of the enterprises entrusted to its care.

The legislative activities of independent agencies are derived from the fact that they establish rules, specifications, and procedures. For all practical purposes these decisions amount to law, and in most cases an agency can enforce its own laws. While anyone can appeal to the Supreme Court, this is rarely practical and therefore is unusual, and generally avoided. An agency can subpoena, initiate its own investigations, enforce its own finding if it feels its own rules have been violated, and can pass on its own decisions. Brief discussions of the nine independent agencies follow.

CIVIL AERONAUTICS BOARD—Formed in 1938 as the Civil Aeronautics Authority, the name of this board was subsequently changed to Civil Aeronautics Board, usually referred to as the CAB. Its purpose is to encourage and foster the development of civil aeronautics and air commerce. This includes wide powers over the licensing of civil airways; thus it can grant or deny operating certificates to flag carriers for both domestic and foreign operation. Its authority covers the regulation of landing areas and other navigational aids and facilities; the rates of the carriers and their compensation for air mail service; filing on charges of unfair competition in the industry; approval or disapproval of business deals between companies, such as contracts, agreements, or mergers; and the establishment of safety rules and regulations.

FEDERAL COMMUNICATIONS COMMISSION—Created in 1934 for the purpose of regulating interstate and foreign commerce by wire and radio, this agency licenses radio and television stations and prescribes their frequencies. It can revoke or modify licenses and it regulates certain telephone and telegraph rates.

FEDERAL POWER COMMISSION—This commission was formed in 1930 to provide for the development and improvement of navigation and the development, transmission, and utilization of power on streams, subject to federal jurisdiction, upon lands of the United States and at government dams. More important, its powers also embody a comprehensive scheme for the regulation of electric utilities and gas utilities engaged in interstate commerce. In regulating these companies it passes on rates, the issuance of securities, and the export or import of power to or from foreign countries. Its jurisdiction covers government power projects as well.

FEDERAL RESERVE BOARD—Described in a separate chapter, the "Fed," as it has come to be called, has broad powers over the expansion and contraction of credit, the national monetary policy, the establishment of margin requirements in security trading, and the supervision of the twelve regional Federal Reserve banks and all member banks.

FEDERAL TRADE COMMISSION—The FTC was established in 1924 to prevent price fixing agreements, boycotts, combinations in restraint of trade, and other unfair methods of competition. Later its duties were expanded to include jurisdiction over false advertising of foods, drugs, cosmetics, and devices, and jurisdiction over unfair and deceptive acts and practices. The general purpose of the FTC is threefold: to promote free and fair competition in interstate trade; to safeguard the life and health of the consuming public; and to make available, to the President, the Congress, and the public, data concerning economic and business conditions.

INTERSTATE COMMERCE COMMISSION—Created under the 1887 act to regulate commerce, the powers of the ICC were enlarged by the transportation act of 1920 and several subsequent acts. It regulates common carriers engaged in interstate commerce, and in doing so, rules on rates, financing, bookkeeping methods, safety devices, investigation of accidents, discrimination, mergers, abandonment of established lines or the creation of new ones, and virtually everything having to do with the public interest in the operation of common carriers.

NATIONAL LABOR RELATIONS BOARD—When the NLRB was created in 1935, the act creating it affirmed the right of employees to full freedom in organizing and in the designation of representatives of their own choosing for the purpose of collective bargaining. It can designate unfair practices on the part of employers or employees and can order them to be stopped. It conducts bargaining elections and certifies the results.

SECURITIES AND EXCHANGE COMMISSION—The SEC is described in a separate chapter. Its field covers all phases of trading in securities and the conduct of national securities exchanges and those connected therewith.

FEDERAL MARITIME BOARD—This agency regulates and controls rates, services, practices, and agreements of common carriers by water, and awards shipping and shipbuilding subsidies.

There are many other government organizations that have a direct bearing on the conduct of business and therefore our financial markets, and they are referred to regularly in the financial sections of newspapers. The impact the government has on our daily lives can be realized when the work of these agencies is coupled with the power of the government to tax.

OTHER FEDERAL AGENCIES

A complete list of federal bureaus may be obtained from the Superintendent of Documents, Washington, D.C. An abridged list of a few of the more important ones in business and finance, in addition to the above independent agencies, follows:

ATOMIC ENERGY COMMISSION—The federal commission given power to store, produce, and guard the atomic bomb and to conduct research on the hydrogen bomb and other nuclear weapons.

BUREAU OF FOREIGN AND DOMESTIC COMMERCE—Created in 1912 to foster, promote, and develop the foreign and domestic commerce of the United States. In doing so it provides the businessman with an intimate knowledge of business at home and abroad, a storehouse of information and statistics which are evaluated and interpreted, and a constant scrutiny of trends through which the changing needs of business are anticipated and special helps are created.

BUREAU OF LABOR STATISTICS—Formed in 1913 and charged with the duties of acquiring and diffusing useful information on subjects connected with labor—especially its relations with capital—hours of labor, earnings of laboring men and women, and the means of promoting their material prosperity.

COUNCIL OF ECONOMIC ADVISERS—Established in 1956, it analyzes the national economy and its various segments. It advises the President on economic subjects, appraises the federal government's economic programs and policies, assists in the preparation of economic reports of the President to Congress, and makes recommendations for economic growth and stability.

EXPORT-IMPORT BANK—Organized in 1934 to aid in financing and facilitating exports and imports and the exchange of commodities between the United States and other countries.

FARM CREDIT ADMINISTRATION—Formed to provide a complete and coordinated credit system for agriculture by making long-term and short-term credit available to farmers.

FEDERAL DEPOSIT INSURANCE CORPORATION—Created in 1933 to insure the deposits of all banks, to pay off the depositors of insured banks that have become bankrupt, to act as receiver for all suspended national banks and for suspended state banks when appointed by state authorities, and to prevent the continuance or development of unsafe and unsound banking practices.

FEDERAL HOUSING ADMINISTRATION—This is one of the chief units of the National Housing Agency. Its purpose is to insure private lending institutions against loss on loans secured by mortgages on one- to four-family dwellings, or on large scale rental housing projects, and on loans for property repair or improvements.

OFFICE OF ALIEN PROPERTY CUSTODIAN—Established in the Office of Emergency Management, authorized and empowered to control or vest foreign-owned property, which property shall be held, used, administered, liquidated, sold, or otherwise dealt with in the interest of the United States.

SOCIAL SECURITY ADMINISTRATION—Created in 1935, this board is now under the jurisdiction of the Department of Health, Education and Welfare. It was designed to administer federal old-age and survivors' insurance, and to conduct studies and make recommendations on the most effective method of providing economic security through social insurance.

TENNESSEE VALLEY AUTHORITY—Created in 1933 to provide for the development of the Tennessee River and its tributaries in the interest of navigation, the control of floods, and the generation and disposition of hydroelectric power.

UNITED STATES TARIFF COMMISSION—Created in 1916 to investigate tariff matters, this agency is charged with investigating customs law operations and foreign and domestic tariff relations; surveying domestic and foreign industries; investigating domestic and foreign manufacturing costs; studying import invoices; and investigating allegations of unfair methods of competition and unfair acts in the importation or sale of articles in the United States.

14

~~~~~~

SEC: ORGANIZATION

THE SECURITIES AND EXCHANGE COMMISSION IS AN independent, quasi-judicial agency of the United States government which was established in 1934 to administer certain federal laws designed to protect the interests of the investing public.

The health and vitality of the nation's economy are dependent in large measure upon the growth and stability of its industries, which provide gainful employment to millions whose products contribute so much to our high standard of living and whose securities provide a profitable return to investors. The opportunity for industry to grow and prosper is dependent in large part upon its ability to obtain money for plant expansion, new equipment, research, and working capital. The availability of funds for such purposes in turn is dependent upon the investing public's confidence in securities as a safe and profitable medium for the investment of their savings.

During the decade following World War I some $50 billion of new issues of corporate securities were sold in the United States, of which approximately one-half had proved worthless by the middle 1930s. Many abuses of the investing public occurred, including misrepresentation and fraud in the sale of securities to the public, and manipulation, or "rigging," of the securities markets. These contributed in no small measure to the 1929 stock market crash and the resulting losses of billions of dollars of investors' savings. As a further consequence, investors lost confidence in the integrity of our securities markets, and the issuance of new corporate securities and trading in outstanding securities reached a low ebb.

Passage of the federal securities laws was a direct outgrowth of these abusive practices. The laws, commonly referred to as the "truth in securities" laws, sought to re-establish investor confidence. They outlawed fraud, manipulation, and other abusive practices in interstate securities transactions, and placed on issuing companies, their management officials, underwriters, and others engaged in the securities business the responsibility for fair dealings in their securities transactions with the investing public. This included continuing disclosure of financial and other information, upon the basis of which investors may make an independent evaluation of securities bought and sold.

Secondly, they provide for commission surveillance of the securities markets to the end that just and equitable principles of trade will be fostered, and misrepresentation, manipulation, and other fraudulent practices curbed. Finally, they gave the commission investigative and enforcement powers in respect of securities violations, coupled with sanctions which may be imposed upon those who defraud investors or otherwise engage in unlawful securities transactions; and they provide important rights which investors may pursue to recover losses sustained in their purchase of securities if they have been defrauded.

Administration of the securities laws, both federal and state, coupled with more effective self-policing by the securities industry, have gone far toward the re-establishment of investor confidence in the basic integrity of the securities markets.

In the intervening years since the 1929 crash and the economic depression which ensued, industrial expansion has moved steadily upward with only moderate interruptions. For instance, plant and equipment expenditures by business corporations, which averaged $4.5 billion a year for 1934–1936, moved to an average of $10 billion for 1944–1946, and $30.2 billion during the years 1954–1956. By the close of 1962 such expenditures had risen to about $38 billion, as shown by the accompanying chart prepared by the Federal Reserve Bank of New York and based on data of the Federal Reserve System, the SEC, and the Department of Commerce. A McGraw-Hill survey

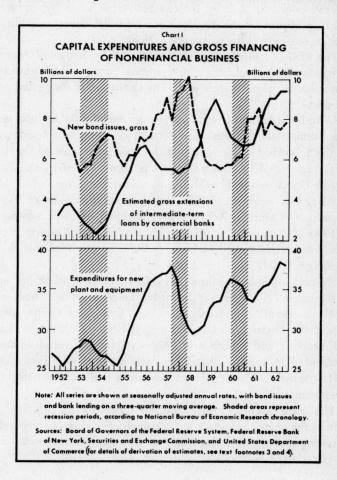

Chart I

CAPITAL EXPENDITURES AND GROSS FINANCING OF NONFINANCIAL BUSINESS

Billions of dollars

New bond issues, gross

Estimated gross extensions of intermediate-term loans by commercial banks

Expenditures for new plant and equipment

1952 53 54 55 56 57 58 59 60 61 62

Note: All series are shown at seasonally adjusted annual rates, with bond issues and bank lending on a three-quarter moving average. Shaded areas represent recession periods, according to National Bureau of Economic Research chronology.

Sources: Board of Governors of the Federal Reserve System, Federal Reserve Bank of New York, Securities and Exchange Commission, and United States Department of Commerce (for details of derivation of estimates, see text footnotes 3 and 4).

early in 1964 estimated $42.4 billion for that year. Later the same year a government survey, issued by the Department of Commerce, upped the estimate to $43.2 billion, which would make it 10 per cent above the 1963 figure.

Part of such expenditures is financed by funds internally generated by the business, part by intermediate-term loans by commercial banks, and part by the flotations of new bond issues, in addition to such equity capital the corporations might raise.

The SEC is composed of five commissioners, not more than three of whom may be members of one political party; and the term of one commissioner expires each year. The chairman is designated by the President.

In addition to the Securities Exchange Act of 1934, the commission also administers the Securities Act of 1933 (both acts are described in the following chapter) which, for one year prior to the formal establishment of the commission, was administered by the Federal Trade Commission. The SEC also administers the Public Utility Holding Company Act of 1935, the Trust Indenture Act of 1939, the Investment Company Act of 1940, and the Investment Advisers Act of 1940. It also renders advisory assistance to federal courts in corporate reorganization proceedings under Chapter X of the National Bankruptcy Act.

Its work is conducted through various divisions and offices, subject to direction, review, and approval by the commission. These consist of three operating divisions, plus the Division of Corporation Finance, the Division of Corporate Regulation, Division of Trading and Markets, and the Office of Program Planning. Activities are supplemented in various phases by nine regional and seven branch offices, which constitute the investigation and enforcement arm of the commission.

The commission's general counsel serves as its principal legal officer; the chief accountant is the principal adviser on corporate accounting matters; and the Office of Opinion Writing assists in the preparation of decisions in contested cases.

OFFICE OF OPINION WRITING

Working independently of the commission's three operating divisions and responsible directly to the commission, this office assists the commission in the review of records in those administrative cases which come before the agency for decision in the exercise of its quasi-judicial functions, and in the preparation of the commission's decisions in such cases (its findings, opinions and orders).

In many instances these cases arise from applications filed with the commission under the provisions of a particular act. For example, such a case might involve an application under the Holding Company Act for approval of a plan of reorganization or merger or for the issuance and sale of securities; or the decision may involve a proceeding to revoke the broker-dealer registration of a securities firm for fraudulent securities transactions, which would bar its continued conduct of a securities business in interstate commerce.

When hearings are concluded in such a proceeding, the parties thereto (including counsel for the participating SEC division) are given the opportunity to file "Proposed Findings of Fact and Conclusions of Law" which they wish to urge for adoption by the hearing examiner and, ultimately, by the commission. Unless this opportunity is waived, the hearing examiner, upon the basis of the evidence developed at the hearing and the proposed findings and conclusions so filed, prepares a recommended decision. The parties then have an opportunity to file "exceptions" to the recommended decisions together with supporting briefs, and to be heard in oral argument before the commission.

Thereupon, the commission, assisted by the Office of Opinion Writing, makes a thorough and independent review and analysis of the record and the arguments of the parties as set forth in their written submissions and at the oral argument. Upon the basis thereof, and aided by the said office, the commission prepares and issues its decision in much the same manner as a federal court. These decisions set forth the findings of the commission as to the facts and evidence established by the record; its conclusions of law based thereon; and the resulting action to be taken, such as the approval or disapproval of the reorganization or of issuance and sale of securities, or revocation of the firm's broker-dealer registration.

Persons aggrieved by decisions of the commission have a right of appeal to the appropriate United States court of appeals.

OFFICE OF THE GENERAL COUNSEL

The general counsel is the commission's chief legal officer. The office coordinates all the legal activities of the commission, providing advice and assistance to the operating divisions, regional offices, and the commission with respect to interpretation, rule-making, analyses of proposed legislation, and other legal problems arising in the administration of the several laws.

It generally directs and supervises all contested civil litigation in the district courts (other than certain enforcement proceedings under the Holding Company Act) and represents the commission in all cases in the appellate courts, filing briefs and presenting oral arguments in behalf of the commission. It also reviews all investigation reports recommending reference to the Department of Justice for criminal prosecution and advises the commission with respect thereto.

THE CHIEF ACCOUNTANT'S OFFICE

Since much of the information filed with the commission is in the form of financial statements, their value is directly dependent on the soundness of the accounting principles and practices observed in their preparation, and the adequacy and reliability of the work done by public accountants who certify to their accuracy. Consequently, a major objective of the commission has been to improve accounting and auditing standards, and to maintain or raise the standards of professional conduct observed by certifying accountants.

To this end the commission has adopted a basic accounting regulation governing the form and content of most of the financial statements currently filed under the acts administered by the agency; and this regulation prescribes accounting practices which have become generally accepted in the field of corporate accounting. It also has promulgated uniform systems of accounts for public utility holding and service companies; has given careful consideration to accounting problems presented in particular cases, culminating in some instances in formal commission decisions; and has published a number of accounting opinions of its chief accountant.

These accounting rules, decisions, and opinions, taken in conjunction with authoritative pronouncements by professional accounting societies and by other governmental agencies, have achieved a substantial clarification and improvement in the accounting and auditing principles and practices generally followed in the preparation of financial statements. In addition, the ethical standards customarily observed by certifying accountants have been fortified by the commission's requirement that an accountant be independent of his client, as well as by the commission's right to disbar an accountant from practicing before it because of unprofessional conduct.

The chief accountant is the commission's chief consulting officer on accounting matters, advising it in connection with accounting problems which arise in the administration of the several acts, particularly in matters involving new accounting policy determinations. He is also charged with supervision of the procedures to be followed in audits or accounting investigations conducted by the commission's staff.

PUBLIC INFORMATION

As indicated, the various corporate and other reports filed with the commission become public immediately upon filing and are available for public inspection. In the case of new security offerings under the Securities Act, the financial and other information is disseminated through the required distribution of the prospectus to dealers and its delivery to purchasers of the securities.

While there is no comparable means for dissemination of the financial and other information contained in the annual and other periodic reports filed by companies whose securities are listed on exchanges, the information is available for inspection, both at the exchanges and at the commission; and photocopies thereof may be purchased at nominal cost. By this means, most of the data filed with the Commission finds its way into the various securities manuals issued by private organizations, which are used extensively by brokers and dealers, investment companies, investment advisers, trust departments, and others. In addition to the public reference room maintained at its headquarters office, where these reports may be examined, the commission maintains a similar service in its New York and Chicago regional offices.

All commission decisions, orders, rules, and regulations are published initially in the form of releases, copies of which are mailed to persons who have asked to be placed on the list for particular types of SEC releases. Bound volumes of printed decisions and reports of the commission may be obtained from the Government Printing Office. Also available from the GPO are monthly reports of trading by "insiders" in listed stocks as well as certain periodic reports of statistical and economic studies made by the commission (which, in certain areas, are also distributed by the commission).

SPECIAL STUDY OF SECURITIES MARKETS

A particularly valuable storehouse of information concerning the entire securities business is contained in the three thousand pages of the SEC's *Special Study of Securities Markets,* published by the Government Printing Office in 1963 (Eighty-eighth Congress, First Session, House Document 95).

This report, with its 176 recommendations concerning the SEC and the industry, took almost two years to prepare. It was undertaken at the direction of Congress, and was carried out by a staff of sixty-five experts. Findings were digested by a separate professional staff of lawyers, economists, analysts, and statisticians, drawn from within and outside the SEC. The report was issued to the public in three sections, in 1963, and covered a wide range of problems which beset the market place and the conduct of attracting the savings of the public into channels of productive industry.

The group's recommendations, in and of themselves, did not bind the SEC to any course of action, but it set a blueprint of action which would guide the commission, on the executive side of government, and Congress, on the legislative.

Subjects dealt with, many of which are discussed in more detail elsewhere in this volume, included salesmen and broker-dealer relationships, new issues and so-called hot issues, reporting requirements, specialists on national security markets, odd-lot trading, floor trading by members for their own account, stricter control of short selling, institutional buying, off-board trading in listed securities, mutual funds, over-the-counter trading, security credit, conflict of interest, market advisory services, market letters, advertising, and efforts of the financial community toward self-regulation.

Many of its suggestions led to quick action by the exchanges. Other recommendations will have to await action by the SEC itself or legislative action by Congress, giving the commission the necessary added powers.

Even speechmaking by New York Stock Exchange brokers, on securities, was brought under control of the stock exchange for the first time, when the exchange moved quickly, in September 1963, to comply with recommendations of the Special Study report.

The stock exchange, which had issued a set of rules in 1962 and again early in 1963 clarifying its standards for communications between brokers and the public, expanded its rules on this subject for member firms, possibly prompted in part by the charges in the Special Study that some brokers had been guilty of "irresponsible dissemination of advice" and misleading information to the public.

Included in its expanded rules were:

Tighter requirements, for member firms recommending securities in market letters and research reports, on disclosing their own dealings in such issues

A "reasonable basis" for any claims by a member firm that it is equipped to provide clients with research services

A specification that if reports and recommendations are prepared by someone other than the firm, such as by its public relations agent, the source must be identified

A requirement that market recommendations and wires from the firm conform to the rules covering market letters sent to the public

In line with principles of full disclosure, the New York Stock Exchange also issued a rule providing that a firm's recommendation to buy or sell a security, "must have a basis which can be substantiated as reasonable," and that the report show the market price of the stock at the time the recommendation was made.

THE ISSUE OF "HOT ISSUES"

The Special Study contained an especially scathing indictment of the so-called hot issue market.

This was most prevalent during the period 1959–1961, but there was a somewhat similar period of feverish speculation, on a smaller scale, in the late 1920s, shortly before the panic of 1929. This earlier one centered chiefly on the formation of investment companies which sold new shares to the public and invested the proceeds deemed advisable by the sponsors.

When such a proposition came along, backed by good names, there was a rush of buying from uninformed investors; and frequently by the time payment was due for new shares subscribed, the market had placed a value on them whereby an automatic profit could be obtained without having first deposited more than a token payment for the shares.

The hot issue market of 1959–1961 differed in that in this later period of speculative fever the securities were those of a closely held or family corporation which was "going public." The closely held shares would be bought by the sponsoring firm, or firms, which then planned to offer the shares to the public. Word would get around that so-and-so is bringing out a "hot" new issue.

This information would spread quickly by grapevine, possibly with a little help from interested parties. A big demand would develop, and applications for the new shares, price still unknown, would soar so that those requesting a modest hundred shares would feel lucky to get ten. Favored customers and other insiders had the best chance to receive a good allotment.

The study devoted a 164-page section to this subject of "going public," and cited various devices used to choke off the trading supply in such new issues, a practice which contributed to an artificially high price. It noted among other things that in some firms registered representatives had opened fictitious accounts in which they had an interest in the eventual allotments of shares in a hot issue.

The report also charged that some firms offered unlisted shares which had "the slimmest chance of survival" and therefore their stock "could be sold by their underwriters only through questionable or clearly illegal techniques."

The offering of new securities is a necessary and thoroughly legitimate part of the business of financing industry. The economy could not function without it, nor without there being a market place for such securities after they get into the hands of the public. But the wave of questionable and even manipulative offerings of that era is what caused the blistering attack by the group that made the special study.

In most cases this questionable brand of new issues moved quickly to a premium after the announcement that they were being offered, only to fall back later, some of them to disappear through liquidation or bankruptcy.

The study took a look at twenty-two that went public between 1959 and 1961, and which immediately enjoyed an advance in price. At the time of the study only seven were still above their offering price, one was even, and thirteen showed a loss.

Another analysis by the SEC, this one covering 792 unseasoned issues sold in 1961, showed that 85 per cent went to a premium but only 22 per cent were still being traded in by September 1962. An even broader study, covering 960 small companies that went public between 1952 and 1962 showed that in December 1962, 37 per cent were either inactive, dissolved, in bankruptcy or reorganization, or could not be found after "diligent efforts."

The study on this hot issue problem prompted the group to call for certain specific actions, including:

1. Prompt delivery of stock certificates to investors
2. A brief ban on trading after the effective (offering) date

3. Limits on underwriters' solicitation of purchasers in the immediate after-market

4. Stronger NASD enforcement of its ban on "free-riding," which is the buying of new shares with the intent of selling them within a brief period without having risked a true investment of funds.

15

~~~~~~

SEC: REGULATORY POWERS

SECURITIES ACT OF 1933

THIS LAW WAS DESIGNED BY CONGRESS TO COMPEL disclosure of pertinent financial and other information concerning securities offered for public sale in interstate commerce or through the mails, so that investors might exercise an informed judgment in evaluating the worth of such securities. There are certain exemptions from the registration requirement, such as municipal securities, offerings which are confined to residents of the state in which the issuing company is organized and doing business, offerings to a limited number of persons, and offerings not exceeding $300,000 in amount (subject to conditions, as discussed below).

Disclosure of the required facts with respect to securities offered for public sale is obtained through the filing of registration statements with the Securities and Exchange Commission. Moreover, a prospectus containing the salient information reflected in the registration statement, including certified financial statements, must be delivered to purchasers of the securities. A condensed version of the prospectus may be distributed in the offering of securities, after the filing of the registration statement, subject to SEC rules and provided the recipient is advised that a prospectus containing the detailed facts may be obtained upon request.

Special forms have been prescribed by the commission for the registration of securities, which vary in their requirements depending upon the nature of the issuing company and of the securities being offered. Each form is designed to disclose the material facts and information concerning: the organization and operations of the issuing company; the significant terms and provisions of the securities being offered; the proposed use of the proceeds of their sale; and the results of the issuer's operations. This last includes certified financial statements, as well as disclosures with respect to management, compensation, stock options, and similar information—so that investors may have the facts upon which to evaluate the securities.

These registration statements become public immediately upon being filed with the commission. They are examined by the SEC Division of Corporation Finance for compliance with the applicable disclosure requirements. If the statement appears materially misleading, inaccurate, or incomplete, the issuing company usually is informed by letter of such deficiencies and given an opportunity to file appropriate corrective or clarifying amendments.

Often, informal and preliminary advisory suggestions from the staff have helped to make approval smoother and more rapid. When appropriately amended the registration statement becomes effective, either by lapse of time or by SEC order, whereupon the securities may be sold.

The SEC has no power to pass upon the merits of securities registered with it—in other words, it may not deny registration of securities and their public sale merely because the securities may be of questionable value, overpriced, or otherwise. Instead, Congress wisely left to the wisdom and judgment of investors, individually and collectively, the responsibility for appraisal of the merits of securities offered for public sale. The commission's function under the Securities Act is to see that all material facts essential to a proper evaluation of the securities and the exercise of an informed judgment as to their worth are made available to investors so that they may make discriminating and prudent investment decisions. Thus, investor self-protection is no less important to the act's scheme of investor protection than is the SEC's responsibility for seeing that the disclosures are complete and accurate.

However, the commission is empowered to refuse effectiveness to, or suspend the effectiveness of, a registration statement if it finds, after an opportunity for hearing, that the registration statement is false and misleading in respect of material facts. In appropriate situations, the commission may resort to this administrative sanction, particularly if there appears not to have been a bona fide effort to meet the statutory disclosure requirements or if fraudulent misrepresentations are indicated. The issuance of such a "stop order," it should be noted, is not a permanent bar to the sale of the securities; the order must be lifted and the registration statement made effective (thereby qualifying the securities for public sale) if and when the statement has been properly revised and corrected.

One of the exemptions from registration applies to smaller offerings of securities not exceeding $300,000 in amount, subject to such terms and conditions as the commission may prescribe for the protection of investors.

In its Regulation A exemption for such offerings, the commission still requires, among other things, that an offering circular containing certain basic information be delivered to persons to whom the securities are offered for sale.

The Securities Act also contains prohibitions against fraud in the sale of securities, whether or not registered; and it empowers the commission to investigate complaints or other indications of fraud or other unlawful activities in connection with the sale of securities. The commission also may institute actions in federal courts to enjoin such unlawful activities; and it may refer evidence of fraud or other willful violations to the Department of Justice with a recommendation for criminal prosecution. These investigations and enforcement activities are conducted through the regional and branch offices of the SEC under supervision of the Division of Trading and Markets and the commission. The office of the general counsel advises the commission with respect to proposed references to the Department of Justice for criminal prosecution.

Furthermore, the law provides important recovery rights if investors suffer losses in the purchase of securities (whether or not registered) which were sold through fraudulent or other unlawful means. Such rights must be asserted in the appropriate federal district courts, since the commission is not empowered to rule on money damages or otherwise serve as a collection agency. Its law enforcement activities, however, frequently result in voluntary restitution to investors where losses have been sustained in the purchase of securities sold by unlawful means.

SECURITIES EXCHANGE ACT OF 1934

In this law, Congress provided the mechanism for regulating trading practices in securities—both on national securities exchanges (such as the New York Stock Exchange) and in the over-the-counter (OTC) market—to protect the investing public by promoting the establishment and maintenance of just and equitable principles of trade in the securities markets, by outlawing fraudulent misrepresentations, manipulation, and other improper practices, and by requiring the continuing disclosure of corporate information.

Under this act, national securities exchanges and national associations of OTC brokers and dealers must be registered with the SEC. To be eligible for registration they must show that they are so organized and conducted as to insure fair dealings, promote just and equitable principles of trade, and protect the interests of investors (including provision for disciplinary powers over their members for unethical practices). In addition, brokers and dealers engaged in an OTC securities business must be registered with the commission and must conform their business practices to the standards prescribed in the law and the commission's regulations thereunder for the protection of investors.

This act complements the disclosure requirements of the Securities Act by providing for the filing of registration statements and subsequent periodic reports, both with the commission and with exchanges, by companies whose securities are listed on exchanges. Through the filing of such reports, important information concerning the issuing corporation, including certified financial statements, are disclosed for the information of the investing public. These data receive widespread dissemination through the medium of the financial press, securities manuals, and other services.

These disclosure requirements are supplemented by provisions governing the solicitation of proxies from the holders of listed securities. Under the commission's proxy rules, disclosure of all pertinent facts must be made to holders of these securities when their proxies are solicited, whether by the management or by a nonmanagement opposition group. Where a proxy contest for control of the management of a company is involved, the rules require disclosure of the names and interests of all persons participating in the solicitation of proxies. The commission is empowered to seek court orders enjoining any solicitation made in violation of its rules, or the voting of proxies obtained through such unlawful solicitation.

In addition, this law seeks to curb improper use of corporate information by management officials or other "insiders," by requiring officers, directors, and 10 per cent stockholders to file initial reports of their holdings of all equity securities of companies which have an equity security listed on an exchange, plus subsequent monthly reports of any changes in such holdings. Furthermore, the law provides that any profits resulting from their purchases and sales (or sales and repurchases) of any such equity securities within any six-month period may be recovered by the issuing company or by any security holder in its behalf. Such a recovery action must be asserted in the appropriate district court.

Although, as indicated, the periodic reporting provisions of this act apply to most companies which register securities for public sale under the Securities Act of 1933, the reporting, proxy soliciting, and insider trading provisions of the law do not otherwise apply to the several thousand companies whose securities are not listed on exchanges but are traded in the OTC market (except that similar provisions are applicable to companies subject to the commission's jurisdiction under the Holding Company Act and the Investment Company Act, whether or not their securities are listed on exchanges).

In 1946 the commission presented a report to Congress entitled *A Proposal to Safeguard Investors in Unregistered Securities.* This proposal recommended the application of such protective provisions to securities of the larger American corporations not fully listed on exchanges. From time to time, legislation to that effect has been proposed by members of Congress. In a further report filed with the Congress in May, 1956, the commission supported, in principle, the enactment of such a bill, subject to certain reservations; and in a supplemental report filed on February 6, 1957, the commission advocated that insurance companies should not be exempted therefrom.

The *Special Study of Securities Markets* of the SEC reaffirmed in 1963 the need for disclosure in the OTC market, noting that the overwhelming preponderance of fraud cases before the commission in the preceding years had involved securities of companies not subject to the commission's reporting requirements. In an unusual display of government-industry cooperation, the SEC and the brokerage community endorsed legislation to extend disclosure requirements to larger companies the securities of which are actively traded in over the counter.

Of equal importance to the disclosure and related provisions of this law is the work of the commission in policing the securities markets. The commission is empowered to make investigations of complaints or other indications of law violations in connection with the purchase and sale of securities. A staff of trained investigators, operating primarily out of the commission's regional and branch offices and under the general supervision of the Division of Trading and Markets, conducts hundreds of investigations each year for the purpose of determining whether fraud or other law violations may have been committed in the purchase and sale of securities.

An important aspect of this law enforcement program is the commission's practice of making surprise inspections of the books and records of brokers and dealers to assure that their trading practices are proper, that their dealings with customers are fair, and that their net capital position is such as not to endanger securities held for, or the free credit balances of, their customers.

Thus if it appears to the commission, upon the basis of a complaint or otherwise, that securities are being offered, sold, or traded in in violation of the registration, antifraud, or antimanipulative provisions of the federal securities laws, the commission's regional and branch offices undertake the conduct of a fact-finding inquiry or investigation to develop all facts pertinent to a determination of that question. These investigations normally are conducted privately, in much the same manner as the Federal Bureau of Investigation conducts its investigations.

If it appears that the securities laws have been violated, the commission is empowered to pursue any one of several courses of action, or a combination thereof. For example, it may institute a federal court action to enjoin any transactions, acts, practices, or courses of conduct in connection with the purchase or sale of securities considered to be violative of the securities laws. In any such action it has the burden of proving to the satisfaction of the court that the defendants have been or are about to violate the law and that their actions should be enjoined by court order.

In addition, facts developed in an SEC investigation which evidence fraud or other willful violation involving the purchase and sale of securities may be referred by the commission to the Department of Justice with a recommendation for criminal prosecution. If the Justice Department is satisfied that the evidence warrants such action, United States attorneys (occasionally with the assistance of SEC lawyers) lay the facts before a federal grand jury and seek an indictment.

Moreover, if the evidence tends to show that a registered broker-dealer or a member of a national securities exchange or of the OTC security dealers association has committed fraud or otherwise willfully violated the securities laws, the commission may institute an "administrative proceeding" for the purpose of determining whether, in fact, such a violation occurred and, if so, whether it is in the public interest to revoke the subject's registration or to suspend or expel it from membership in the exchange or the national securities association. Here again, counsel for the SEC staff has the burden of proving the violation through the introduction of evidence before an SEC hearing examiner; and the respondent has the same right of cross-examination and to introduce evidence in its defense as prevails in a regular court trial.

If in the opinion of the commission the evidence establishes such a violation, and if it concludes that the public interest so requires, the commission may revoke the broker-dealer registration or suspend or expel the respondent from such membership. Such decisions and orders represent an exercise of the commission's quasi-judicial functions. They may be appealed to the appropriate circuit court of appeals.

The very existence of the commission's investigative powers operates as an important retstraint upon those who might otherwise prey upon innocent and uninformed investors. On numerous occasions the commission's investigations have resulted indirectly in restitution to investors for losses suffered in the purchase of securities sold by unlawful means.

Likewise, many segments of the securities industry embarked on major programs of reform and more intensive self-regulation when the Special Study group of experts began its investigations.

From time to time there is an outbreak or "rash" of fraudulent promotions and operations which severely taxes the ability of the SEC and other securities administrators to provide the degree of protection which investors may be entitled to expect. Notable among these were: (1) the sale of millions of dollars of Canadian securities of little or no value during the early 1950s; (2) the uranium stock boom, which reached its height in 1955; and (3) in 1957, an outbreak of "boiler room" activities, emanating largely from New York, involving the peddling over the long distance telephone of securities of questionable value—a "high pressure" sales campaign involving fraudulent misrepresentations as to the company, its property and operations, the value of its securities, profits to be realized from their purchases, and similar data.

Primarily as a result thereof, the commission issued the following ten-point guide to investors:

1. Think before buying.
2. Deal only with a securities firm which you know.
3. Be skeptical of securities offered on the telephone from any firm or salesman you do not know.
4. Guard against all high pressure sales.
5. Beware of promises of quick spectacular price rises.
6. Be sure you understand the risk of loss as well as the prospect of gain.
7. Get the facts—do not buy on tips or rumors.
8. Request the person offering securities over the phone to mail you written information about the corporation, its operations, net profit, management, financial position, and future prospects. Save all such information for future reference.
9. If you do not understand the written information, consult a person who does.
10. Give at least as much thought when purchasing securities as you would when acquiring any valuable property.

It is a sad fact that the leaflet listing the above cautions did not receive wider distribution or acceptance. There were 100,000 printed —an insignificant number when one considers the millions of investors who could have profited by reading these words of wisdom. And of the 100,000, probably through an oversight, only 30,000 were distributed.

PUBLIC UTILITY HOLDING COMPANY ACT OF 1935

The Public Utility Holding Company Act of 1935 was enacted as the result of an investigation conducted by the Federal Trade Commission, which began in 1929 at the direction of the United States Senate, and related congressional investigations. During these investigations it was found that various abuses and evils existed in the field of public utility holding company finance and operation which were inimical to the best interests of the public and of investors and customers.

Some of the evils uncovered were: (1) issuance of securities upon the basis of fictitious or unsound asset value; (2) issuance of securities under circumstances which subjected the public utility companies to the burden of supporting an overcapitalized structure and tended to prevent voluntary rate reductions; (3) impositions upon subsidiary companies of excessive charges for services, construction work, equipment, and materials; (4) control by holding companies over the accounting practices and rate, dividend, and other policies of public utility companies, which complicated and obstructed state regulation, or the exertion of such control through disproportionately small investment; (5) growth or extension of holding company systems bearing no relation to economy of management and operation, nor to the integration and coordination of related operating properties; and (6) lack of economy of management and operation of public utility companies, or lack of efficiency and adequacy of service rendered, or lack of effective public regulation.

The act was designed to eliminate these evils and abuses. To that end, it subjected public utility holding company systems in the electric utility business, or in the retail distribution of natural or manufactured gas, to regulation by the Securities and Exchange Commission in accordance with standards prescribed by Congress. In furtherance of this policy, the act requires: (1) the registration of public utility holding companies; (2) the geographic integration and simplification of holding company systems; (3) the simplification of corporate and capital structures and the equitable redistribution of voting power among security holders of such companies; and (4) commission regulation of the financial and related transactions of system companies.

Generally speaking, the congressional mandate requires each system to be limited in its operations to a single "integrated public utility system." Under certain circumstances, however, additional utility systems and other incidental businesses are retainable. One of the governing standards of the act is the requirement that the retainable system, or combination of systems, must not be so large as to "impair the advantages of localized management, efficient operation, or the effectiveness of regulation."

Attainment of the objectives of the act may be had through voluntary action by the companies affected, subject to commission approval of their plans as meeting the prescribed standards of the act. Similarly, voluntary compliance also may be had with the requirement for simplification of corporate and capital structures and equitable redistribution of voting power among security holders, again subject to commission approval as fair and equitable to investors and as necessary to accomplish the statutory objective.

If there is no voluntary action taken by the companies within a reasonable period, the commission is required, after appropriate notice and opportunity for hearing, to order the companies to take whatever action may be required to bring about compliance with the statute.

Recapitalizations, mergers, and consolidations of public utility holding companies and their subsidiaries must be approved by the commission as fair and equitable to affected security holders. If such a company is undergoing reorganization in a federal court under the Bankruptcy Act, its reorganization plan must be passed upon by the commission before it is submitted to the court for approval.

This act also provides for regulation of the issuance and sale of securities by holding companies and their subsidiaries. Among other things, the commission must find that the new security is reasonably adapted to the security structure and earning power of the issuer and that fees and commissions paid in connection therewith are reasonable.

If an issue of securities of a subsidiary operating company has been approved by the state commission of the state in which the subsidiary is organized and doing business, and if the proceeds from its sale are solely for the purpose of financing the company's business, the act provides an exemption of the issuance and sale of such securities, subject to such terms and conditions as the SEC may impose for the protection of investors, consumers, and the public.

To implement these objectives and to eliminate investment banker control and assure maintenance of competitive conditions in the sale of these securities, the commission's rules require (with minor exceptions) that issuers invite sealed, competitive bids for the purchase of their securities.

The purchase and sale of utility securities and utility properties also are subject to prior approval by the commission as meeting standards of the law designed for the protection of investors and consumers, including reasonableness of the consideration paid or received, maintenance of competitive conditions, and similar matters.

When the Public Utility Holding Company Act became law, in 1935, 15 holding company systems controlled 80 per cent of all electric energy generation, 98.5 per cent of all transmission of electric energy across state lines, and 80 per cent of all natural gas pipeline mileage in the United States. In 1938, 53 holding company systems, comprising 1,620 companies, were registered with the commission under the act. Since that date, additional systems have registered, with the result that 2,314 companies have been subject to the act as registered holding companies or subsidiaries throughout the eighteen-year period from 1938 to 1956.

Included in the total were 216 holding companies, 998 electric and gas utility companies, and 1,100 other companies engaged in a wide variety of activities. Among the latter were brick works, laundries, experimental orchards, motion picture theaters, and even a baseball club.

The picture is vastly different today, reflecting the action of the SEC in enforcing the provisions of the Public Utility Holding Company Act. On June 30, 1963, the date of the latest annual report of the commission available at this writing, only 17 public utility holding company systems were still registered with the commission. These 17 had previously comprised 19 registered holding companies which functioned solely as holding companies and 6 which were engaged in substantial public utility and related operations; 164 electric and gas utility companies; and 111 nonutility companies —a total of 302 companies. (Some holding company systems have within them intermediate holding companies which may or may not also be operating public utility companies.)

The effect has been to separate the major portion of the electric and gas utility industry from holding company control, so that most public utility companies today are independently owned and managed.

In writing the statute, however, the Congress concluded that groups of electric and gas utility properties which constituted physically integrated systems and were not too large or too sprawling to meet the standards in the act offered operating efficiencies which justified holding company control. The approximately sixteen systems expected to remain subject to the act will have complied with these standards. It is estimated that they will comprise over 160 companies with assets (less valuation reserves) of some $8.5 billion. These continuing systems account for approximately 20 per cent of the aggregate assets of the privately owned electric and gas utility and gas pipeline industries of the nation.

The Division of Corporate Regulation assists the commission in administration of this act. It may be noted that the Federal Power Commission, not the SEC, exercises federal jurisdiction over the rates of electric and gas utility companies. Furthermore, the FPC, not the SEC, has regulatory jurisdiction over financings by any electric or gas utility company which is not a subsidiary of a registered holding company.

TRUST INDENTURE ACT OF 1939

This act further buttresses the provisions of the disclosure requirements and fraud prohibitions contained in the Securities Act of 1933. It provides that bonds, notes, debentures, and similar debt securities, issued under indentures under which more than $1 million in principal amount of securities may at any time be outstanding, may not be offered for sale to the public unless the trust indenture conforms to specific statutory standards designed to safeguard the rights and interest of the purchaser.

Among these are provisions relating to the indenture trustee which require an "independent" corporate trustee, free of certain conflicts of interest; minimum combined capital and surplus; high standards of conduct and responsibility to preclude the preferential collection of certain claims owing to the trustee; and provision for reports and notices by the trustees to investors.

The Division of Corporation Finance aids the commission in the administration of this act.

INVESTMENT COMPANY ACT OF 1940

Investment companies, particularly the so-called mutual funds, have become very popular as a medium of investment for a portion of the public's savings in recent years. They are designed to provide the vehicle by which the savings of a large number of investors, who may be inexperienced in investment and finance, may be brought together in one pool of capital, which is then invested by managers of the investment company, reputedly skilled in the art of investment.

The mechanics are simple: An investor purchases the securities of an investment company, which in turn uses those funds, together with the funds invested by others, for the purchase of securities of industrial and other companies which are expected to yield a profitable dividend return coupled with capital growth. Purchasing a variety of securities reduces the risk that would be involved by putting all of one's eggs in one basket. Normally a selling commission is charged the purchaser of an investment company security of the open-end, or mutual fund, type. This is referred to as the *load*. In some cases this charge runs as high as 7 to 8.5 per cent. In addition there is a service charge, usually around one-half of 1 per cent a year, for managing the fund.

The phenomenal growth of investment companies over the past years attests to the popularity of investment company securities (see Chapter 8).

Under this act, the activities of companies engaged primarily in the business of investing, reinvesting, and trading in securities are subject to regulation by the commission. Investment companies must register with the commission; their affairs must be conducted in accordance with the applicable provisions of the act, including compliance with the commission's proxy regulations; and various of their transactions, including those between affiliates, are prohibited or made subject to commission approval, under prescribed statutory standards. However, the commission has no control over the investment policies of investment companies.

The commission, under the act, may prepare special reports for security holders upon the fairness of plans of reorganization, merger, or consolidation of investment companies, and may apply to courts for orders enjoining the consummation of any plans considered grossly unfair to security holders. The commission also may apply to courts for orders enjoining acts and practices of investment company managements involving gross misconduct or gross abuse of trust, and for orders seeking the removal of officials responsible for such misconduct or abuse of trust.

The Division of Corporate Regulation assists the commission in the administration of the regulatory provisions of this act. The various disclosure and reporting requirements, including proxy soliciting and insider reporting provisions, are similar to those prescribed by the Securities Exchange Act; and the Division of Corporation Finance assists the commission in their administration. It should be noted that securities of investment companies offered for public sale must be registered under the Securities Act in order that investors, through such registration and the required delivery of a prospectus, may exercise an informed judgment with respect to their purchases of such securities.

In 1962 the Wharton School of Finance and Commerce submitted a 595-page *Study of Mutual Funds* to the SEC. It did not challenge the fundamental soundness of mutual funds but it was critical of control over boards of directors and management fees.

INVESTMENT ADVISERS ACT OF 1940

This act provides for registration with the commission of persons engaged in the business of advising others on security transactions, and imposes upon them the duty of conducting their affairs in accordance with the standards prescribed in the act by Congress.

The antifraud provisions of the act, which are similar to those under the Securities Act of 1933 and the Securities Exchange Act of 1934, prohibit investment advisers from "employing any device, scheme, or artifice to defraud" any client or prospective customer. Furthermore, if an investment adviser acts as a principal for his own account in connection with any transaction with a client, he must disclose to the client, in writing, the capacity in which he is acting, and obtain the client's consent.

In 1962 the commission adopted a new rule regarding advertising by investment advisers. It was intended to curb certain flamboyant types of advertising which might tend to mislead or deceive the public. The Division of Trading and Markets, with the assistance of regional offices, aids in the administration of this act.

BANKRUPTCY ACT

Under Chapter X of the Bankruptcy Act, the commission serves as an independent, expert adviser to federal courts in connection with proceedings for the reorganization of debtor corporations in which there is a substantial public interest. It renders advice and assistance to the courts on all phases of such proceedings, but particularly with respect to the fairness of the terms and provisions of proposed plans of reorganization to the affected security holders, and with respect to the feasibility of such plans.

Its services under this act may be broadened. In February 1964, William L. Cary, former chairman of the SEC, told a House commerce subcommittee that amendments to the Bankruptcy Act appeared to be necessary to provide more adequate protection to customers in the event of a broker's insolvency.

He was referring to the case of the Allied Crude Vegetable Oil Refining Company headed by one Anthony (Tino) DeAngelis, which failed to meet an $18.5 million call for margin from the New York Stock Exchange firm of Ira Haupt and Company. The firm subsequently was forced to liquidate; but those of its customers with cash or securities left on deposit were saved from loss through action by the stock exchange which, for the first time in history, made good the loss. Otherwise these customers would have had to stand in line along with other general creditors of the bankrupt vegetable oil concern.

In the Haupt case the SEC chairman testified that the absence of significant margin levels exposed the firm to serious risks and that the firm had been put in double jeopardy in that in addition to advancing loans on securities to its customers, it had also advanced money to Allied Crude on warehouse receipts which the government contended were forged.

16

〰〰〰〰〰〰〰〰〰〰〰〰〰〰〰〰

THE COMMODITY
MARKETS

Commodities, as referred to in the financial section, are the raw materials and provisions from which the world makes what it needs. In the financial community they are traded in on a spot basis, that is, for cash and immediate delivery, or on a futures basis, which calls for delivery in some specified month in the future.

In considering price movements in this field, and indeed in all of the world primary markets, the student is called upon to appraise not only such factors as demand and supply, weather conditions, crop blights, and the stage of the trade cycle, but also the influence of the government. And not alone the influence of the United States government, for most of the governments of raw material producing countries have taken a hand, in one way or another, in regulating the supply of commodities.

They have restricted or encouraged production, formed marketing organizations, granted loans on easy terms so that output might be withheld from the market, subsidized their exporters, and altered tariff barriers and fixed quotas so that their own domestic markets might be sheltered. They have endeavored to fix prices by fiat and to maintain ceiling prices during wars or other periods of intensive inflation, thus, at times, contributing to the creation of vast black markets.

Futures markets have been organized in New York and other cities for dealing in the principal commodities. Many of them were closed during World War II and were only reopened gradually. The New York market is not the primary one in all of the commodities. In cotton futures it is of the very first importance, and New York also has major futures markets in coffee, sugar, cocoa, cottonseed oil, rubber, hides, copper and zinc, wool, and potatoes. It is outranked by Chicago, Winnipeg, Liverpool, and Buenos Aires in the grain markets, by Chicago in provisions, Kansas City in millfeeds and lard, and Memphis in cottonseed and cottonseed meal. Boston has an important spot market in wool tops and wool but no futures market in them.

The New York Cotton Exchange remained active during World War II and dealt in cotton, while wool and wool tops were traded in during this period on the New York Wool Top Exchange, an affiliated organization. Other New York futures markets include the New York Coffee and Sugar Exchange, the New York Produce Exchange, the New York Cocoa Exchange, the Commodity Exchange, Incorporated—for dealing in rubber, hides, and metals—and the New York Mercantile Exchange.

The Chicago Board of Trade has long been known as the leading grain futures market of the world, although in cash business Kansas City and Minneapolis both exceed it. Other major commodity futures markets frequently referred to in the financial section include the Kansas City Board of Trade, Winnipeg Grain Exchange, and the Memphis Board of Trade.

CONTRACT MARKETS

These several futures markets are known as contract markets; that is, they deal in commodities for future delivery. On a commodity exchange, future-delivery contracts are agreements for the purchase or sale of a definite amount of the actual commodity deliverable during a specified future period—usually a month—the day of delivery, the place of delivery, and the grade to be delivered, where a choice exists in the contract, being at the option of the seller. This type of contract-dealing in commodities began to come into vogue in grain in Chicago around 1850, and rules governing futures contracts were adopted by the Chicago Board of Trade in 1865. Future-contract trading in cotton began on the New York Cotton Exchange in 1870.

There are many cash or spot exchanges in cotton, wheat, and other grains, but as a rule the futures markets are few in number. For example, Chicago, Minneapolis, and Kansas City each do business both in cash grain and in grain futures; whereas in places like Peoria, Sioux City, and Indianapolis there is much business done in cash wheat but none in futures.

Cash commodities are sold for *forward* delivery as well as for *immediate* delivery. Futures contracts can be sold for delivery in the current or a future month.

HEDGING

The use of futures contracts for the delivery of commodities makes possible the practice of hedging. This term, as applied to commodity trading, means the taking of such action as will result in offsetting possible losses in transactions previously or about to be entered upon. As illustrated by the *Commodity Year Book,* published by Commodity Research Bureau, Incorporated, hedging, when expressed in terms of action, involves one of the following:

1. The sale of one or more futures contracts in a commodity to eliminate or lessen the adverse effects of a possible decline in value of a spot purchase of an approximately equal amount of the same commodity. *Example:* A grain elevator man buys 10,000 bushels of wheat from a farmer. He sells futures contracts in the equivalent of 10,000 bushels on, say, the Chicago Board of Trade. Assuming that prices move in the same direction, he is protected in the following manner. Losses due to price declines on his actual wheat will be offset by gains from the sale of futures contracts (he can repurchase the contracts at a lower price than that at which he sold). If the

price of wheat rises, the gain will be offset by the loss on the futures transaction.

2. The purchase of one or more futures contracts in a commodity to eliminate or lessen the adverse effects of a possible advance in the value of the spot commodity needed to fill a forward sale of the commodity or a product thereof. Example: A miller sells flour for delivery two months after the date of sale. He does not have wheat on hand to fill the order, and he may have no intention of acquiring it until shortly before grinding and delivering the flour. He buys futures contracts in the amount of wheat necessary to fill his flour contract. In this way, he hedges against the risk that the price of wheat may rise before he buys it and thus wipe out the milling profit that he expected to make on the flour, or even result in a dead loss.

It should not be necessary to point out that not all of the trading which is handled on the principal commodity exchanges is strictly trade business. There is a great deal of speculative trading, and the Commodity Exchange Authority collects figures as to the amount in the case of those commodities under its supervision, generally agricultural commodities. A trader may buy thousands of bushels of wheat, although he does not accept delivery of the actual wheat; a trader may sell wheat, although he never saw a wheat farm.

Yet these speculators perform a function. They increase the volume of dealings in a commodity on both sides of the market, and thus they facilitate the legitimate business of hedgers by making it possible for them to trade on a narrower margin of profit. Trade accounts in a commodity market are individuals, partnerships, associations, or corporations whose main business is in the raw material field. These would include farmers and producers, merchants and shippers, importers, mills or manufacturers, warehousemen and dealers, processors, ginners, and distributors.

Speculation in commodities is usually considered more highly specialized than speculation in securities. Most people are willing to admit their lack of virtuosity in commodity trading, but almost everyone who is solvent, and many others who are not, believes that

How Cottonseed Oil Futures Contracts Are Traded Without Money or Collateral

By a WALL STREET JOURNA

NEW YORK—How are
worth of cottonseed oil, repr
contracts," traded on the
Exchange without any mor
up by customers?

The answer lies in a s
the exchange that applie
refiners and others engag
oil business. These peopl
in futures without any n
fulfill a prime purpose
minimize risks in ownin
lowing "legitimate hedg

To understand this
trading, consider the
a cottonseed oil process
one tank car, or 60,0
cents a pound. His
the risk that his inven
because of a price d

One way to protec
by entering the futur
tracts are agreement
at a specified future
this hypothetical ca
short" a futures con
say, 12½ cents a p
buyer has agreed
for 60,000 pounds o

What If Price Falls

Consider what
days, the cash p
½ cent to 9½ ce
$300 in inventory
ordinarily fall or
cash prices. So
the futures ma
for May delive

He now own
and another to
made a profit o
contracts, offse

What happe
oil cash and f
case the proce
inventory, but
losses in the fu
buy a future c
"pay off" his o
at 12½ cents.

The New Y
specify that onl
cottonseed oil f
no initial cash
security. These
tual inventories
of crude or refi

... tallows, fats, waxes or
... increase in

wipe out
roker money,
ve to put up
a loss.
k purchases
although the
er. The Fed-
ium percent-
70%, as the
nimum cash
isted on ex-
d credit on
based on a
required for

Futures Prices

Thursday, March 5, 1964

CHICAGO—WHEAT

	Open	High	Low	Close	Change	Season's High	Season's Low
Mar	203	204	199½	200-200¼	−1¼to1	224	182½
May	201	202½	198⅞	199-199½	−1¼to¾	219⅞	177¾
July	162	163¼	161⅞	162-162⅛	unch to +⅛	179½	150½
Sept	164⅜	165	163⅝	164⅛-164	+⅜to¼	181⅛	152
Dec	169⅝	170⅛	169	169¼	+⅝	185	167½

CORN

	Open	High	Low	Close	Change	Season's High	Season's Low
Mar	119	119¾	119	119½-⅝	+⅞to1	129	114⅝
May	121⅛	121⅞	121⅛	121¾-⅝	+¾to⅝	131	116⅞
July	123⅜	124	123¼	123¾	+⅝	131⅛	119
Sept	123⅛	123⅝	123⅛	123⅜	+¼	127⅛	120⅝
Dec	120⅝	121¼	120⅝	121¼	+⅜	121⅛	116

OATS

	Open	High	Low	Close	Change	Season's High	Season's Low
Mar	65	65⅝	65	65⅜	+⅜	75½	63⅞
May	66⅛	66¾	66⅛	66½-⅜	+⅜to¼	75⅞	65½
July	65⅝	65⅞	55⅝	65¾	+⅛	72¼	64½
Sept	67⅝	67¾	67⅝	67¾	+⅜	69¾	65⅞
Dec	69½	70	69½	69⅞	+¼	72	68¼

RYE

	Open	High	Low	Close	Change	Season's High	Season's Low
Mar	132¾	133¾	132¾	133¼-⅛	+½to⅜	169	127½
May	137	137⅝	136⅝	136¾	+¼	168	129¼
July	135¼	135¾	135	135½	+½	155½	127⅜
Sept	134¾	135½	134¾	135½	+¾	149	132¾
Dec	138¼	138½	138	138	+½	148¼	136½

SOYBEANS

	Open	High	Low	Close	Change	Season's High	Season's Low
Mar	269¼	269⅝	268½	269½-⅜	+⅝to½	298¾	250
May	268¾	269¼	267¾	268⅝-½	+¼to½	302¾	259
July	268	268⅝	267⅛	267⅞-⅞	−⅜to½	304½	260½
Aug	264½	264½	263⅜	263⅝-¾	−¾to⅝	299¼	260¾
Sept	255½	255⅝	254⅛	254⅝-¾	−⅝to½	273½	247
Nov	254½	254½	252⅝	253⅛-253	−⅝to¾	264½	252
Jan	257½	257½	256⅛	256¾	−⅝	262⅞	256⅛

SOYBEAN OIL

	Open	High	Low	Close	Change	Season's High	Season's Low
Mar	7.76	7.79	7.75	7.76	+ .01	10.62	7.30
May	7.98	7.99	7.96	7.97	− .01	10.73	7.45
July	8.18	8.20	8.16	8.17	− .01	10.83	7.95
Aug.	8.25	8.25	8.22	8.21b	− .02	10.77	7.85
Sept	8.28	8.28	8.27	8.27	− .01	10.44	7.91
Oct	8.41	8.43	8.39	8.39b	− .02	10.50	8.30
Dec	8.55	8.55	8.55	8.55	− .03	8.82	8.55

SOYBEAN MEAL

	Open	High	Low	Close	Change	Season's High	Season's Low
Mar	69.00	69.00	68.10	68.15-.10	− .75to.80	80.00	61.15
May	71.00	71.00	70.25	70.30	− .55	80.35	63.90
July	71.25	71.25	70.75	70.90	− .25		
Aug	70.70	70.70	70.45	70.50b			
Sept	67.20	67.[illegible]					

POTATOES (MAINE)

	Open	High	Low	Close	Change	Season's High	Season's Low
Mar	2.27	2.28	2.26	2.26	− .01	2.55	2.15
Apr	2.40	2.40	2.37	2.38	.....	2.76	2.27
May	2.70	2.71	2.65	2.69	.....	3.16	2.46
Nov	2.18	2.18	2.17	2.18	− .01	2.20	2.15

Sales: 598 contracts.

WOOL FUTURES

	Open	High	Low	Close	Change	Season's High	Season's Low
Mar	155.7	155.8	155.7	155.8	+ 1.0	155.8	119.2
May	150.5	150.7	150.3	150.3b	+ 0.5	150.7	122.4
July	148.3	148.7	148.0	148.7	+ 1.1	148.7	124.0
Oct	147.7b	147.9	147.5	147.7b	+ 0.6	147.9	124.8
Dec	146.9	147.4	146.8	147.0b	+ 0.7	147.4	125.7
Mar	145.6b	146.0	145.9	146.0b	+ 0.9	146.0	129.5
May	144.6	145.0	144.5	144.7b	+ 0.7	145.0	138.5
July	142.8b	143.5	143.5	143.5b	+ 0.8	143.5	140.4

Spot: 156.0n.

WOOL TOPS

	Open	High	Low	Close	Change	Season's High	Season's Low
Mar	180.0b	181.0	181.0	180.5b	+ 0.6	188.0	161.0
Dec	181.0b	181.7	181.7	181.0b	+ 0.2	181.7	176.4

Spot: 181.0n. Closings: May 182.7b, July 182.0b, October 182.2b, March 181.0b, May 179.9b, July 178.8b.

LEAD

	Open	High	Low	Close	Change	Season's High	Season's Low
May	12.50b	12.50	12.50	12.50b	.....	12.65	9.37
Oct	12.55b	12.55	12.52	12.50b	− .05	13.00	11.34

Sales: 3 contracts. Closings: March 12.15b, July through March 12.50b.

ZINC

	Open	High	Low	Close	Change	Season's High	Season's Low
Dec	13.15b	13.10	13.10	13.05b	− .15	13.50	13.00

Sales: 12 contracts. Closings: March 12.50b, May 12.60b, July 12.70b, September 12.80b, October 12.90b, January and March 13.10b.

COPPER

	Open	High	Low	Close	Change	Season's High	Season's Low
May	34.10	34.35	33.90	34.35b	+ .03	35.28	29.07
July	33.65	33.93	33.38	33.93	+ .11	34.65	29.22
Sept	33.00	33.41	32.90	33.40b	+ .08	34.55	29.25
Oct	32.75	33.05	32.66	33.00b	+ .08	34.38	29.60
Dec	32.60	32.87	32.40	32.87	+ .15	34.15	29.91
Jan	32.35b	32.50	32.25	32.52b	+ .07	33.75	30.05
Mar	32.10b	32.40	32.10	32.42b	+ .10	33.50	31.85

Sales: 255 contracts. Closing: March '64, 34.35n.

SILVER

No sales: Closings: March 129.25b, April and May 129.40b, June 129.50b, July 129.55b, August 129.65b, September 129.80b, October 129.85b, November 129.90b, December and January 130.10b, February 130.15b.

RUBBER

	Open	High	Low	Close	Change	Season's High	Season's Low
Mar	24.25b	24.[illegible]0	24.60	24.40b	+ .15	27.70	23.00
Sept	[illegible]5	24.15	24.15b		+ .10	25.40	23.20

...cts. Closings: May 24.20b, July 24.15b, ...ry 24.10b, March 24.05b.

10.35	10.35b	− .11			
10.55	10.55b	+ .07		15.70	9.32
				14.60	9.65

...s. Closings: October 10.65b, January

What Commodities Cost

Cash prices in primary markets—Monday, March 16, 1964

Commodity and unit	Monday	Friday	Highs High	Highs Date	1963-1964 Lows Low	Lows Date
FOODS—						
Wheat (No. 2 hard, c.i.f.), bu	$2.57	$2.56	$2.85⅞	3/29	$2.32	7/25
Corn (No. 2 yellow), bu	1.54¼	1.54¾	1.74⅛	9/25	1.44⅝	11/22
Oats (No. 2 white), bu	.86¼	.86¼	.98⅛	1/ 3	.83¾	8/20
Rye (No. 2 Western, c.i.f.) bu	1.78	1.79⅝	2.01¾	9/25	1.64¾	8/12
Flour (spring patents), 100 lbs	*6.55	*6.55	7.30	1/ 2	6.10	8/ 5
Cocoa (accra), lb	*.23½	*.23⅞	.29	5/ 1	.21⅛	1/ 2
‡Steers, Chic (Prime 1100-1300 lbs.)	22.50	22.62½	30.50	1/ 9	21.37½	x2/19
‡Steers, Chi (Choice 1100-1300 lbs.)	21.50	21.75	29.50	1/ 8	20.62½	x2/19
‡Hogs, Chic (g'd-choice 180-220 lbs.)	15.62½	15.37½	20.00	7/24	14.35	4/ 8
Sugar (granulated), lb	.1185	.1185	.169	5/23	.098	1/ 2
Coffee (No. 4 Santos), lb	*.50	*.50¼	.52½	x3/ 3	.32¾	8/ 9
Butter (92 score), lb	.58⅝	.58⅝	.62	10/ 1	.58⅜	10/24
Eggs (No. 1 medium white), doz	.32½	.32½	.42¼	x1/15	.22½	5/16
TEXTILES—						
Cotton (middling 1 inch), lb	*.354	*.354	.3595	4/ 5	.3495	1/ 2
Print cloth (64-60; 38½"—5.35), yd	.14¾	.14¾	.15	12/13	.13½	1/ 2
Silk (20/22, "2A") lb	*5.58	*5.55	8.20	4/ 5	5.47	x1/30
METALS—						
Steel billets (Pittsburgh), ton	84.00	84.00	84.00	11/13	80.00	1/ 2
Iron (No. 2 fdry., Swedld), ton	63.50	63.50	65.50	1/ 2	63.50	8/ 7
Steel scrap (No. 1 Hvy., Pitts.) ton	28.50	28.50	31.00	3/31	24.50	6/19
Lead (spot), lb	.13	.13	.13	x1/ 2	.10	1/ 2
Copper (elec.), lb	.31-.32	.31-.32	.32	x3/13	.31	1/ 2
Tin (Straits), lb	1.35½	1.35⅝	1.59	x2/25	1.08⅛	2/20
Aluminum (ingot), lb	.23½	.23½	.24	x1/20	.22½	1/ 2
Quicksilver (per flask, 76 lbs.)	*267.50	*268.00	268.00	x3/ 9	183.00	7/16
Zinc (prime West E. St. L. basis), lb	.13	.13	.13½	x1/28	.11½	1/ 2
Silver, oz	1.293	1.293	1.293	9/ 9	1.21	1/ 2
MISCELLANEOUS						
Rubber (rib-smoked sheets), lb	*.25¾	*.25½	.32	1/23	.23	9/ 9
Hides (Butt Brand Steers), lb	.06¼	.06¼	.10½	1/ 2	.06	x3/ 6
Calfskins (Midwstn light) lb	.30	.30	.37½	1/ 2	.25	9/26
Crude Oil (Bradford, Pa.), bbl	4.48	4.48	4.63	1/ 2	4.48	x1/13
Crude Oil (Mid Cont 36 36.9 grav.) bbl	2.97	2.97	2.97	1/ 2	2.92	4/ 8
Gasoline (Tank Wagon), gal	.162	.162	.162	1/ 2	.162	1/ 2
§Coal (furnace), ton	29.25	29.25	29.25	x2/12	25.00	5/ 1
Moody's Commodity Index	368.3	369.7	393.2	5/23	357.0	8/28
Reuter's U. K. Commodity Index	474.8	476.0	496.2	11/15	435.2	1/ 2

Prices listed are for the New York market unless otherwise noted. *Nominal. †Not available. ‡Based on 100 lbs. §Manhattan. x1964.

he knows something about selecting a stock for purchase. For the
unconvinced and the uninitiated, however, it can be said that the
full unit of trading in the grain markets in this country is 5,000
bushels of wheat, oats, corn, rye, or barley. All futures trading is
done on margin. Original margins vary according to the market,
the credit of the customer, and the nature of the price swings.

Grain quotations are in cents and eighths of a cent a bushel, and
each change of one-eighth cent a bushel on a 5,000-bushel contract
is equal to $6.25 on the contract. The hours of trading on the Chi-
cago Board of Trade are from 10:30 A.M. to 2:15 P.M., New York
time. In the cotton market the contract unit on the New York Cotton
Exchange is 100 bales, or 50,000 pounds, and quotations are in cents
and hundredths of a cent a pound. Each single point change is equal
to $5 on a 100-bale contract, and each change of one cent a pound is
equal to $500 a contract.

Other commodities are traded in on these and other exchanges,
and the contract units and the units of fluctuation vary with the
commodity. The exchanges willingly give out information on these
technicalities of trading.

Government crop reports are published monthly on the grains
and cotton during the planting and growing season. The crop year
for wheat in the United States is from July 1 to July 1, and in cotton
from August 1 to August 1. Detailed reports and tables are also
carried on the other principal commodities, with fewer details being
given to those of lesser importance. An attempt is made, therefore,
to give a broad news coverage to all of the leading staples and most
of the lesser commodities, excepting only those of very remote
interest.

Commodities which figure in world commerce are numbered by
the hundreds, and it would be impossible, as well as undesirable,
to give reports on all. There are many commodities, such as asbes-
tos, copra, tea, platinum, and many obscure minerals and agricultural
products of industrial importance, which are dealt in for cash.

The usual daily reports on commodities are supplemented by
more elaborate reports on novel or important situations which may

develop in a given commodity. In recent years the United States farm program, involving parity prices, and government price support and purchase programs, has been most important to the market.

An infestation of boll weevils of unusual proportions in southern cotton fields will, of course, have an important bearing on cotton prices, and accordingly such a story is of economic importance. Drought or rains in the wheat fields of the West or Argentina will naturally influence wheat prices. Legislation in various countries may also have an effect. Threats of war affect virtually all commodities.

In addition to the direct and more elementary influences on commodity prices there are more abstract influences, such as the rates for money and credit and trade agreements.

17

CONSTRUCTION AND USE OF INDEXES

An index in the field of statistics is used to measure volume, price, or activity. It consists of a compilation of figures, which is averaged and may be weighted, and is designed to point out, indicate, or disclose the ratio of one condition to the general condition in a comparable field.

In the construction of an index the aim is to select a group of variables, the changes of which will be representative of the field covered. It is a difficult task, for no matter how much care is put into the original work of construction, the index must cover a long period to be of value, and in a long period of years conditions change so radically that usually the original selection of factors must be judiciously revised.

No student who compiles an index should ever claim that he has hit upon the perfect measure. It may be as near to perfect as he can make it; it may be fairly representative of the field he wishes to measure. It will always be subject to the fallibility of human judgment. He can offer no guarantee that his is the perfect index and that it gives an exact picture of the over-all condition he wishes to depict. Consequently, no one is ever completely satisfied with indexes; but they are a valuable tool in the hands of the student, businessman, and financier.

SELECTION OF FACTORS

When the statistician starts the construction of an index, he selects a wide variety of factors, the average of which he thinks will be representative of the field. Once selected, he must then decide how much weight should be given to each individual factor. For instance, if he is compiling an index of agricultural prices, how many percentage points of the 100 per cent shall he accord to the price for potatoes, string beans, or soybeans?

He must decide, and he will have to be arbitrary about it. If he takes, say, twenty agricultural products and decides that an average of these twenty will be fairly representative of the price situation in agriculture, this will be an arbitrary decision, as it must be. Someone may say he left out two or a dozen or several dozen other products that should have been included. It will be a matter of judgment, with no one able to say what is correct.

Then when he has selected the twenty, shall he give each one of them a consideration of 5 per cent in the compilation of his index? Or should he give potatoes 7.5 per cent, string beans 4.75 per cent, soybeans 2.375 per cent—or use some other figures?

The agricultural motif has been used here merely because it illustrates the point. The same problem is encountered in the construction of any index. If one would make an index of the stock market, what should be called the proper proportion between the so-called blue chips and the so-called cats and dogs? Should a change of an eighth point in the common stock of a bankrupt railroad have the same influence on the index as an eighth-point fluctuation in United States Steel?

PURPOSE OF AN INDEX

The first step in the construction of the index is to define the purpose for which it is to be used. Generally the aim is either to measure changes in the price level, the degree of activity in business, or the volume of physical output.

The personal judgment of the compiler must be relied upon when he first constructs the index and throughout the life of the index, for changes must be made continuously. Clara K. Grey, of the Chase Manhattan Bank's Department of Financial and Business Research, in a study made for the bank, pointed out that an index designed to be a trade barometer would obviously require different construction from one used in computing a deflator for the national income. A "deflator" is a divisor used to eliminate the element of price change from changes in dollar values.

She pointed out that the computation of an index is an expensive and laborious task, that the important indexes have been designed for widespread use in various problems, and that they have the relatively vague aim of measuring changes in the price level. Moreover, as it is impossible to collect every price involved, it is necessary to select a sample giving approximately the result which would be obtained if all prices were covered. This means the selection of representative data for the different classes, such as farm versus nonfarm products, consumers' versus producers' goods, and many others.

COLLECTION OF PRICES

Professor Wesley C. Mitchell, in *Making and Using of Index Numbers,* a bulletin which he wrote for the United States Department of Labor, Bureau of Labor Statistics, held that the collection of prices is a much more difficult task than the problems of weighting and averaging, because a choice must be made from among the many prices which exist at any one time for a commodity. Even on the same level of trade, he pointed out, prices differ as the result of such factors as varying grades, large lots and small lots, different localities, and imperfections in competition. When the field worker has collected data for an index number, Professor Mitchell added, he:

must select from among all those different prices for each of his commodities the one or the few series of quotations that make the most representative sample of the whole. He must find the most reliable source of information, the most representative market, the most typical brands or grades, and the class of dealers who stand in the most influential position.

He must have sufficient technical knowledge to be sure that his quotations are for uniform qualities, or to make the necessary adjustments if changes in quality have occurred in the markets that require recognition in the statistical office.

He must be able to recognize anything suspicious in the data offered him and to get at the facts. He must know how commodities are made and must seek comparable information concerning the prices of raw materials and their manufactured products, concerning articles that are substituted for one another, used in connection with one another, or turned out as joint products of the same process.

He must guard against the pitfalls of cash discounts, premiums, rebates, deferred payments and allowances of all sorts; and he must know whether his quotations for different articles are all on the same basis, or whether concealed factors must be allowed for in comparing the prices of different articles on a given date.

RUNNING AVERAGES AND WEIGHTS

Two devices frequently used by statisticians in the compiling of an index include what are termed *running averages* and *weights*. The purpose of both is to make the index portray as accurately as possible a picture of the field that is being charted.

For instance, suppose we are compiling an index of business, and one of the important factors in this index is the rate of operations in the steel industry. For a number of weeks, we will assume, the industry has been operating around 90 per cent of its capacity. Over the previous five weeks the operating rates, we will assume, have been 88, 87, 90, 92, and then 93 per cent. This averages 90 per cent, so the statistician uses 90 rather than 93 per cent as the factor on steel in his index of business.

The reason he does so, rather than taking the current week, is to soften sudden ups and downs which might temporarily affect the operating rate but actually would not signify any vital change in business conditions.

For instance, let us suppose that after the week in which operations were at 93 per cent we had a legal holiday. The plants are closed and consequently the new week's operations average only 68 per cent of capacity. To show them at 68 per cent would indicate that conditions in the industry had suddenly turned extremely dull. This factor would bring a decline in the business chart which would not portray actual business conditions.

The statistician would strike a running average of the new five-week period, that is, 87, 90, 92, 93, and 68 per cent. This would give him 86 per cent for the steel factor against 93 the previous week, thus depicting the drop caused by the legal holiday, but avoiding the precipitous drop which would be misleading.

CONSUMER PRICE INDEX

The Bureau of Labor Statistics of the United States Department of Labor compiles many indexes, and two of them rate as probably the most familiar indexes among the many thousands in existence. They cover wholesale prices and the prices paid by consumers for food, housing, fuel and utilities, household furnishings and operation, apparel and upkeep, transportation, health and recreation, and a few miscellaneous items.

This latter index is frequently a page-one story in the newspapers, as it is of vital interest to the wage earner, unions, economists, landlords, students, and virtually all businessmen. It reflects the cost of living and is called that in headlines and in conversation although its official name is Consumer Price Index for Urban Wage Earners and Clerical Workers.

There are 2.3 million wage earners working under agreements which provide for periodic adjustments in their pay linked to the changes reported by this index. Unions and managements alike, at their bargaining table when a new contract is under negotiation, take into consideration this cost-of-living factor, basing claims for or against a rise in pay on the figures issued by the Bureau of Labor Statistics.

Among unions that have negotiated cost-of-living escalator clauses in their contracts are the United Automobile Workers, the United Steelworkers, and the United Packinghouse Workers. Settlement of labor contracts frequently includes a provision for a deferred pay increase under which workers will get a few cents an hour more in the second and third years of a contract to adjust for the gradual uptrend in the cost of living.

This index is ideally suited to its role in determining escalator terms as it reflects the expenditures of industrial workers and their families, a group that represents 40 per cent of the population and 56 per cent of the urban population.

Aside from its use in labor-industrial relations it has also been used in certain long-term rental contracts, insurance policies, and alimony agreements.

As with all indexes, this familiar one has undergone revisions at various times over the years since it was originated in 1913 to reflect changes in the buying habits of industrial workers. A major revision became effective January 1, 1964, supplanting one that had been in use since 1953. In this period wage earners averaged a 20 per cent rise in real income.

As a consequence the bureau's investigations found these consumers were spending relatively less of their income on food and more on housing and medical care, about the same on apparel, and slightly more on transportation, health, and recreation. Adjustments accordingly were made in the new series.

The basic concepts were not changed, but the weighting factors and price data base were updated, a more comprehensive index was developed, and certain improvements in statistical procedures were introduced. The number of individual items in the market basket was increased to 400 from 325, and a few of the former items were eliminated. Examples of those that were dropped included lemons, women's nightgowns, men's pajamas, an appendectomy, and a sewing machine. Among new items added were between-meal snacks, hotel and motel rooms, demountable air conditioners, garbage disposal units, moving expenses, parking fees, taxicabs, airline and intercity bus fares, outboard motors, phonograph records, golf fees, college tuition and textbooks, music lessons, legal services, and funeral expenses.

The accompanying table shows weights given by the bureau to the major divisions of expenditures and the items in each division.

Relative Importance of Consumer Price Index Components, New and Old Series (Per Cent)

Components	New Series	Old Series[a]
All items	100.00	100.00
Food	22.43	28.18
Food at home	17.89	23.11
Cereals and bakery products	2.45	3.27
Meats, poultry, and fish	5.63	6.43
Dairy products	2.80	3.81
Fruits and vegetables	3.02	4.46
Other food at home	3.99	5.14
Food away from home	4.54	5.07
Housing	33.23	30.71
Shelter	20.15	18.34
Rent	5.50	6.16
Hotel and motel rates	0.38	–
Home ownership	14.27	12.18
Home purchase and financing	9.11	7.51
Taxes and insurance	2.13	1.61
Maintenance and repairs	3.03	3.06
Fuel and utilities	5.26	4.91
Fuel oil and coal	0.73	1.21
Gas and electricity	2.71	2.11
Other utilities	1.82	1.59
Household furnishings and operation	7.82	7.46
Furniture	1.44	1.55
Appliances	1.36	1.71
Other	5.02	4.20
Apparel and upkeep	10.63	10.58
Men's and boys'	2.86	2.79
Women's and girls'	4.08	3.67
Footwear	1.51	1.41
Other apparel	2.18	2.71
Transportation	13.88	11.65
Private	12.64	9.98
Automobiles and related goods	9.02	7.38
Automobile services	3.62	2.60
Public	1.24	1.67
Health and Recreation	19.45	18.03
Medical care	5.70	5.88
Personal care	2.75	2.27
Reading and recreation	5.94	5.57
Other goods and services	5.06	4.31
Miscellaneous[b]	0.38	0.85

SOURCE: United States Department of Labor, Bureau of Labor Statistics
[a] Individual items reclassified into groups and subgroups according to new series classification; [b] Not actually priced; imputed to priced items.

WHOLESALE PRICE INDEX

The bureau's wholesale price index likewise requires a similar amount of detail, research, and judgment. This is designed to measure the percentage change, once a month, in the wholesale cost of a list of important commodities from their average wholesale cost in the period 1947–1949.

It is a weighted index of actual prices. The bureau covers about 900 commodity series, and usually it prices several grades and markets, so that in all it gets about 10,000 quotations. It does not include wholesale services, with the exception of electricity and gas. This eliminates transportation. Also excluded are real estate, buildings, and securities.

Roughly this index contains about 29 per cent raw materials, 8 per cent semimanufactured articles, and 63 per cent finished products which require no further fabrication. Quotations are obtained from primary markets when possible, and from first-hand transactions.

Raw material prices, for instance, are obtained from the respective commodity exchanges—that is, wheat from the trading floors in such cities as Chicago, Kansas City, and Minneapolis, and cotton prices from the trading floor in New York. With the finished products and semimanufactured products the bureau usually uses f.o.b. factory prices unless the trade practice is to quote delivered prices. In general the prices represent what the wholesaler actually pays, rather than list prices.

Of the 900 prices used, only six are contract prices, the others being market prices. Most of these prices are obtained weekly, but many are taken daily and a few biweekly. In cases where a price is fairly stable, it is taken only once a month. About 60 per cent are obtained directly from the manufacturers, and the effort of the bureau is to increase this percentage.

There are vast complications in the compilation of such an index which there is no need to enlarge upon here. There must be an effort to keep quality constant, or else adjust for a lowering or an improvement in quality. At times substitutions must be made, either because an article has disappeared or because it is no longer representative of the market covered. Then there must be an adjustment for the difference in price between the article that is dropped from the index and the new one that is added.

There are a number of business indexes compiled by government agencies, which receive particular attention in the press and in public discussions because they center largely on measuring our economic activity and health. No organization produces more statistics than the government.

Terms such as gross national product, national income, personal income, and gross private domestic investment are common and are described in another chapter in this book. They, and many others, are statistical compilations, and from them indexes are constructed to give us a cue as to where we are going and how fast.

THE MANY INDEXES

The student who follows the financial section of a newspaper will find himself confronted with an endless number of indexes. While that on the cost of living is certainly the most familiar, there are others that are followed by those in the market place and anyone else who is seeking to peer into the future. Only a few can be mentioned here, but in general their purport is self-explanatory.

One of the oldest is the weekly figure on freight car loadings. This was started in 1918 by the Association of American Railroads, and its weekly figure was a "must" in newspapers which published a complete financial section. The trend in carloadings provided an index of the volume of goods that was moving from the manufacturer to sales outlets and to consumers.

This is still published in a number of newspapers, but the old index has been supplemented. The reasons are obvious. One is that railroads, which for decades carried the bulk of heavy freight, have been subjected to greater competition from other methods of transportation, notably trucks, the private automobile, barge lines, and oil pipelines. The second reason is that the railroads themselves, and the makers of freight cars, have improved a freight car's capacity.

The freight car of today is a far different vehicle than it was in

1918. It is built lighter, and it can carry more. In addition the cars are loaded more heavily. Thus a carload of some years ago would represent far less tonnage and far less revenue than the carload of today.

Recognizing this change of pattern the Association of American Railroads, starting in 1963, publishes in addition a figure on ton-miles of freight handled. It still publishes the old figure on carloadings, and both figures can be found in the financial press, but the car today is different. Whereas the average carrying capacity of a freight car in 1922 was 43.1 tons, it increased to 47 tons in 1932, then 53.2 tons in 1952, and 56.3 tons in 1962. There went the former significance of a venerable index of business activity. The net ton-mile compilation has assumed greater significance; yet even it does not measure the flow of trade, because of the inroads of competing forms of transportation.

Another factor distorting the traditional carloading figure has been the growth of so-called piggyback cars. These are highway trailers loaded on a flat car. The railroad carries a piece of freight a part of the distance and a truck picks up the trailer for later haulage. Both get a part of the transportation revenue.

The oil industry, through the American Petroleum Institute, is another major supplier of an index that reflects general business. It issues to the press weekly a statistical record of oil production in the United States, the amount of crude oil run to stills, gasoline production, the rate of operation of refineries, the inventory of light fuels used mostly for heating homes, the amount of heavy fuels, and the stocks of unfinished oils. It breaks all this down into geographical areas, with daily averages and comparisons with previous periods.

Much the same is done for the power and light industry by the Edison Electric Institute. This is an index of business, for the more power that is used, the greater the over-all operation of industry. The institute breaks down its kilowatt-hour figures weekly, and gives comparisons, on a regional basis.

The National Machine Tool Builders Association has an index, and this too is watched, because if industry is buying more machine tools, apparently it foresees a need for them. The number of housing starts, reported by the Census Bureau, is yet another, for if more family units are started, presumably the home builders are optimistic. Paperboard output is another one, for it is used by retailers to send goods to customers. If they need a lot of it, the indication is the customers are buying more goods.

Then there are the indexes of manufacturers' inventories and new orders, published monthly by the Department of Commerce. Along with manufacturers' sales, the two constitute an important economic barometer. An inventory gain or loss is closely watched to see if manufacturers are building up their inventories through producing more than is called for by current orders, or are permitting their inventory to run off, anticipating a time of poorer demand. The threat of a strike in a basic industry, such as steel, is usually accompanied by a rush of buyers to build inventories.

This is far from being a complete list of the important indexes that are contained in financial sections of newspapers and that are watched avidly by businessmen and economists. There is an index for virtually every economic indicator that exists, a good bulk of them compiled and issued by governmental agencies and others by trade associations.

18

THE WORLD BANK

THE INTERNATIONAL BANK FOR RECONSTRUCTION AND Development, generally called the World Bank, is an international cooperative financial agency owned by the eighty-five member countries which have signed its Articles of Agreement or Charter and subscribed to its capital.

The charter of the bank was drawn up in July 1944 at the United Nations Monetary and Financial Conference in Bretton Woods, New Hampshire, at which forty-four allied governments were represented. Among other things, the delegates were concerned with the problem of financing the enormous foreign exchange costs which would be required for postwar reconstruction and development. Part of the answer was the World Bank, which can and does draw on both governmental and private capital to finance its international lending operations. Some of the principal purposes of the bank, as described in its charter, can be summarized as follows:

1. To assist in the reconstruction and development of its member countries by facilitating the investment of capital for productive purposes, and thereby promote the long-range growth of trade and the improvement of living standards

2. To promote private foreign investment by guarantees of and participations in loans and investments by private investors

3. When private capital is not available on reasonable terms, to make loans for productive purposes out of its own funds or out of funds borrowed by it in the investment market

In carrying out its purposes the bank's operations have developed along three principal lines: the lending of funds for productive purposes, the borrowing of funds in various investment markets to supplement its capital and finance an increased volume of loans, and technical assistance to member countries in the planning and carrying out of development.

LENDING OPERATIONS

By March 31, 1963, the bank had made 338 loans in sixty-one countries, amounting to the equivalent of $6,758 million. In a broad sense they can be divided into reconstruction loans and developed loans.

Early in the bank's operations, the most pressing need for its services was in Western Europe, whose productive plant had been seriously damaged and disrupted by the war. Consequently, the first loans were in that area and helped to finance a part of the famed "dollar gap." The first bank loan of $250 million was made in France on May 9, 1947. The following August, the bank lent $195 million to the Netherlands, $40 million to Denmark, and $12 million to Luxembourg for reconstruction. With the advent of the Marshall Plan in 1948, the bank withdrew from the financing of European reconstruction, a field which was in any case far too large for its resources.

The bank then turned to the financing of economic development. The first two loans in this field went to Chile in March 1948, and consisted of a loan of $13.5 million for electric power development and a loan of $2.5 million for agricultural development. Since then, development lending by the bank has ranged widely and covers fifty-nine countries on five continents, in every stage of economic development. The scope is indicated by Table A.

A. Distribution of Development Loans, March 31, 1963

Area	Number of Countries	Number of Loans	Amount (millions)
Africa	17	44	$ 971
Asia	12	102	2,220
Australasia	1	7	418
Europe	12	65	1,001
Western Hemisphere	19	120	1,651
Total	61	338	$6,261

The bulk of the bank's development loans are related to the financing of specific projects. In general, they meet the foreign exchange costs arising as a result of the installation of facilities basic to increased industrial and agricultural production. The bank's loans fall into a number of categories (see Table B).

B. Purposes of Development Loans

Purposes	Number of Countries	Amount (millions)
Electric power	38	$2,283
Transportation	40	2,161
Communications	4	27
Agriculture and forestry	19	516
Industry	14	1,067
General development	4	205
Water supply	1	2
Total		$6,261

The power loans are financing facilities that on completion will aggregate a generating capacity of some 15 million kilowatts and will add thousands of miles of distribution and transmission lines to carry the additional power. In Latin America alone the bank has lent $960 million for power development, including the addition of 8.4 million kilowatts to generating capacity, which more than doubles the amount of power available in the entire region at the end of the last war. In Asia bank-financed projects are adding some 3 million kilowatts to generating capacity.

Included in transportation loans are investments of $1,059 million in railway improvements in nineteen countries. In India alone the bank has lent $379 mililon for a broad modernization and expansion program for the railways; this is the largest amount the bank has made available to a single enterprise. A further $672 million of transportation loans is assisting highway construction, improvement, and maintenance programs. In Latin America some 30,000 miles of highway projects are being assisted by bank loans; Iran is employing $72 million of the bank's funds to construct or improve 1,800 miles of her national highway network; and the Japanese borrowed $80 million to finance a new high-speed toll highway serving major cities on the island of Honshu.

Other major categories of transportation lending include $297 million for port development in Belgium, Burma, Ecuador, India, Israel, Nigeria, Nicaragua, Peru, the Philippines, Turkey, Thailand, the Sudan, and Yugoslavia. Also included in this figure are funds for improvement of the Suez Canal by the United Arab Republic and for improvement of Belgium's inland waterways. The bank has also lent $64 million for oil and gas pipelines in the Sahara, Pakistan, and Trinidad; and $57 million for purchase of aircraft and for airport improvements.

The bulk of the agricultural loans have financed basic projects for irrigation, flood control, land clearance, and mechanization. Irrigation and flood control account for some $318 million of agricultural lending. Largest loan in this category was one for $90 million in connection with the financing of works in the Indus Basin, arising from the treaty settling the dispute over the use of the Indus waters between India and Pakistan. The loan was made to Pakistan. The bank was also active as the friend of both sides during the eight years required to negotiate the Indus Settlement, and is serving as fiscal agent for the governments of Australia, Canada, Germany, India, New Zealand, the United Kingdom, and the United States, which are contributing about $800 million to the financing of the Indus program.

Loans for industry have virtually all been for the benefit of private enterprises. A wide range of production has been financed. More than $350 million in loans is assisting iron and steel producers, with $314 million going to the private steel companies in India and Japan to enable them both to increase ingot production and to improve and diversify their finished and semifinished lines. Mining enterprises have borrowed $203 million from the bank, including $101 million in the African Republics of Mauritania and Gabon for development of iron ore and manganese deposits. Development and modernization of coal mines in India and Chile account for $76 million of the bank's lending for mining ventures.

A further $139 million has been lent by the bank for modernization and expansion of the pulp and paper industry in Finland, Chile, and Pakistan. Fertilizer and chemical producers are using $82 million of the bank's loans, including the Dead Sea works in Israel which borrowed $25 million to expand its production of potash.

Private enterprise has also benefited materially from services rendered to it by government-owned power stations, railways, highways, and other facilities financed by the World Bank. Even in the service field private companies have been substantial borrowers from the bank. In Japan, for example, the bank has lent about $150 million for power projects with a combined generating capacity of nearly 1.4 million kilowatts, nearly all of which has been or is being installed by privately owned power companies.

FINANCING THE BANK

The financial and credit base of the bank is the capital subscriptions of its eighty-five member countries, totaling $20,729,800,000. One per cent of this sum, totaling about $208,000,000 has been paid in by the members in gold or United States dollars and is freely at the disposal of the bank; and 9 per cent, equivalent to $1,852,000,000, has been paid in the various member currencies and can be used for loans only with the consent of the country concerned. Total usable funds from capital to March 31, 1963, amounted to $1,678,000,000, including the 1 per cent portion paid in gold or United States dollars by all members, and the 9 per cent portion, equivalent to

$1,456,600,000 in various currencies, released to the bank for lending.

The remaining 90 per cent of subscribed capital is not paid in and cannot be used for loans or operations of the bank. It is callable only to meet obligations arising from sales of bank bonds to investors or from guarantees by the bank of the obligations of others. Consequently, the 90 per cent of unpaid capital, amounting to the equivalant of $18.6 billion, represents a pooling of the credit of the eighty-five member countries to establish and support the credit of the bank.

By March 31, 1963, bank borrowing in world investment centers aggregated about $4 billion, of which the equivalent of about $2.5 billion was outstanding on that date as follows: $1.9 billion of United States dollar bonds and notes, and roughly $620 million of bonds and other obligations denominated in Swiss francs, sterling, Canadian dollars, Netherlands guilders, West German marks, Belgian francs, and Italian lire. Of the outstanding issues it is estimated that some $1.1 billion were held by institutional investors in the United States, while the equivalent of about $1.4 billion, including $800 million of dollar bonds, were estimated to be held in more than thirty-five other countries.

To supplement available capital, the bank has developed a broad market for its bonds in the United States and other countries. Of necessity this market has to be international, since to satisfy the needs of its borrowers the bank lends in various currencies, principally United States and Canadian dollars and the currencies of Western Europe.

Further supplements to the bank's finances have been obtained from sales of parts of its loans, and from repayments to the bank by borrowers. To March 31, 1963, sales to investors of parts of loans aggregated about $1.5 billion; and borrowers' repayments to the bank, $628 million.

TECHNICAL ASSISTANCE

The technical assistance activities of the bank grew out of its investigations related to prospective loans, especially in the less developed countries. Frequently bank loan missions find it necessary to advise borrowers on such matters as priorities between competing projects; modifications of project plans, leading to reduced costs or greater efficiency; and problems of administration and management. Of special importance is advice on the planning and carrying out of the financing of the local costs of projects, a responsibility of the borrowers, since the bank in general lends only foreign exchange requirements.

A broader service has developed in the form of "general survey missions" organized by the bank at the request of member countries. Such missions survey development possibilities and problems of countries and make recommendations concerning them. General survey missions to date have reported on British Guiana, Ceylon, Colombia, Cuba, Guatemala, Iraq, Italian Somaliland, Jamaica, Jordan, Kenya, Libya, Malaya, Nicaragua, Nigeria, Spain, Surinam, Syria, Tanganyika, Thailand, Turkey, Uganda, and Venezuela.

In addition to general survey missions, the bank has helped organize a number of special missions to study various aspects of the economies and development requirements of member countries.

In 1961, in recognition of the urgent need for continuing assistance in planning and carrying through development, the bank established a Development Advisory Service, whose function is to recruit senior financial advisers and economists to advise the governments of less developed countries. The service has sent members of its staff to advise the governments of Chile, Ghana, Libya, Nigeria, Pakistan, and Thailand on economic and financial matters related to their development.

The bank also carries on a program of feasibility and sector studies designed to assist and speed the preparation of development projects and programs. These studies have included, among others, studies of a highway project in Burma, the transport system of Ecuador, a river crossing at Calcutta and a coal transport project in India, a road program in Nigeria, an irrigation project in Peru, waterworks and sewerage projects in the Philippines, a school construction program in Tunisia, and a capital study in Chile.

Through operation of the Economic Development Institute in Washington, D.C., the bank is helping to raise the level of competence of senior officials concerned with development in the less developed areas. More than two hundred officials from more than sixty countries and territories have attended the eight regular six-month courses and the special courses of the institute. Within the bank fifteen general training programs for junior government officials have been carried through. One hundred thirty participants from sixty-two member countries have attended these seven-month courses.

All powers of the bank are vested in the board of governors, to which each country appoints a representative. The governors meet annually to review and comment on the policies and operations of the bank, but have delegated virtually all authority to the executive directors.

There are eighteen executive directors, five appointed by the five largest subscribers to capital—the United States, the United Kingdom, France, India, and Germany—and thirteen elected by the eighty other member governments. The executive directors sit as a board and function in a manner similar to the directorate of a private corporation. They appoint the president who selects the other officers and staff and directs the day-to-day operations of the bank. Action on loans and bond issues and other operational matters are initiated by the president and staff and require the final approval of the executive directors.

Up to date there have been no defaults by any of the bank's borrowers on payments of interest or of principal on loans, and the bank's reserves from earnings and commissions amounted to $783 million on March 31, 1963.

19

~~~~~~

THE INTERNATIONAL DEVELOPMENT ASSOCIATION

THE INTERNATIONAL DEVELOPMENT ASSOCIATION, which was established in September 1960, is an affiliate of the World Bank. Its purpose is to assist underdeveloped member countries whose ability usefully to employ foreign capital for development is beyond their present ability to service further foreign indebtedness obtained on conventional terms.

To carry out its objectives the association makes available to the underdeveloped countries "development credits" whose terms are such that they do not bear as heavily on the recipient countries' balance of payments positions as do conventional loans, including World Bank loans.

Development credits by IDA have all had a term of fifty years to final maturity and they bear no interest. Repayment of principal is due in foreign exchange, with amortization beginning after a ten-year grace period. Thereafter 1 per cent of the principal is repayable annually for ten years; and 3 per cent is repayable annually for the final thirty years. To defray IDA's administrative costs a service charge of three-quarters of 1 per cent a year is payable on amounts of the credit withdrawn and outstanding.

The funds employed by IDA have been contributed by the seventy-five countries holding membership in it. Authorized capital is currently $1 billion of which $968,250,000 has been subscribed. Capital subscriptions are divided into two classes. Part I, which is fully convertible and amounts to over $739 million, consists of the subscriptions of the highly developed countries of Western Europe plus those of the United States, the United Kingdom, Australia, Canada, Japan, and the Republic of South Africa. The Part I countries, being in an advanced state of development, are not eligible for credits from IDA, though their dependent or associated territories may be.

The Part II subscriptions to capital, received from sixty countries, all eligible for IDA credits, are paid 10 per cent in convertible currencies or gold and 90 per cent in national currencies. The latter, however, are convertible in connection with IDA credits only with the contributors' consent. In all the association has some $762 million equivalent in usable, convertible funds that have been or are available for its credit operations. In addition supplemental contributions equal to more than $10 million have been received from Sweden, and raise usable funds to over $771 million.

In general the purposes of IDA credits are similar to those of World Bank loans, which they are intended to supplement. IDA lends over a wider range of purposes than the bank, and its activities could extend into the social field, including the financing of projects for sanitation, pilot housing, education, or other projects of high developmental priority whether or not they are revenue producing or directly productive.

To March 31, 1963, the association had made thirty-six development credits available in eighteen of its underdeveloped member countries. The following tables indicate the areas of IDA operations and their purposes.

All of the IDA credits for electric power development have been made for projects in India and Turkey that extend facilities for which the World Bank has previously lent money. Included in transport credits are three loans aggregating $145.5 million to India, and

DISTRIBUTION OF IDA DEVELOPMENT CREDITS, March 31, 1963

Area	Number of Countries	Number of Credits	Amount (millions)
Africa	4	4	$ 34.30
Asia and Middle East	5	22	338.80
Europe	1	2	6.70
Western Hemisphere	8	8	70.35
	18	36	$450.15

PURPOSES OF IDA CREDITS

Purpose	Amount (millions)
Electric power	$ 37.70
Transportation	247.35
Communications	42.00
Agriculture and forestry	92.20
Industry	16.50
Water supply	9.40
School construction	5.00
	$450.15

they directly and indirectly supplement previous transport lending by the bank. One loan of $60 million is for construction and improvement of highways in India; another, for $18 million, is for the enlargement and improvement of the port of Bombay; and the third loan, of $67.5 million, will help to carry forward further improvement and expansion of India's railways in which the World Bank has already invested over $375 million.

A further $67.4 million of transport credits have been made for highway projects located in Chile, Colombia, Costa Rica, El Salvador, Haiti, Honduras, and Paraguay. With the exception of Chile the World Bank had initially been involved in the planning and financing of the projects. In addition, in the case of the credits for highways for Chile, Colombia, and Costa Rica, the World Bank and IDA acted in concert with the former, making a loan simultaneously with IDA's credit operation.

All of the $42 million in the telecommunication category was comprised in a single credit to India for improvement of her communication system. Of the $92.2 million in agricultural credits more than $56 million also went to India for six projects concerned with either irrigation or flood control. A further $18.7 million in agricultural loans went to Pakistan for two irrigation projects; and $13 million to the Sudan for the Roseires dam and irrigation project on the Blue Nile. In the case of the Roseires credit, the World Bank simultaneously lent $19.5 million for the same project.

The other categories of credits include loans for industrial development banks in China and for industrial estate development in Pakistan; for development and improvement of the water supplies of Amman, Jordan; Managua, Nicaragua; and Taiwan, China; and for construction of secondary and technical schools in Tunisia.

The organization of the association is virtually the same as that of the World Bank. To become a member of IDA, a country must first be a member of the bank. Each member country of IDA is represented by the same governor and executive director as represents it for the bank, and IDA and the bank share the same management and staff. The assets, liabilities, and capital of the two organizations, however, are wholly separate.

~~~~~~

20

THE INTERNATIONAL
FINANCE CORPORATION

THE WORLD BANK HAS FOUND THAT LOANS TO PRIVATE enterprise have been limited by the requirement in its charter that such loans must bear a government guarantee. This has discouraged some private borrowers from coming to the bank, for fear that government guarantees would mean government interference in their affairs. Governments have also been reluctant to grant guarantees to private borrowers on the grounds that they may be charged with discrimination between private concerns or in favor of private projects over public projects.

It was partly because of these limitations that the bank supported proposals for a new international organization—the International Finance Corporation—whose function would be to make investments in privately owned productive enterprises, without government guarantee. The International Finance Corporation came into existence as an affiliate of the World Bank in July 1956. By the end of March 1963, seventy-three governments had become members and had contributed—entirely in gold and United States dollars—$98,198,000 to its capital.

The corporation always invests in association with private investors; serves as a clearing house for bringing together investment opportunities and private investors; and helps to enlist managerial skill and experience where they are not readily available, as in the case of the less developed countries.

The IFC has greater flexibility in its operations than does the World Bank. It is able to accept all kinds of securities, including equities, straight debt, convertible bonds, and bonds or notes with profit participation or other special features. In making investments the corporation can and does accept various combinations of investment instruments.

The corporation helps to spur local capital market development in member countries through underwritings and stand-bys covering the sale and distribution of industrial securities and equities. It also seeks private international participation in its investments, underwritings, and stand-bys; and further channels private international investment into industrial development through sales of items from its investment portfolio.

As of March 31, 1963, IFC had made fifty-nine investment commitments in twenty-four countries, aggregating over $82 million, including underwriting and stand-by commitments amounting to $8.1 million. Participations and sales of loans and equity investments out of portfolio totaled $15.4 million on that date, and a further $2.4 million had been sold out of underwriting and stand-by commitments. The corporation's investment and other commitments are distributed as follows:

Area	Number of Countries	Number of Commitments	Amount
Africa	3	3	$ 7,786,000
Australia	1	2	975,000
Asia and Middle East	5	9	12,814,000
Europe	4	6	6,884,000
Western Hemisphere	11	39	53,815,000
	24	59	$82,274,000

The purposes for which IFC has invested in private industrial enterprises are as follows:

Purpose	Amount
Manufacturing enterprises	$37,862,000
Processing enterprises	30,633,000
Mining enterprises	3,100,000
Service enterprises	520,000
Private industrial financing institutions	10,159,000
	$82,274,000

Included in recent investments by the corporation are investments in an automotive electrical equipment company in Spain, fertilizer companies in Greece and Tunisia, a steel plant in Mexico, a textile company in Colombia, a bearing company in India, a pulp and paper producer in Chile, a seamless steel pipe plant in Mexico, and in private industrial development institutions in Morocco, the Philippines, and Spain.

Since 1962 IFC, through its Department of Development Bank Services, has been acting on its own and the World Bank's behalf in connection with the financing and servicing of industrial development banks or institutions. These organizations, which are privately owned and organized, provide a vehicle for both domestic and foreign investment in private industry in underdeveloped countries; serve as focal points for domestic capital formation and for establishment of local capital markets; and are centers for technical and managerial advice to developing industry.

These development institutions are also important to the World Bank and IFC in that they offer them a medium by which they can help to finance small and medium-sized industrial development—the kind usually encountered in the underdeveloped countries.

Within the last year IFC has acted as adviser to the World Bank in connection with about $55 million in loans to private industrial development institutions in Austria, Morocco, Pakistan, and the Philippines. In the case of Morocco, Pakistan, and the Philippines the corporation also invested or agreed to invest in shares of the development institutions that had received World Bank loans. The corporation, in these instances, played a complementary role with the World

Bank, with the latter helping the development institutions to meet their needs for borrowed funds and the IFC helping to broaden the capital bases on which their credit is founded. In addition, in the case of the Philippine institution the IFC worked with its organizers in establishing its legal and corporate framework, and has committed itself to a stand-by covering an offering of the institution's shares.

Though an affiliate of the World Bank, the IFC is an independent and separate organization. It has its own management and staff and its capital, assets, and liabilities are completely divorced from those of the bank. The president of the bank, however, is also president of IFC. To become a member of the corporation, a government must first be a member of the bank; and the executive directors of the bank, who represent countries that have become members of IFC, constitute the corporation's board of directors.

The International Finance Corporation has operated at a modest profit since its establishment. All earnings and securities profits are credited to a reserve against losses; and on March 31, 1963, this reserve stood at nearly $16 million.

21

THE INTERNATIONAL
MONETARY FUND

THE INTERNATIONAL MONETARY FUND IS AN INDE-
pendent international organization with a membership, at May 15,
1963, of eighty-six countries. The fund holds and administers resources totaling more than $15 billion in gold and national curren-
cies, created from the quota subscribed by each country upon joining
the fund. Potential access to an additional $6 billion is provided
through the fund's general arrangements to borrow.

The purposes, organization, and method of operation of the fund
are laid down in its Articles of Agreement, prepared at the United
Nations Monetary and Financial Conference held at Bretton Woods,
New Hampshire, July 1–22, 1944. The principal objective of the
fund, as described by Article I of the agreement, is to promote a
freer system of world trade and payments as a means of helping its
members to achieve economic growth, high levels of employment,
and improved standards of living. The $15 billion which the fund
holds in its resources provides a reserve on which members may
draw, with its agreement, to meet foreign payments obligations,
thus gaining time in which to solve balance of payments difficulties
without resorting to the imposition or intensification of exchange and
payments restrictions.

The highest authority of the IMF is exercised by the board of governors, on which each member country is represented by a governor and an alternate governor. The board of governors usually meets once a year, and has delegated many of its powers to the board of executive directors. The executive board is on continuous call at the fund's headquarters in Washington, D.C., and conducts the regular business of the fund. Of its present eighteen members, the executive board has five members appointed by the five member countries with the largest quotas—the United States, the United Kingdom, France, West Germany, and India—and thirteen elected by the remaining members. The executive board, and a staff of more than five hundred persons from fifty-seven countries, are presided over by a managing director.

Cooperation with other international agencies is provided under the IMF Articles, and this involves frequent contacts with agencies dealing with problems that have significance for the fund. An Agreement of Relationship with the United Nations outlines a program of mutual assistance between the UN and the fund, as an independent organization. There is continuous coordination with the work of the contracting parties to the General Agreement on Tariffs and Trade (GATT). Close ties exist between the fund and the International Bank for Reconstruction and Development. Executive directors of the fund in some cases also serve as directors of the bank. Membership in the fund is a prerequisite to membership in the bank.

The fund seeks to fulfill its basic objectives through three distinct but closely interrelated spheres of activity. The first is through the continuing process of regular consultation with member countries. The fund conducts annual consultations with each member to review its foreign exchange restrictions, if any, and major developments in the member's economic situation and policies.

The second and most familiar aspect of the fund's work lies in the provision to members of short-term financial assistance from the fund's $15 billion resources. Member countries may, with the fund's agreement, draw foreign exchange in exchange for their own currency. Currencies drawn from the fund may be used in a flexible way to relieve the member's payments difficulty, but are not intended to be used for military purposes or for programs of economic development. Countries that are pursuing national development programs may use the fund if they experience temporary payments difficulties such as would ordinarily entitle a member to fund assistance. Amounts drawn are related to the size of the member's quota, the seriousness of the situation, the member's economic performance and outlook, and other relevant factors. Members are expected to repay their drawings within three, or at the outside, five years. Assistance may also be granted to a member in the form of a stand-by arrangement under which the member is authorized to draw up to a specified amount during an agreed period of time, usually one year, should the need arise.

Research and technical cooperation comprise a third area of IMF activity. By collating and assessing the mass of information received from members and other sources, the fund keeps abreast of trends and developments in international trade, prices, production, costs of living, and other economic indicators. An active program of research examines the theoretical as well as the practical side of economic developments and problems. The fund's program of publications makes generally available a wealth of economic data and information of current importance. Fund staff experts are sent, at the request of individual members, to give advice on such matters as the modification of central banking machinery or simplification of exchange systems. Another form of technical cooperation is provided through the fund's training program, conducted for selected staff members of finance ministries and central banks of member countries.

The fund's financial assistance is extended through foreign exchange transactions with its members. The fund sells foreign currency to a member which pays for it with its own national currency at a par value agreed with the fund. In reversing a transaction, the member repurchases its own currency from the fund with a payment of gold or some currency acceptable to the fund. To maintain the revolving nature of the fund's resources, members are expected to repay their drawings within three, or at the outside, five years.

Upon joining the IMF, each member is assigned a quota, the size of which is based upon its holdings of reserves, international trade, and other economic factors. The United States quota, at $4,125 million, is the largest. A member's quota approximately determines its voting power and the amount of foreign exchange it may draw from the fund. The subscription of each member is equal to its quota and is payable 25 per cent in gold and 75 per cent in the member's own currency. If a new member's gold reserves are insufficient to permit the 25 per cent of quota gold payment, the member may subscribe in gold a total of 10 per cent of its total gold and convertible currency reserves, and the balance of the quota in national currency. When this is done, the member is expected, as its reserves increase, to substitute gold for its currency until the fund's holdings of its currency are reduced to 75 per cent of the quota.

To be eligible to use the fund's resources, a member must show that it has a current payments difficulty.

A member requesting assistance is given virtually automatic access to the fund's resources for amounts up to the value of its gold subscription. The fund's attitude toward drawing up to an additional 25 per cent of a member's quota is a liberal one, provided the member requesting such a drawing is making reasonable efforts to solve its payments problems. Requests for larger drawings must be related to well-balanced programs directed toward the stability of the member's currency, at realistic rates of exchange.

The fund collects certain charges on the use of its resources and is thus able to finance itself from operations, eliminating the need for special assessments on members. There is a service charge of one-half of 1 per cent on each transaction. An additional charge is applied to amounts purchased in excess of a member's gold subscription. It becomes effective three months after each transaction, when the rate starts at 2 per cent per annum. The rate rises with the amount of money purchased relative to the member's quota, and with the length of time the drawing is outstanding.

From the beginning of exchange operations, on March 1, 1947, to March 31, 1963, forty-seven members had drawn the equivalent of $6,820 million in Argentine pesos, Austrian schillings, Belgian and French francs, Canadian and United States dollars, Danish kronor, West German marks, Italian lire, Japanese yen, Netherlands guilders, pounds sterling, Spanish pesetas, and Swedish kronor. Repayments for the same period totaled $5,111 million, reducing the amount outstanding to $1,641 million. An additional $5,683 million had been provided in stand-by arrangements, of which $1,634 million was actually drawn.

The fund agreement came into force on December 27, 1945, after being signed by twenty-nine governments, representing 80 per cent of the original quotas in the fund. An inaugural organizational meeting of the board of governors was convened at Savannah, Georgia, on March 8, 1946, at which time the By-Laws were adopted, the site of the headquarters (Washington, D.C.) was agreed upon, and the first executive directors were elected. The executive directors met for the first time on May 6, 1946. On March 1, 1947, the fund stated its readiness to commence exchange transactions.

Comparatively little use was made of the fund's resources in the first years of its existence, when progress toward its objectives was limited by the severity of postwar economic difficulties, and exchange restrictions and other import controls were widely used. The international payments situation, which was characterized by a large, continuing surplus earned by the United States in its trade with other countries, suggested a greater need for grants and long-term credits than for the short- to medium-term financing of the fund. The Marshall aid program, which was established to meet these unusual needs, become a channel for large amounts of United State foreign assistance from 1948 through January 1951.

During this period and later, substantial economic recovery was achieved in the United Kingdom, Western Europe, and Japan, with favorable effects upon the world economy as a whole. Production increased in many countries, inflationary pressures were met with firmer policies, and governments began to relax their restrictions on the international flow of goods and services.

As members moved toward its objectives, the IMF found opportunities for supporting their efforts in a variety of circumstances. During one twelve-month period of high activity, which began in December 1956, the fund's transactions increased by the equivalent of $1 billion.

The heavy demand upon the fund during this period was taken into consideration during a subsequent review by the executive directors of the adequacy of its resources. It was concluded that the fund's holdings of gold and currencies should be enlarged by means of a general 50 per cent increase in members' quotas. Increases of 100 per cent were agreed for Canada, Japan, and West Germany; and additions above 50 per cent, for some members that had small quotas relative to their economic positions at the time of the quota review. There followed an increase in the fund's total quotas from $9,200 million at the beginning of 1958 to $15,224 million on March 31, 1963.

This enlargement of quotas was virtually completed in 1960, and recent increases in the total have resulted chiefly from additions to the fund's membership. In the meantime, however, the advent of convertibility of some of the world's major currencies has increased the possibility of large international movements of short-term capital. To strengthen its resources in such a contingency, the IMF in January 1962 approved an agreement whereby ten industrial countries undertook to lend the fund up to the equivalent of $6 billion if this should be necessary to forestall or cope with an impairment of the international payments system. The borrowing arrangements became effective in October 1962, by which time eight of the participating countries, with maximum commitments equivalent to $5,560 million, had formally notified the fund of their adherence to the agreement. The arrangements remain in effect for four years from the date of full ratification, and there are provisions for extension.

22

THE INTER-AMERICAN DEVELOPMENT BANK

THE INTER-AMERICAN DEVELOPMENT BANK IS A HEM-ispheric financial institution created in December 1959 by nineteen Latin American republics* and the United States to help speed up the economic development of the member countries individually and collectively. It represents the culmination of Latin American efforts going back seventy years to create an inter-American institution in whose policies they would have a strong voice and which would focus on the needs of the hemisphere. It was not until August 1958, however, that the United States pledged its support. Negotiations on the bank's charter began in January 1959 and were completed in April; and by the end of the year the required number of countries had ratified it. Shortly after, in October 1960, the Inter-American Bank formally opened for business.

The basic functions of the bank, as set forth in its charter, are:

1. Promote the investment of public and private capital for development purposes

2. Utilize its own capital, funds raised in financial markets, and other available resources to finance development projects in member countries, giving priority to those loans and guarantees that will contribute most effectively to their economic growth

* Cuba is not a member.

[184]

3. Encourage private investment in projects, enterprises, and activities contributing to economic development and supplement private investment when private capital is not available on reasonable terms and conditions

4. Cooperate with the member countries to orient their development policies toward a better utilization of their resources in a manner consistent with the objectives of making their economies more complementary and of fostering the orderly growth of their foreign trade

5. Provide technical assistance for the preparation, financing, and carrying out of development plans and projects, including the study of priorities and the formulation of specific project proposals

In carrying out these functions, the bank cooperates with national and international institutions and with private sources supplying investment capital.

CAPITAL STRUCTURE

The bank's Charter provided the bank with two completely separate sets of resources: the ordinary capital and the Fund for Special Operations.

ORDINARY CAPITAL RESOURCES

The initial subscriptions to the ordinary capital stock amount to $813,160,000, taken up in varying proportions by the twenty members.

Of this amount, $381,580,000 corresponds to the bank's paid-in capital; and $431,580,000, to its callable capital. The latter is subject to call only if required to meet bank obligations and enables the institution to borrow in the capital markets.

One-half of the paid-in subscriptions of each country were paid in gold or dollars and the other half in the respective domestic currencies. As the $150 million paid-in subscription of the United States was paid wholly in dollars, the initial ordinary lendable resources of the Bank included $265,790,000 in dollars and the equivalent of $115,790,000 in Latin American currencies.

These lendable resources were increased by nearly $100 million in

1962 through the sale of two bond issues, one for $24.2 million in freely convertible lire placed in Italy and a second for $75 million sold in the United States.

Within the over-all minimum target of the Alliance for Progress (see next page) of an annual flow of $2 billion in external funds to Latin America during the present decade, the bank set as a goal annual commitments of approximately $150 million from its ordinary resources. The board of governors in March 1963 voted to recommend an increase of $1 billion in the callable capital stock. Looking to the possible admission of new members to the bank, the board of governors also voted to recommend a $300 million increase in the authorized capital to be available for such eventuality.

FUND FOR SPECIAL OPERATIONS

In addition to the ordinary resources, the Charter provided the bank with a Fund for Special Operations, amounting initially to $146,316,000 contributed by the twenty member countries in proportional quotas paid half in dollars and half in domestic currencies. This fund is handled completely separately from the bank's ordinary resources and is employed to make "soft" loans, on terms and conditions appropriate for dealing with special circumstances arising in specific countries or with respect to specific projects. Initially, the fund consisted of $123,158,000 in dollars (including a $100,000,000 United States contribution) and $23,158,000 in Latin American currencies. The board of governors of the bank also voted in 1963 to recommend an increase of $73.2 million to be paid into the fund by the twenty members by means of proportional quotas based on the original contributions.

THE SOCIAL PROGRESS TRUST FUND

In July 1960, President Eisenhower, in his "Newport Declaration," stated that the United States was prepared to give financial assistance for social development programs in Latin America, if the Latin American countries would undertake institutional reforms. The formal basis of such commitment was set forth in the 1960 Act of Bogota, in which the United States pledged a Special Inter-American Fund for Social Development, with the Inter-American Bank as the primary mechanism for its administration.

In March 1961 President Kennedy launched the Alliance for Progress program as a hemispheric cooperative plan "to transform the 1960's into an historic decade of democratic progress," under which the United States would be disposed to provide resources based on the willingness, intention, and capacity of the Latin American countries to mobilize their own resources. In June, the United States Congress appropriated $500 million to create the Special Inter-American Fund, of which $394 million, termed the Social Progress Trust Fund, was turned over to the Inter-American Bank for administration; $100 million went to the former International Cooperation Administration; and $6 million was assigned to the Organization of American States for collaboration in the preparation of national development programs.

Subsequently, in August 1961, at a special meeting of the Inter-American Economic and Social Council held in Punta del Este, Uruguay, the Latin American members of the bank and the United States agreed formally to establish the Alliance for Progress. Under this plan, the Social Progress Trust Fund became part of a goal to channel $20 billion in external aid to Latin America over a ten-year period.

LENDING OPERATIONS

According to the origin of the resources it uses, the bank's activities are classified as ordinary, Special, or Trust Fund operations (see table on page 189).

With the ordinary resources the bank, as of June 30, 1963, had made sixty-nine loans amounting to $295 million to help finance private enterprises or governmental projects in the fields of industry, agriculture, electric power, transportation, and water supply. These loans are repayable in the currencies lent and generally finance no more than 50 per cent of the total cost of the individual project. The terms are comparable to those extended by other international financial institutions granting "hard" loans. The interest rate has been 5.75 per cent annually, including a 1 per cent commission allocated to the bank's special reserve.

With the Fund for Special Operations, the bank, as of June 30, 1963, had granted thirty-three loans for a total of $116.9 million to help finance projects in fields similar to those covered by the ordinary resources. The fund enables the bank to engage in the financing of private or public projects that make no immediate or direct contribution to the improvement of the balance of payments but that are considered important to the economic growth. Terms of repayment are easier, including longer amortization periods, possible repayment in domestic currency, and lower interest rates than those applying to ordinary loans. An interest rate of 4 per cent per year has predominated on these loans.

With the resources of the Social Progress Trust Fund, the bank had made, up to June 30, 1963, sixty-four loans amounting to $347.9 million for projects in four specific socio-economic fields: land settlement and improved land use, housing for low-income groups, water supply and sanitation facilities, and advanced education and training related to economic development. These loans have been made in dollars, for periods ranging between twenty and thirty years and at rates of interest of 1.25 and 2.75 per cent, depending on the type of project. The bank also requires on these loans a service charge of 0.75 per cent, payable in dollars, on principal amounts outstanding. Principal and interest payments can be made in dollars or local currency, at the borrower's option.

TECHNICAL ASSISTANCE

The bank is authorized by its Charter to provide technical assistance to its member countries and to private firms within the countries for the preparation of specific development plans and projects and the formulation of loan proposals and, on a more general level, for the development of advanced training through seminars and other instruction of personnel specializing in the preparation of

INTER-AMERICAN DEVELOPMENT BANK, Approved loans up to June 30, 1963
(dollars in thousands)

Country	Ordinary Capital		Fund for Special Operations		Social Progress Trust Fund		Grand Total	
	Number of Loans	Total Amount	Number of Loans	Total Amount	Number of Loans	Total Amount	Number of Loans	Total Amount
Argentina	12	$ 66,554	2	$ 6,207	2	$ 35,000	16	$107,761
Bolivia			4	21,960	2	10,500	6	32,460
Brazil	11	41,140	3	21,765	7	52,860	21	115,765
Chile	7	36,789	3	8,919	7	23,638	17	69,346
Colombia	7	28,908	2	3,208	4	31,337	13	63,453
Costa Rica	4	11,502	1	1,000	1	3,500	6	16,002
Dominican Republic					2	6,500	2	6,500
Ecuador	1	2,343	3	8,462	5	23,515	9	34,320
El Salvador	3	3,959	1	183	4	11,640	8	15,782
Guatemala	3	5,300			3	11,300	6	16,600
Haiti			1	3,500			1	3,500
Honduras	2	510	3	9,210	3	5,650	8	15,370
Mexico	7	49,645	1	3,800	5	18,600	13	72,045
Nicaragua	1	2,000			3	7,885	4	9,885
Panama			1	2,900	2	10,362	3	13,262
Paraguay	2	2,750	5	16,450	1	2,900	8	22,100
Peru	3	7,912			4	26,300	7	34,212
Uruguay	3	14,443	1	640	2	10,500	6	25,583
Venezuela	3	21,211	1	2,700	6	53,000	10	76,911
Central American Bank for Economic Integration			1	6,004	1	2,925	2	8,929
Total	69	$294,966	33	$116,908	64	$347,912	166	$759,786

development plans and project studies. The technical assistance may be in the form of grants and loans, or by providing advisory services by bank officials. Up to June 30, 1963, the bank had authorized close to $14.2 million in reimbursable technical assistance and about $6.1 million in technical assistance grants from both its own resources and those of the Trust Fund.

MANAGEMENT OF THE BANK

The highest authority of the Inter-American Bank is its board of governors, composed of twenty governors representing each of the member countries. The governors meet regularly once a year. The board of executive directors, the president, and the executive vice president of the bank have been delegated the day-to-day management of the institution by the board of governors. The board of directors is composed of seven members, one appointed by the United States and six elected by groups of Latin American countries. The board of directors serves for three-year terms. Its members cast the number of votes of the countries they represent, which are proportional to the shares of ordinary capital subscribed.

DEFINITIONS OF TERMS

EVERY BUSINESS AND PROFESSION HAS A LANGUAGE PEculiar to itself. Wall Street is no exception, and in the financial press these terms are used frequently, on the assumption everyone knows their meaning.

While various terms have been defined in preceding appropriate chapters, there are others with which the reader of the financial news should be acquainted. They are well known in the financial community but may seem strange to the casual reader, just as would the words one might overhear in a discussion in a classroom where students are interested in chemistry, the theater, politics, atomic energy, or electronics.

An explanation of a selected group of financial terms is presented for that reason.

ACCEPTANCE—Bankers' acceptances, for the most part, are bills covering exports, imports, and domestic shipments which have been "accepted" by a bank. The bank thus backs up the credit of the purchaser of the goods. Thus accepted, the acceptance is negotiable and can be traded in on the open market. More specifically:

a. *Bank Acceptance*—The Federal Reserve Board describes a bank acceptance as "a draft or bill of exchange, whether payable in dollars or some other money, of which the acceptor is a bank or trust company, or a firm, person, company or corporation engaged generally in the business of granting bankers' acceptance credits." They are used in international trade and in domestic transactions involving major staple commodities. They are the highest form of commercial credit—the credit risk has been virtually eliminated, since the responsibility for payment rests upon the banks, whose credit is widely known and firmly established. The credit of the bank has been substituted for that of its customer. Of course the customer meets the acceptance by depositing the necessary funds with his bank before the maturity of the obligation.

b. *Trade Acceptance*—Bill of exchange drawn by the seller of goods at the time of the sale and accepted by the purchaser. In order to be eligible for rediscount, the acceptance must certify that it was so drawn by the seller on the purchase of the goods. The usual form is a notation to the effect that "the obligation of the acceptor of this bill arises out of the purchase of goods from the drawer."

ACCRUED DIVIDENDS—Dividends are dependent upon earnings of a corporation and do not constitute a debt of the corporation until declared by directors. In the case of cumulative preferred stocks, where the rate is fixed and payment comes prior to payments on the common, the dividends are said to have accrued if they are due but have not been paid.

ACCRUED INTEREST—The amount of interest that has accrued on a bond since it last made a payment. In most cases, where the bond pays regularly, a buyer of a bond pays the going market price plus accrued interest and the seller receives this amount. There are exceptions when the interest is in doubt, in which case the bond is said to be selling "flat," which means without any adjustment for accrued interest. There are also exceptions in the case of "income bonds," in which a corporation is obligated to pay interest only when earned.

ACCUMULATION—In financial parlance it refers to the quiet purchase of a security in large quantities. This may be done in order to secure a large block of the security before the market rises. The motive is a long-term profit rather than a show of strength to support the market.

AD HOC ARBITRATOR—An arbitrator for one specific grievance. The term means the same as "temporary arbitrator," since the individual is a third party selected for a single case or a specific group of cases.

ADJUSTMENT BONDS—Bonds issued in a reorganization or in order to bring several issues of bonds of a corporation into one class at a uniform interest rate. They have most often been used in the case of reorganization of railroads. The term is virtually synonymous with income bonds; in other words they rank low in the matter of security, they have a stated par value and maturity date, and are usually secured by a mortgage. But whether the issue can be refunded at maturity depends upon the credit of the corporation and the amount of obligations in the corporation's debt structure ranking prior to it. Interest on such adjustment bonds is payable only when earned and declared by directors, as in the case of dividends on stocks.

A.D.R.—AMERICAN DEPOSITORY RECEIPTS—This is a method of facilitating investment by Americans in the securities of foreign corporations. The A.D.R. is a certificate, similar to a stock certificate, registered in the name of the holder. It represents the right of the holder to a specific number of shares of the foreign corporation. These shares usually are deposited with a European bank that acts as agent for the American banks that sponsor the issuance of the depository receipts. An A.D.R. enjoys a ready market and the owner receives the same dividends, notices, proxies, and reports as do the direct owners of the foreign shares; and they are eligible for listing on our exchanges. When listed, all fees such as issuance, listing, transfer, custody, and expenses involved in the disbursement of dividends are paid by the foreign company. When traded over the counter, the sponsoring bank charges a fee to the investor for issuing the certificates. Red tape that is frequently involved when an American investor is entitled to dividends on foreign securities held directly is avoided through A.D.R.'s, as the foreign bank makes dollars available to the American deposition bank. If the foreign company issues rights, the holder of an A.D.R. may exercise them only if the foreign company has registered under the Securities Act of 1933. If not registered, however, he can sell them abroad, and the proceeds will be paid to him through the American sponsoring bank.

There are about two hundred issues of A.D.R.'s from about a dozen countries, largely European or British Commonwealth countries.

AD VALOREM—Value, used in connection with the levying of a tariff on imports. These tariffs are either based on the number of articles imported or their weight (in which case the duty is described as a *specific duty*), or if the levy is based on the value of the article, the duty is an ad valorem duty.

AIR POCKET—A market term meaning abrupt or extreme weakness, during which time the security sinks in value without encountering any nearby bids.

ALLOTMENT—The portion of a new issue of securities awarded to a purchaser by an offering syndicate when subscriptions to the issue exceed the amount available.

AMERICAN BANKERS ASSOCIATION—The leading association of commercial banks in the United States, founded in 1875. All banks are eligible for membership.

AMORTIZATION—A term applied to the gradual paying off of a long-term debt by the installment or sinking-fund method. It is also applied to the gradual writing off of a premium paid for a bond selling above par at the time of the purchase. As this premium represents a part of the investment cost and will not be returned to the purchaser when the bond matures, he must apply a portion of the cash interest received to a reduction of the premium. The bookkeeping method of accomplishing this is to charge to the interest account on each interest date the amount of amortization for the period and to make a corresponding credit to the bond account.

AND INTEREST—Closely allied with accrued interest. It means the extra price paid by the purchaser of a bond, and received by the seller, over and above the market price of the bond. It represents the accumulation of interest since the previous coupon was paid.

APPRAISAL—The act of estimating the value of personal or real property.

APPROPRIATION—A sum authorized and set aside for a specific purpose.

ARBITRAGE—Buying an identical or similar security in one market and selling it in another, in order to take advantage of a temporary disparity in price. The transaction may conceivably be carried out by using more than two markets, and the term is applied to transactions in stocks, bonds, gold, silver, foreign exchange, bills of exchange, and all commodities. More often, arbitrage is used in the case of the purchase of convertible bonds or convertible preferred stocks and the sale of an equivalent amount of common stock.

ARREARS—A debt that is due but unpaid. It is also applied to dividends on issues of cumulative preferred stocks which have become due but remain unpaid.

ASSENTED SECURITIES—The securities which have been pledged by their owners in favor of some change, such as a reorganization in which the status of the securities will be altered.

ASSESSMENT—A levy made on a security in order to raise additional capital.

ASSETS—The property, and claims against others, owned by an individual, business, or corporation. They may be tangible or intangible and are classed as fixed, current, and deferred.

AT THE MARKET—Term used in brokerage transactions, the customer authorizing his broker to buy or sell at prevailing prices. If the customer does not wish to buy or sell at the market, he may place a price at which he will buy or sell and authorize the broker to transact business "at or better" than the said price.

AUTOMATION—Fundamentally it means applying the science of mechanics to jobs that previously were performed by hand labor. It is as old as the industrial revolution, but has received a new importance in recent years as technological improvements have enabled manufacturing plants to supplant human labor with mechanical labor.

BABY BONDS—Bonds issued in denominations of $50 or $100 in order to attract investors of comparatively small means. Ordinarily, bonds are issued in $1,000 denominations.

BALANCE OF PAYMENTS—The relationship of the money flowing into and out of a country. It is directly affected by a country's foreign trade, travel, foreign aid, foreign investment, and remittances. This is discussed more fully in a separate article in this book.

BALANCE OF TRADE—Difference in money value between a country's imports and exports. The nation's balance is said to be favorable if total exports exceed total imports and unfavorable if the imports exceed the exports.

BANKING SYNDICATE—A group of banks associated together to underwrite and sell a new issue of securities.

BANK OF ISSUE—Any bank that is authorized to issue paper money in the form of bank notes.

BANK RATE—The rate of discount fixed by the Bank of England or other central bank in Europe as distinguished from the open market rate. The equivalent in the United States is the rate of discount fixed by the Federal Reserve, which is usually, but not always, the same in the twelve Federal Reserve districts.

BANK RESERVE—The proportion of cash or balances with other banks which a bank is required by law to maintain against the total of deposits in its own institution. Member banks of the Federal Reserve System keep their reserves with the Federal Reserve bank of their district. State banks and trust companies, not members of the system, keep reserves in the form prescribed by state law.

BARREL—This familiar container has a somewhat different meaning in the oil industry than elsewhere. It means 42 gallons. That is the way oil is measured, even though an actual barrel, or drum, holds 50 gallons. The 42-gallon measure came into being in 1866 when a group of producers got together and issued a proclamation that they would sell no oil by the barrel, or package, but by the gallon only, and that an allowance of two gallons, in favor of the buyer, would be made on the gauge for each and every forty gallons. While they specified the gallon as the measure, the 42-gallon barrel gradually emerged as the accepted unit.

BASE RATE—The regular rate of pay, excluding overtime, bonuses, and premiums.

BASING POINT—A system used in quoting prices of articles sold over a wide market, particularly in the case of heavy products such as finished steel, where the freight rate is an important factor in the cost. The steel industry for years quoted a price f.o.b. a designated point, or basing point, which may or may not have been the point of production. A multiple basing point system is based on a number of price-standard cities as distinguished from a single basing point system in which there is only one city. For some years Pittsburgh was the principal place for which f.o.b. prices of steel products were quoted. Under this system buyers of steel figured costs on the basis of the quoted price plus freight from Pittsburgh, even though the steel which they bought might have been fabricated at some nearer or more distant point.

BASIS—A term used to describe the spread between the price for future cotton as established by a futures contract on an exchange and the price for spot cotton as established in a spot transaction.

BEAR—A trader who expects to be able to buy securities or commodities at a lower level. He may sell short in anticipation of the decline, in which case he becomes a prospective buyer.

BEAR MARKET—Term applied to the market when the influence of the bears is predominant and the price trend is downward.

BEAR RAID—Heavy selling of a security to depress the price suddenly, the bears taking advantage of a weakened technical condition of the market.

BEDEAUX SYSTEM—An efficiency system introduced by Charles Bedeaux which sets a standard amount of production per minute for each job.

BID AND OFFER—The prices respectively at which a prospective buyer will purchase and a prospective seller will sell.

BIG BOARD—A term applied to the New York Stock Exchange.

BILATERAL ACTION—Action agreed to by both the employer and the union bargaining agent.

BILLS DISCOUNTED—The aggregate of notes, acceptances, and bills of exchange which a bank has discounted for its customers—as distinguished from loans.

BIMETALLISM—Free concurrent coinage of two metals, usually gold and silver, at an established ratio between the two, into coins of full legal tender value.

BIS—BANK FOR INTERNATIONAL SETTLEMENTS—The institution formed as part of the Young plan to effect a revised settlement of various financial claims among creditor nations growing out of World War I. It was opened in May 1930, at Basle, Switzerland, under the official control of Germany, Belgium, France, Great Britain, Italy, and Japan.

BLANKET MORTGAGE—A mortgage covering all the property of a corporation, given to secure a single debt.

BLIND POOL—Funds pooled by a group of speculators who place the management of the fund in the hands of one person for a specified period.

BLOCKED CURRENCY—Currency designated for a specific use as distinguished from currency that circulates freely and may be used in any manner. It arises out of efforts by various governments to withhold payment from various classes of creditors and is used as a means to control exchange and trade movements. As it cannot circulate freely, the exchange market quotes such currency at a discount from the regular currency of the country in question.

BLUE CHIP—Common stock of a company that has an acknowledged reputation for the quality of its goods and services and its ability to make money in lean years as well as when business is booming. Usually these well-seasoned shares sell at relatively high prices and a high price-earnings ratio.

BLUE LIST—A daily publication listing offerings of municipal securities. It includes the name of the bond, the number of bonds available, the coupon rate, the maturity date, and the dealers who have bonds for sale. It is, in effect, a catalogue of municipal bonds for sale, and gives an indication of the inventory of unsold bonds which dealers have on their shelves and in which they are prepared to make secondary offerings. It is published by the Blue List Publishing Co., Inc., New York, N.Y.

BLUE-SKY LAWS—Laws enacted by various states to regulate the issuance of securities, the sale of a particular block of securities, or the business of dealing in securities.

BOARD LOT—Same as round lot. The unit of trade on any exchange. On the New York Stock Exchange a board lot is 100 shares of stock or $1,000 par value in a bond, except in special instances.

BOARD ROOM—The room for customers in a brokerage office, where quotations are published and business transacted with the customers.

BOBTAIL POOL—A pool in which the members act independently instead of as a unit. Each member closes out his own commitments as he wishes.

BOILER ROOM—A room in which a group of fast-talking salesmen of securities of doubtful merit phone the unsophisticated in an effort to peddle their stocks. The salesmen use sucker lists. If they make a sale, their profit is outrageously high.

BOND—A formal evidence of a debt, whereby the borrower promises to pay the lender a specified amount with interest at a fixed rate payable on specified dates. In most cases the bond is secured by a definite mortgage on property. It differs from a stock in that it constitutes a debt of the issuing corporation rather than a share in the business of the corporation; it constitutes a contract, the terms of which must be complied with before the stock receives dividends.

BOND CROWD—The members of an exchange who specialize in trading in bonds, frequently transacting orders for other members of the same exchange.

BONUS STOCK—Stock issued to purchasers of securities or the underwriters when a new venture is being launched; usually such stock consists of common shares given to every purchaser of preferred shares.

BOOK—A brokerage term describing the memorandum book in which the specialist keeps an account of prospective buying and selling orders which have been placed with him for execution.

BOOKS, CLOSED AND OPEN—Transfer books of a corporation are usually closed at a specified date prior to the payment of a dividend so that the transfer agent may determine to whom dividends should be sent; no new transfers of ownership of stock are recorded while the books are closed. On a specified date the books are reopened and transfers made.

BOOK VALUE—The actual money value of all of a corporation's assets, such as plant, equipment, inventories, accounts receivable, cash, etc., minus all its liabilities. The difference is divided by the number of equity shares outstanding to obtain the book value per share. There is no necessary correlation between a stock's book value and market value, as many other factors enter into determining the latter.

BOOM—A fast advance in prices or in business.

BROKERS' LOANS—Loans made to brokers by banks on approved collateral, representing roughly the amount of money necessary to carry the floating supply of speculative securities. Both the Federal Reserve and the New York Stock Exchange compile regular totals of such loans.

B.T.U.—British thermal unit, used as a measure of heat. It is the heat necessary to raise the temperature of one pound of water one degree fahrenheit. The term is frequently used in newspapers in stories about gas companies.

BUCKET SHOP—A dishonest brokerage house in which orders placed by a customer are not executed but are held by the broker, who chooses to gamble that his customer is wrong. The bucket-shop operator thus takes a position in the market opposite to that of his customers.

BUCK ROGERS—Stocks that enjoy a sudden rise in a short period of time.

BULGE—A small and quick advance in prices.

BULL—A trader who has purchased securities or commodities in anticipation of a rise in value. He is a prospective seller.

BULLION—Metal in bulk form, such as gold or silver in the form of bars, lumps, or ingots.

BYRNES ACT—A federal statute which prohibits interstate transportation of strikebreakers.

CABLE RATES—In the foreign exchange table, the rates quoted for a cable transfer as distinguished from the check or demand draft rate, or the rate for thirty-, sixty- or ninety-day bills of exchange. The cable rate is always higher than the others.

CALL—

    a. Demand for payment of money due.

    b. A contract entitling the holder to buy specified securities or commodities at an agreed-upon price within a specific period of time. Opposite of a "put," which entitles holders to deliver such securities or commodities at a specified price within a designated period.

    c. The procedure of opening trading on most commodity exchanges, with an attendant calling out each delivery month and members making their respective bids and offers. After the call, trading proceeds in all deliveries simultaneously.

CALLABLE BONDS—Bonds which may be redeemed by the issuing company prior to the maturity date. Usually the redeemer has to pay an agreed-upon premium over the face value if he avails himself of the privilege.

CALL LOAN—A loan which either the borrower or lender may terminate at will. Such loans usually apply to New York Stock Exchange collateral and are frequently referred to as street loans or stock exchange loans.

CAPITAL—Net worth, or the excess of assets over liabilities. In a corporation it is represented by the various capital stock accounts, surplus, and undivided profits.

CAPITAL GAIN OR CAPITAL LOSS—The profit or loss realized from the sale of a capital asset. If the asset has been held for less than six months and a day, it is said to be short-term and is taxed at the individual's full income tax rate. If held for more than six months and a day, it is long term; and the income tax is at a maximum of 25 per cent.

CAPITALIZATION—The total amount of the securities issued by a corporation. If this includes bonds and debentures, they are usually carried on the books of the corporation at their par or face value. Common and preferred stock may be carried at par or stated value, the latter being an arbitrary figure determined by the directors at the time the securities were first issued.

CAPTIVE—A mine or plant, the product of which is used entirely by a parent company instead of being sold to the public. A large user of coal, cement, paper, or oil, which is not in the business of marketing these products but is a large user of them, may own and operate captive mines, wells, or mills.

CARRYBACK—A term used in corporate taxation. Should a corporation sustain a deficit in 1964 after having paid a tax on its earnings in 1962 or 1963, it is permitted to carry back the 1964 loss as an expense, and thus get a rebate from the government on the tax it paid in the previous years.

CARRYOVER—Stock of a staple commodity which is not consumed during the year of production and is carried over to the next year.

CARTEL—An international combination within one industry, similar to a trust. Its aim is to stabilize prices by allocating territory between its various units and by limiting production.

CASH FLOW—A corporation's earnings after taxes and dividend disbursements, plus noncash charges such as the funds it is able to set aside for capital consumption allowances, including especially depreciation and depletion reserves. The total represents internally generated funds which are available for the corporation's expansion and thus tend to relieve it of the necessity of going to the capital market to raise new money through the issuance of additional securities. It is money that flows into a corporation and does not necessarily have to flow out.

CASH GRAIN—Same as spot grain, which is grain for immediate delivery.

CATS AND DOGS—A stock market term referring to securities of doubtful value which cannot be used as collateral for a loan and which are held as an acknowledged speculation.

C.D.—Time certificates of deposit issued by banks. They cover interest-bearing time deposits and are attractive to big investors such as large corporations, over short periods, as they offer higher yields than Treasury bills and are readily negotiable in an active secondary market. At the close of 1962 there were $6.2 billion in C.D.'s outstanding, thus topping the volume of $6 billion in commercial paper and $2.7 billion in bankers' acceptances. While large corporations are the chief buyers of C. D.'s, state and local governments also are purchasers.

CENTRAL BANK—The bank holding the main body of bank reserves of a country and having the note-issuing power.

CERTIFICATED STOCK—Used in commodity dealings to indicate a commodity that has been classed and found tenderable, and for which a certificate has been issued declaring that it is tenderable.

CERTIFICATES OF DEPOSIT—Negotiable instruments, usually with maturities of three, six, or nine months, which attest that a large depositor has a stated amount of money on short-term deposit at a certain bank. New York money market dealers stand ready to buy and sell such certificates in open trading. These certificates bear a relatively low rate of interest.

CHECKOFF—The collection of union dues by the employer from the pay envelopes of the union members. In some cases the employer performs this service for the union automatically, and in other cases the deduction must be specifically authorized by the employee.

C.I.F.—Cost of the article, plus insurance during transportation, plus the freight charges to the point of destination (cost, insurance, freight).

CLASS I RAILROADS—Railroad companies having gross annual operating revenues in excess of $1 million.

CLASS SYSTEM—A term occasionally applied to the stagger system of electing directors. Only a portion of the board has to stand for election in any one year. Each director's term runs for more than one year, so only one class of directors, or one portion of the full board, must win stockholder support at any one annual meeting.

CLEARING HOUSE—A voluntary association of banks in a city or county joined together to facilitate their daily exchange of checks, drafts, and notes.

CLEARINGS—The volume of checks and drafts processed for collection by the banks in a given period.

CLOSED MORTGAGE—A mortgage covering indebtedness on property which cannot be further increased.

CLOSED SHOP—A place of employment where only union members may be hired or retained in employment.

CLOSED UNION—A union which unreasonably withholds union membership.

COLLATERAL—Security deposited with a lender by the borrower as a pledge for the repayment of the loan.

COMMERCIAL BANK—A bank that accepts deposits payable on demand, has checking accounts, and makes short-term loans to business. It maintains its reserves in quickly convertible forms, thus differing from a savings bank.

COMMERCIAL CREDIT—Credit furnished to producers, wholesalers, jobbers, and retailers. It is for those engaged in the production and distribution of goods, as distinguished from personal, banking, public, agricultural, or investment credit.

COMMERCIAL PAPERS—Short-term negotiable instruments, such as notes, bills, and acceptances, that arise out of commercial transactions, as distinguished from speculative, real estate, personal, or public transactions.

COMMISSION—Charge made by banks and brokers for handling a piece of business. On most exchanges the minimum rates for commissions are established by the exchanges, the charge being graduated according to the selling price of the security handled. Dealers do not charge a commission, as they take a position in the market and trade with their customer, not for him.

COMMITMENT—Pledge or contract involving financial responsibility to take up securities or commodities bought at the agreed time, or to make delivery of same if sold.

COMMODITY—Raw materials and provisions. They are quoted in the newspapers both on a cash basis, meaning for immediate delivery, and on a futures basis, meaning for delivery in some specified month in the future.

COMMON STOCK—The junior security of a corporation. It receives no protection in the event of failure of the corporation until all prior obligations have been met and preferred dividend obligations have been cared for. It represents the ownership of an equity in a business after all other claims.

COMMUNITY PROPERTY—The opposite of separate property. It comes from Spanish law, and prevails in various forms in eight states. Under it spouses have equal interests in earnings, profits, and wealth obtained during marriage; on the death of one, only half of the community property (plus all of his or her personal property, if any) passes under the will. The survivor's half is not affected. Usually the husband is the manager of the community property. In most cases community property does not include earnings or wealth accumulated before marriage, although in some cases the earnings received on such private property become part of the community after marriage.

CONSOLS—A government bond which has replaced and consolidated other loans. They are perpetual, i.e., they have no stated maturity. The term was originally applied to the 3 per cent consolidated annuities of Great Britain.

CONSUMER PRICE INDEX—A measure of the average changes in prices of goods and services typically bought by city families of wage earners and clerical workers, based on the prices of four hundred items believed to be representative of all urban places in the country.

CONTINGENT FUND—A fund set aside out of earnings of a corporation to provide for emergencies.

CONTINGENT LIABILITIES—Liabilities for which a business may be held, but which are not certain.

CONTRACT—An agreement between two or more parties enforceable at law. When applied to commodities, it means an agreement to accept or deliver a specific amount of the commodity on a specific date.

CONTRACT GRADE—The grade of a commodity required to be delivered on a futures contract.

CONVERTIBLE SECURITIES—Bonds or stocks that may be exchanged for other securities of the issuing corporation, usually common shares, at the option of the holder.

CORNER—Applied to stocks, the concentrated ownership of a sufficient proportion of the outstanding shares so that shorts may not borrow the shares except from the owner group. In commodities, sufficient ownership of the commodity to control or dictate prices.

COST OF LIVING—This usually refers to the Consumers Price Index, compiled and published monthly by the Bureau of Labor Statistics of the Department of Labor.

C. AND F.—COST AND FREIGHT—Used in importing and exporting to mean that the price quoted includes the cost of the merchandise plus the freight to the point of destination. It does not include insurance. If insurance is also included, the abbreviation used is C.I.F.

COUPON BONDS—Bonds not registered in the name of the holder, but which have coupons attached to them which may be clipped and cashed as they mature. Each calls for a specified amount of interest.

COVENANT—A formal agreement which binds one to a contract or makes a stipulation.

COVER—Buying a security that previously had been sold short.

CRAFT UNION—A union that restricts its membership to workers having a particular skill but admits members having that skill regardless of the industry in which they work or the company that employs them.

CUMULATIVE—Usually applied to preferred stocks, and provides that if the dividend is not paid in any one quarter, the payment is carried over and remains a debt that must be satisfied before the common stock receives a dividend.

CUMULATIVE VOTING—A method whereby the holder of a certain number of shares of stock may concentrate his entire voting strength at a meeting of stockholders for the election of one candidate or may distribute his votes among as many candidates as he desires.

CURRENT ASSETS—The assets of a corporation that are immediately available, or can be made available in a short time. Included would be the cash on hand, government securities held, trade receivables, and inventories that are readily marketable.

CURRENT LIABILITIES—The liabilities of a corporation that fall due within a short period, usually regarded as within twelve months. This would include bond or note issues falling due within that time, sinking fund requirements, short term loans, and bills payable.

CUSTOMER'S REPRESENTATIVE—Employees of security firms who are regularly employed in the solicitation of business or the handling of customers' accounts, or who advise customers about the purchase or sale of securities.

DAY ORDER—An order given by a customer to his broker, good for one day only. If the order is to remain open for a longer period it is marked G.T.C., i.e., good 'til countermanded. Or it may be limited to a week or a month.

DEADHEADING—Transportation for which no fee is paid. In railroading it would include the shifting of a train crew from one point to another, or the transportation of the holder of a pass. In communications it would include the sending of unpaid company messages.

DEBENTURE—Long-term debt secured only by the assets and general credit of the obligor, rather than by a mortgage. Usually the term is used in connection with a bond issue, but it is sometimes used with debenture stock. In the latter case, the debenture stock is in the nature of a prior preference stock, ranking above the preferred and common issues. In the case of debenture bonds, the bonds are not secured by a mortgage or any specific pledge of assets.

DEFENSIVE ISSUES—Securities on which earnings have been relatively stable for a number of years and which, while they may not advance much in a bull market, are believed to be relatively secure from heavy selling pressure in bear markets.

DEFLATION—A condition characterized by rapidly falling prices and dull business. Normally it takes place when the amount of goods produced far exceeds the ability or willingness of people to buy. There is a sharp contraction of credit, price wars become frequent, individuals and corporations cut their expenses, and unemployment mounts.

DEFLATOR—A deflator is a divisor used to eliminate the element of price change from changes in dollar values. It is used in the construction of some indexes to balance or eliminate the effect of a changed dollar value.

DELIVERY—The term is applied to both securities and commodities. If a purchase is made for cash, delivery must take place on the day of the transaction. If the purchase is made in the ordinary way, the rules of the stock exchange provide that delivery must take place not later than the fourth business day following the transaction. In the case of commodities, a certain day is set by the exchange for the delivery of contracts falling due in a certain month.

DEPLETION—Gradual exhaustion of the value of an asset. Usually a charge is made on the books of a corporation to balance the loss of its assets.

DEPRECIATION—Gradual shrinkage in the value of an asset due to physical wear and tear, obsolescence, or a sudden decline in the market value of the asset.

DIGESTED SECURITIES—Securities which have largely been placed with investors who may reasonably be expected to hold them for a long term.

DILUTION—Usually applied to a reduction in per share earnings caused by the issuance of a block of shares for properties that fail to maintain the previous rate of earnings. For example, if a company is earning $4 a share on its stock and then issues additional shares in the acquisition of a property or business which is unable to maintain this same per share rate of earnings, then the stock is said to have been diluted. If, on the other hand, the new acquisition proves to be a wise one, and more than $4 a share is produced on the extra block of stock, then the stock has been enhanced rather than diluted.

DISCOUNT RATE—The fee Federal Reserve banks charge for loans to member commercial banks on notes, acceptances, and bills of exchange. The rate varies according to conditions in the money market and is changed by a Federal Reserve bank whenever it believes bank credit should be tightened or relaxed. The rate strongly influences general interest rate patterns.

DISCRETIONARY ORDERS—Orders given to a broker to purchase or sell securities for a customer according to his own judgment, but at the risk of the customer.

DISMISSAL WAGE—A lump-sum wage payment to an employee whose employment is ended through causes beyond his control. It is usually based on years of service and is the same as discontinuance wage or severance pay.

DISTRIBUTION—The term used in business to embrace all the activities employed in finding customers for goods and services, and in moving goods geographically and through the channels of trade. Distribution includes the retail, wholesale, advertising, and service industries, as well as the sales and marketing functions of manufacturing.

DIVIDEND—That portion of the earnings of a corporation paid to stockholders as a return for their investment in the business.

DOLLAR AVERAGING—Periodic investing of a definite number of dollars irrespective of the number of shares involved. For instance, if an investor decides he will invest $1,000 every month, or quarter, or year, in XYZ stock, his dollars may buy a large number of shares one time and then only a few shares at other times. Dollar averaging contrasts with share averaging, in which the investor makes periodic purchases but always buys the same number of shares, irrespective of the number of dollars required.

DOUBLE TAXATION—This refers to the fact that a corporation is taxed on its earnings, and when a portion of the earnings is distributed to stockholders as dividends, the stockholders likewise pay an income tax. Thus the same block of earnings is taxed twice.

DOWNSTREAM BORROWING—The borrowing of money by a corporation through the use of the credit standing of its subsidiaries.

DOW THEORY—A theory for forecasting stock market trends. In large part it was the creation of the late William Peter Hamilton, former editor of the *Wall Street Journal*. Whatever its merit, the theory has a vast following, so its influence on the market is far-reaching. It is based on the chart action of the rail and the industrial averages. For forecasting purposes, it is the contention of the theory's adherents that successive rallies of these two averages which penetrate preceding high points, with ensuing declines halting before they have penetrated preceding low points, constitutes a bullish indication for the market. Conversely, failure of the two averages to penetrate previous high points, with ensuing declines falling below former low points, constitute a bearish signal.

DUE BILL—A notice of an amount due. As used in the securities business, it is signed by the buyer of a security and specifies an amount due the seller under certain conditions. For instance, if a firm sold a stock which had gone ex-dividend but on which the dividend had not yet been paid, it would get a due bill from the buyer, specifying that when the payment date arrives, the money is to revert to the selling firm.

DUE DILIGENCE—Term applied to a meeting of representatives of an underwriting syndicate with officials of the company which is issuing new securities. At such meetings the prospective underwriters question company officials and others connected with the financing on matters relating to the business of the company and the statements appearing in the registration. This is to comply with provisions of the law, which are that the prospective sellers of the new issue must show due diligence. Frequently such meetings are small and the questioning is more or less routine. In a few cases, however, a due diligence meeting furnishes the company with an opportunity to display its products to the bankers and to stir their enthusiasm.

DUMMY—A term used in connection with directors placed on a board who have no financial interest or responsibility in the company, but represent someone who has.

DUMP—Exporting a large quantity of some article to a foreign country for sale at any price, even below the cost of production, in order to avoid unsettling the domestic market. Also applies to the sale of a large quantity of stocks regardless of the price secured.

E.D.R.—EUROPEAN DEPOSITORY RECEIPT—It is patterned after the American depository receipt which was originated in 1927 to facilitate investments by Americans in securities of foreign countries. The European depository receipt was first issued in London in 1963, to facilitate international trading in Japanese securities. It is a negotiable receipt covering certain specified securities which have been deposited in a bank in the country of origin of the securities. Their use in trading eliminates the necessity of shipping the actual stock certificates, thus making transfer of ownership easier, faster, and less expensive. The existence of A.D.R.'s, E.D.R.'s, and the original underlying securities in two or more markets makes possible an active arbitrage market.

EPUNTS—Pronounced "E.P.U. nits." A relatively new European financing technique, or gimmick. The unit of account is a payment guarantee, the value of which is expressed in terms of gold, as are free world currencies. The unit is not a gold obligation itself but has a value based on gold. Each unit represents slightly less than nine-tenths of a gram of gold, the same as the basis of the value of the American dollar. The holder of a matured bond that is expressed in Epunits can request payment in any one of seventeen currencies, irrespective of the kind of currency he used when he made the purchase. If one or more of the seventeen currencies has depreciated, he will ask for payment in another. The same applies to payments of interest on the bond. The name Epunits comes from the European Payments Union, formed in 1947 to facilitate currency exchange, to which seventeen nations belonged. The union no longer exists.

EQUIPMENT TRUST—A trust by means of which rolling stock of a railroad is mortgaged and the purchase of the rolling stock financed through the sale of equipment trust certificates based on the mortgage.

EQUITY—In a margin account, the excess of the value of securities over the debit balance. More often the term is used to indicate the ownership interest in a company held by its common and preferred stockholders.

ESCALATOR CLAUSE—A price adjustment clause inserted in a contract or purchase order as a protection against price uncertainties of the future. Comparatively rare some years ago, this clause became common following the formation of the Office of Price Administration (1941) and the institution of governmental price ceilings. It was found usually in new leases on real estate and in contracts to deliver various types of goods which were subject to ceiling control. The clause simply stated that prices in effect at the time of the signing of the lease or contract might be increased if the ceiling were removed.

Another kind of escalator clause provides for renegotiation of prices at a later date. Usually the buyer retains the right to cancel the deal if he is dissatisfied with the new price level.

When applied to wages, it means a collective bargaining agreement which provides for the adjustment of wages in line with changes in the cost of living.

ESCHEAT—State seizure of property that has no apparent owner, usually the estate of a person who dies without heirs.

ESCROW—An agreement among three parties whereby one party acts as custodian and holds some valuable consideration received from the second party to be surrendered to the third party on the fulfillment of a specified obligation. Usually a bank acts as the custodian and holds stocks, bonds, a deed, or other valuable paper which one individual deposits on the condition that it must be delivered to another individual as soon as he completes his contract.

EURODOLLARS—Dollar deposits or loans in a European country. An example is a deposit of dollars in a London bank which the bank may lend to an individual, or to another European bank. In a similar manner a French bank might have a deposit of sterling which it could lend in France, or in some other country. European banking centers have an active market in the lending and borrowing of foreign deposits. Thus there are Euro-every significant currency in the free world, such as Euro-sterling or Euro-Swiss francs. Their use differs from an ordinary transaction in the foreign exchange market in that the latter is a straight purchase or sale of a foreign currency, for immediate or forward delivery. The Eurocurrency market is one based on the lending and borrowing of a bank balance in a foreign currency. It is a growing international market which is further removed from controls and regulations than is the familiar foreign exchange market in various domestic currencies.

EXCESS RESERVES—The amount of a bank's reserves against its deposits in excess of the amount required by law. The excess may be on deposit with the Federal Reserve, with a designated depository, or in the bank's own vaults.

EX-DIVIDEND—When directors declare a dividend they set a date for taking a record of stockholders entitled to the dividend. After this date the stock is quoted without the dividend—or ex-dividend—as the holder of the stock on the record date will receive the payment even if he sells his shares before the dividend is paid.

FACTOR—A middleman in the field, who has authority to sell, or to consign for the purpose of sale, to buy, and to advance or borrow money with goods as security, when acting for his principal.

FAIR EMPLOYMENT PRACTICE—The policy of hiring and promoting without regard to race or religion.

FANNIE MAY—Nickname for the Federal National Mortgage Association.

FEATHERBEDDING—The imposition, by labor unions, of certain rates of pay for certain specified jobs, irrespective of whether the time required to perform them has been shortened by improved machinery or improved efficiency. The term is usually applied in the railroad industry, where there are literally thousands of cases of runs, or jobs, for which the roads are required to pay a full day's wage for work that takes but a few hours.

FEDERAL FUNDS—Reserves borrowed and lent in transactions between large commercial banks to even out daily reserve positions. One bank, with an excess, will "sell," or lend, to a bank that wishes to "buy," or borrow. This is done through firms specializing in that field. There are no figures on the amount involved, but seventy-five large banks throughout the country are said to be in the federal funds market daily.

FIAT MONEY—Money which a government declares shall be accepted as legal tender, but which is not covered by any available specie reserve. It is inconvertible and irredeemable.

FIDUCIARY—Of the nature of a trust, a confidential relationship; also the individual in whom the trust is placed and who is authorized to act in a confidential capacity.

FIFO—An accounting term meaning first in, first out. The opposite of LIFO which means last in, first out. Both are used in valuing inventory.

FINDER'S FEE—A reward given by an individual, group, or firm to the person or persons who discover and bring to the former a profitable deal. Such fees may run around 5, 10, or 15 per cent of the profit, but they are usually based on word-of-mouth promises and are difficult to enforce legally. Moreover, it is sometimes difficult to determine a fair basis for splitting a finder's fee, as differences of opinion may exist as to just how much any one individual contributed in discovering and delivering the deal.

FISCAL YEAR—The accounting year as distinguished from the calendar year.

FIXED CHARGES—Expenses which are more or less constant despite the volume of business transacted.

FLAT—Term used in bond trading to indicate that the purchase price of the bond includes any interest that may have accumulated. The term is also used in Wall Street in the case of shares loaned to shorts when no interest is paid to the short on the money which he deposits with the lender of the shares.

FLOAT—To sell a new issue of securities. Also applied to the floating account of a bank which holds out-of-town checks which are outstanding and in the process of collection.

FLOATING DEBT—Notes and other short-term indebtedness of a corporation that have not been funded or converted into long-term debt bearing a fixed interest rate.

FLOOR BROKER—A member of an exchange who transacts business for another member of the exchange; usually referred to as a "two-dollar broker."

F.O.B.—Free on board cars, steamships, or other means of transportation.

FOR A TURN—Applied to a speculative purchase or sale made with the intention of securing a quick but small profit.

FORMULA PLAN INVESTING—An objective plan to guide the investor of funds, designed to persuade him to dispose of stocks when they have reached some predetermined level and substitute bonds in their place. There are many different plans, but probably the more rudimentary of two broad types is the fixed ratio plan. Under this the investor determines a fixed percentage of his capital to be placed in stocks, and then if a periodic evaluation of his holdings shows the stock funds to have exceeded their percentage, he sells sufficient shares to bring the proportion down. If they have declined below his limit, he buys more. The variable ratio plan adds to the above formula a change in the percentage of capital placed in stocks and in more stable securities, depending upon the historical level of the market. To determine this, the investor must chart any recognized index of stock prices and examine it periodically to see if the general market is above or below its established zone.

FRANCHISE—A privilege extended to an individual or a corporation by a governmental body, empowering the recipient to do something that otherwise would be illegal, such as to operate without competition from other operators.

FREE RIDE—As used in financial parlance, the term is applied to one's subscription for securities at the time of their original offering to the public. In the few days intervening before payment must be made to the offering syndicate, the price sometimes is enhanced, thus providing the buyer with an opportunity to sell out at the higher market price and buy in at the lower offering price, thus obtaining a free ride. In former years this could be done on occasion without depositing any money, but under the present stricter regulations the subscriber must deposit his money in full before his order can be accepted.

FREE RIDERS—A term applied by the unions to nonmember employees who share in benefits obtained by the union but take no part in union activities.

FROZEN ASSETS—Assets of a corporation that are not readily convertible into cash.

FULL LOT—The unit of trading on an exchange. On the New York Stock Exchange a full lot is 100 shares or $1,000 par value in bonds in virtually all cases.

FUNDED DEBT—Bonded, long-term indebtedness as distinguished from unfunded, floating, or current debt.

FUNDING—The process of converting floating indebtedness into long-term debt. It is accomplished by paying off the nearby obligations with funds raised through the sale of a long-term bond issue or a stock issue.

FUTURES—Contracts in commodities whereby the seller agrees to deliver a specified amount of the commodity at some future date, usually from one to six months hence.

GARNISHEE—A legal action by a creditor, attaching the wages of an employee while they are in the hands of an employer.

GENERAL MORTGAGE BONDS—Bonds secured by a blanket mortgage upon property already subject to prior mortgages.

GILT EDGED—A term denoting highest quality securities.

GIVE UP—A term used in trading. If a customer of one firm wishes to buy or sell a stock but it is not convenient for him to get in touch with his broker's office, he may give the order to another firm that is a member of the same exchange. The second firm may execute the order or may turn it over to the first firm. If the second firm handles the order it "gives up" the name of the one that actually has the individual's account. The commission paid by the investor is not affected. The term is also used if one member acts for another member, and in making a trade with a third member on the floor, "gives up" the name of the one for whom he is acting, rather than his own name.

GOOD DELIVERY—Securities placed with a bank or broker for collateral or for sale must constitute a good delivery; that is, they must be genuine, title must be vested in the owner and have been properly conveyed to him, and they must be in negotiable form.

GRANDFATHER RIGHTS—An Interstate Commerce Commission term under which carriers and freight forwarders that operated between the West Coast and Alaska prior to the date Alaska became a state could continue the same operations without seeking further ICC authority.

GREENBACKS—Inconvertible notes authorized by three acts of Congress, which reflected the Civil War inflation era. They were legal tender for all debts, public and private, except duties on imports and interest on public debt.

GROSS NATIONAL PRODUCT—This is published quarterly and is the most inclusive available measure of our over-all economic activity. It is the nation's total output of goods and services at current market prices. It is compiled by adding together the expenditures for all final products and services bought during a given period. *Final products* are purchases that are not resold. Aside from consumer goods and services they therefore include business purchases of tools and equipment; adjustment also is made for changes in the physical volume of business inventories valued at current prices. This is necessary so that when inventory liquidation occurs, the figure for gross national product can be reduced by an appropriate amount. When inventories are being accumulated by business, GNP is increased. A few items for which the recipient does not pay directly are included in GNP. These are imputed values and include such things as food furnished to employees, food consumed by farmers who produced it, and the rental value of owner-occupied houses.

There are four major component divisions of GNP: consumers, business, government, and foreign. Expenditures by the first group are called *personal consumption.* The sum is the amount of money spent for goods and services by individuals and nonprofit organizations. It includes sales taxes. Business spending and personal spending on houses and farm equipment are termed *gross private domestic investment.* The sum measures the dollar value of new construction, the spending of business for new durable goods, and the net change in inventories. *Government purchases of goods and services* includes the spending by all government units—federal, state, and local. It eliminates payments which do not represent current production, such as social security payments, veterans' benefits, interest, and loans. *Net foreign investment* is the net amount of national output that is sold or given to foreign countries.

GROWTH STOCKS—Shares of companies that show a steady increase in gross earnings and which usually plow back a fairly large percentage of their net for expansion and research.

GUARANTEED BONDS—Bonds on which the principal or interest or both, have been guaranteed by a party other than the original issuer.

GUARANTEED STOCK—Stock issues of one corporation, the dividend payment on which, and sometimes the principal itself, is guaranteed by another corporation. This occurs frequently in the case of railroads, where one large system will make such a guarantee in order to take over or lease a feeder line.

HATCH ACT—A federal statute, amended by the Taft-Hartley Act, which forbids corporations or unions to make contributions or expenditures in connection with the elections for certain federal offices.

HEDGE—A purchase or a sale intended to balance or offset a trading position in any market and to lessen anticipated losses. It amounts to a form of insurance used by dealers in commodities, securities, and foreign exchange, to prevent losses through price fluctuations. It is a method of protecting a transaction entered into because of one's business by another transaction entered into in the speculative market.

HIRING HALL SYSTEM—A system under which the employer agrees to hire only workers supplied by the union except in cases where the union is unable to supply needed replacements.

HOKEY—A nickname given to bonds of the Home Owner's Loan Corporation.

HOLDING COMPANY—A corporation which owns all or a good proportion of the stock of one or more operating companies. Frequently one holding company holds stocks in other holding companies, and the operating company is several times removed from the parent organization. Through this device, the control of vast and widely separated properties may be exercised by one group having comparatively little capital.

HOT ISSUE—A new issue of securities, usually common stock, which is coming to market at an offering price that is considered by speculators to be well below potential value. There is keen competition to buy shares of these new securities at the offering price; and if the speculators have correctly appraised the situation, they are able to sell shares awarded them at a premium over the offering price in a matter of a few days or even on the day the issue is marketed.

HYPOTHECATION—Deposit of securities or other collateral as a pledge for the repayment of a loan.

INACTIVE POST—The post on the floor of the New York Stock Exchange where comparatively inactive securities are traded in in round lots of 10 shares.

IN AND OUT—A term applied to buying and selling a security in a short space of time. This is also referred to as a *round turn,* although the latter may be a purchase and sale over a more extended period.

IBA—Investment Bankers Association of America.

INCOME BONDS—Bonds on which the payment of interest is contingent upon earnings. Interest on such bonds does not constitute a fixed charge, as it is payable only out of such earnings as may remain after all fixed charges have been met.

INDENTURE—The mortgage indenture or deed of trust signifying an agreement between two or more parties.

INDEX NUMBERS—Numbers which may be used to measure the relative level of prices of commodities, securities, or groups of either. Usually the price level which is regarded as normal is given an index number of 100 and fluctuations up or down are measured like percentages.

INFLATION—A condition characterized by rapidly rising prices and active business during which time profits are high in monetary terms but the purchasing power of money steadily diminishes.

INGOT—A bar of metal cast from a mold.

INJUNCTION—A court order which either imposes restraints upon action or directs that action be taken. In either case it is backed by the court's power, and disobedient parties may be held in contempt.

INSTRUMENT—A term denoting any kind of document in writing by which such contract is expressed.

INSULAR BONDS—Bonds issued by any of the insular possessions of the United States.

INTEREST—The rental price paid for the use of money.

INTERIM CERTIFICATES—Temporary certificates issued to the buyers of new issues of securities to be held until the final and engraved certificates can be issued in their place.

INTERIM DIVIDEND—Small nominal dividends paid once or more during the year by a corporation in anticipation of a final dividend at the close of the year.

INTERLOCKING DIRECTORS—Directors of one corporation who are at the same time directors of another corporation in the same or similar line of business.

INTERNAL BONDS—Bonds issued by a government in its own currency for purchase by its investors at home.

INTERNATIONAL SECURITIES—Securities which enjoy a ready market on the principal markets of more than one leading country.

INVESTED CAPITAL—Consists of working capital (current assets less current liabilities), net fixed assets after depreciation, and investments and other assets.

INVESTMENT—Capital put into an enterprise for a long period to yield a moderate return with maximum safety.

INVESTMENT BANKER—A banker who finances the long-term capital requirements of business as distinguished from its seasonal or current requirements. He is a buyer and seller of securities, an originator of new issues, an underwriter of additional issues, a dealer in existing issues, and a distributor of securities.

INVESTMENT CLUB—A group, usually a few friends or close associates, that meets periodically to discuss markets and make investments. Many, but not all, are members of the National Association of Investment Clubs, in Detroit, which has developed a set of rules for guidance in organizing and running a club. Usually the clubs frown on the more speculative issues. The majority appear to favor growth companies, the sales of which tend to increase by at least 10 per cent a year; they collect small sums from their members at periodic intervals, sometimes as little as $10 a month; they usually reinvest their dividends and capital gains instead of making cash distributions to members; and they diversify whenever possible.

INVESTMENT COUNSELOR—A professional who renders advice on investments for a fee.

INVESTMENT DOLLAR—Dollars in London that are available for the purchase of dollar securities. In times of great demand these dollars are quoted at a premium, and the amount of the premium changes daily— once, when the New York stock market was especially buoyant, running as high as 11 per cent. As there are only so many dollars available in the investment pool, the rate charged to secure them changes rapidly throughout any business day, whenever there is an unusual demand for American securities.

INVESTMENT TRUST—A corporation formed to combine the capital of a number of persons to invest it in a variety of securities. The company invests and reinvests the capital entrusted to it in such a way as to secure an income and realize capital profits.

IRISH DIVIDEND—A humorous term for an assessment on a stock instead of a dividend received by the investor.

ISSUE—Bonds or stocks or other obligations marketed for a corporation and constituting one of its liabilities.

JOB EVALUATION—The system of fixing the relative values of jobs as they exist in a plant.

JOURNEYMAN—A worker in a traditional craft who has served his apprenticeship and mastered the kind of work involved in his craft.

JUNIOR BONDS—Bonds which are secondary to other issues of the company. In the event of foreclosure their claims are satisfied only after all prior claims have been met.

JURISDICTIONAL DISPUTE—A dispute between two unions as to which shall represent a group of workers in collective bargaining or as to which union's members shall perform a certain type of work.

KEYNESIAN ECONOMICS—The economic theory propounded by Lord Keynes which looks upon wage rates not only as an element of the cost of doing business but also as a factor in the demand for the products of industry. The theory is frequently used to support proposed wage increases on the ground that higher wages will increase purchasing power and help prevent depressions and unemployment.

LAMB—An inexperienced speculator.

LAWFUL MONEY—Every form of money which is endowed by law with legal tender quality.

LEA ACT—The federal statute forbidding featherbedding in the radio industry.

L.C.L.—Less-than-carload lot, a term used by raidroads to designate freight shipments of less than a carload each.

LEASEBACK—A practice whereby a company or individual sells property and then leases it back from the new owner. In recent years this practice has been growing. Usually the lease runs for a long term and the company, in almost all cases, contracts to pay all taxes and maintain the property, plus paying the stated rental. This assures a good return to a new owner. From the company's standpoint, it is an easy way to raise working capital without the issuance of new securities. Another advantage is that the rent is a deductible operating expense. The rent can conceivably amount to much more than the company would be able to deduct for depreciation had it retained title to the property.

LEGAL BONDS—Obligations with high ratings prescribed by state or federal laws as suitable investments for many fiduciary institutions.

LEGAL LIST—The list of investments of high quality, approved by certain states, in which fiduciaries and institutions may invest. The securities must qualify under legal specifications.

LEGAL TENDER—Money which may legally be tendered for the settlement of a debt unless the contract specifically calls for another type of money.

LETTERS OF CREDIT—Instruments by which a bank substitutes its own credit for that of its customer. It is a letter requesting one person to make an advance to a second person on the basis of the credit of the writer.

LEVERAGE—The power of advantage or disadvantage which accrues to the junior securities of a corporation in a rising or falling market. If a corporation has securities outstanding which are senior to the common stock, earnings which eventually accrue to the common may be drastically affected by even a small change in the company's operations. If the company has no securities except shares of common stock, the earnings per share go up or down in direct proportion to the change in net income. There is no leverage. But if it raises new capital through the sale of bonds or preferred stock on which there is a regular obligation to pay interest or a fixed dividend, or makes a bank loan, and this new money is profitably employed, the earnings on the common are quickly enhanced. It has leverage. If the new money fails to earn enough to meet the new carrying charges, then leverage works against the common.

LIEN—A charge against a property, for the purpose of exacting settlement of a debt.

LIFO—Last in, first out. An accounting term used in evaluating inventory, as, for instance, by a store which is continually buying and selling a certain definite product. The last shipment received before taking inventory may be considered the first sold.

LINE OF CREDIT—The maximum up to which an individual may borrow from his bank at any given time.

LIQUID ASSETS—Among banks it means the assets which may be immediately turned into cash. Among industrial concerns it means current assets.

LIQUIDATION—Termination of a business. In securities it means the sale of securities to realize cash.

LIQUIDITY—A high percentage of assets which may be quickly converted into cash.

LISTED SECURITIES—Securities which have been approved for trading by a stock exchange.

LLOYD'S—An association of English insurance underwriters.

LOAD—Applied to open end investment companies, or mutual funds, it is that portion of the purchase price retained by the sponsoring company to cover commissions and other costs of distribution. Not all mutual funds have a loading charge. It is incurred by the investor only when he makes his purchase, not when he sells. Applied to public utility companies, it means the use to which the facilities of the company may be placed.

LOCKED IN—Placed in a position where one cannot liquidate an investment without a sacrifice. It could apply to an individual in a high tax bracket who has a major paper profit in a stock which he has held for a short time only, the profit on which would be heavily taxed; or it could apply to a long-term capital gain, which is not as severely taxed, but still would advance the individual's income into a higher bracket.

LOMBARD LOANS—A British term meaning loans on bonds and shares. Usually they refer to collateral loans made by the central bank to commercial banks.

LONG—A buyer who is "long" is holding securities or commodities, usually in anticipation of a price rise; a position exactly opposite to that of the short seller.

LONG PULL—An expression indicating that securities have been bought with the intention of holding them for an extended period.

MANAGED CURRENCY—Currency not anchored to gold, but rather controlled or manipulated by the government in an effort to secure a predetermined level of prices.

MANIPULATION—The artificial advancing or depressing of prices irrespective of real value.

MARGIN—A payment on account. It represents the amount deposited by a trader with his broker on the purchase of securities or commodities, the broker lending the added amount which is needed to complete the purchase.

MELON—An expression denoting a large cash or stock dividend.

MERCHANT BANK—The type of financial organization in England that combines the functions of a commercial bank with those of an investment banking firm. The name is derived from the fact that many of these institutions had their origin with merchants of the seventeenth century who also developed a banking business. Successors to these merchants are not members of the London Stock Exchange and do no business with the public. Many still refer to themselves as merchants, instead of bankers. Names such as Rothschild and Baring are typical of the merchant banking families of years ago, and many have been advisers to kings. They originate financial deals, control insurance companies and investment trusts, and handle accounts for large investors, but not the general public. A few have opened offices in Wall Street and other major financial centers.

MILKING—An expression denoting undue exploitation of a business by squeezing out all the profit possible without making due provision for expansion, improvement, and contingencies.

M.I.P.—The monthly investment plan developed by the New York Stock Exchange. It is a pay-as-you-go plan whereby the investor selects the stock of his choosing, makes a monthly payment to his broker—which may be as little as $40 a month—and the broker buys for the customer's account as many shares as his credit balance permits.

MOCK UP—A roughly constructed but full-scale model of a machine.

MONOPOLY—The power to control prices within an industry. It is in violation of the antitrust laws.

NARROW MARKET—A stock market term denoting light trading in an issue in which there are few nearby bids and offers. The same as a *thin market*.

NASD—The National Association of Securities Dealers, an association of brokers and dealers in unlisted securities.

NATIONAL BANK—A banking institution that secured its charter from the federal government. These banks must become members of the Federal Reserve System.

NATIONAL INCOME—A measure of economic activity, published quarterly and compiled by the Department of Commerce. It is the total of income earned in producing the gross national product, such as wages, salaries, income of unincorporated businesses, rental income, net interest receipts, and corporate profits before taxes. It includes an estimated figure of income received by producers; of imputed values for goods and services, such as food produced and consumed by farmers, food furnished employees; and the rental value of owner-occupied homes. National income is always smaller than gross national product as it does not include business allowances for depreciation and capital consumption, and it does not include indirect business taxes such as sales and excise taxes.

NEGOTIABLE—A security that can readily be passed from one person to another. Such securities or certificates must be in writing, carry an unconditional order to pay, be payable at a determinable time and to the bearer, and must indicate the drawer.

NET FREE RESERVES—The funds members banks may use to expand loans and investments.

NOMINAL—Applied to a market, it indicates the probable level of the market, but that level is not based on actual transactions.

NOMINEE—As applied to the securities business the nominee, usually a corporation, is the party holding securities for the benefit of the true owner. The securities are listed in the name of the nominee. The primary purpose is to avoid delays in the transfer of the securities in question. Banks make full use of nominee registration of securities held in trust accounts, as when a bank sells securities from such a trust account it must cite the legal authority under which it acts and in some cases it may be required to obtain court proof of its authority and submit certified copies of a will or trust instrument. In some cases cotrustees are involved, and the signatures of each must be obtained in order for the securities to be "good delivery." By the use of a nominee, costs can be kept down and delays in delivery avoided.

NONCUMULATIVE—A preferred stock on which a corporation is not obligated to pay a dividend unless the amount is actually earned, and upon which unpaid dividends do not accrue.

NOTE—Evidence of a promise to pay, either on demand or on a specified date.

N. R. O. FUNDS—The initials stand for nonresident owned. A common example is open end investment companies, notably in Canada, the shares of which are sold to United States investors.

OBLIGATION—A term applied to all types of indebtedness.

ODD LOT—An amount of stock less than the established unit of trading.

ODD-LOT DEALERS—Members of an exchange who specialize in handling odd lots for regular commission brokers, charging a small differential as compensation.

OECD—Organization for Economic Cooperation and Development, through which the United States has channeled postwar aid to Europe.

OFF-BOARD—A term applied to transactions in unlisted securities. It is also applied to special transactions in listed securities when a block changes hands but the order is not executed on the trading floor of a national securities exchange.

OLD LADY OF THREADNEEDLE STREET—Nickname for the Bank of England.

OPEN-END BONDS—Mortgage bonds in which the amount issuable under the mortgage is left indefinite, the mortgage permitting subsequent issue.

OPEN MARKET—A broad and freely competitive market.

OPEN SHOP—A shop in which membership in a union is not a prerequisite of securing or maintaining employment.

OPERATING RATIO—In railroad bookkeeping, the ratio of operating expenses to operating revenue.

OPTION—A privilege to buy or sell specified securities or commodities at a definite price within an agreed-upon time.

ORDINARY SHARES—The British term for the junior stock issue of a corporation, similar to common stock in America.

OUTLAW STRIKES—Stoppages in work which lack the approval of the national or international union and usually violate either the union constitution or a collective bargaining agreement.

OUT OF LINE—Term used by speculators to indicate that certain securities are selling either too high or too low in comparison with other securities.

OVERCERTIFY—To certify a check for an amount in excess of the balance held on deposit in the account of the drawer.

OVER THE COUNTER—A market—not an organized exchange—for large blocks of high-grade listed securities, inactive securities, and those not listed on an exchange. Transactions are effected between buyer and seller directly, usually at net prices and not, as on an exchange, on a commission basis through brokers.

PACKAGE BARGAINING—Collective bargaining in which demands for wage increases are coupled with other demands.

PAPER—Short-term evidences of debt.

PAPER PROFITS—Unrealized profits.

PAR VALUE—Applied to bonds it indicates the value originally received by the issuer, and it is the amount due the investor at maturity. Applied to stocks it means the face or nominal value, and the amount is engraved on the face of the certificate. In the case of common stocks it is virtually meaningless, which is the reason many companies issue stocks of no par value. On the formation of a new company, the common stock, or at least a large portion of it, is frequently issued to the underwriters as a bonus for their services and therefore does not represent actual cash paid into the company treasury. Or it may be issued to new investors as a bonus. Therefore, it should be ignored by any investor in an equity security.

PARENT COMPANY—A company owning sufficient stock of another company to be able to dictate its control.

PARITY—In foreign exchange, the value of one currency in terms of another as determined by their respective gold backing. In commodities, the price level at which two delivery points are equalized, after expenses of shipping, interest, and insurance have been adjusted. When there is a disparity between the two, one is referred to as being above parity or below parity.

PARTICIPATING BONDS—Bonds which, in addition to being entitled to a stated rate of interest, also share in excess profits of the issuing company.

PARTICIPATING PREFERRED—A preferred stock which, in addition to being entitled to its regular dividend, also participates in the earnings of the company and may therefore receive additional dividends. The basis on which it participates is specified, and usually it receives no additional payments until the common has likewise paid dividends to the extent of the preferred's regular payment.

PARTNERSHIP—A business owned by a small number of individuals, each of whom assumes legal responsibility for the liabilities and the conduct of the business.

PATTERN BARGAINING—Collective bargaining in which the union seeks to apply identical terms, conditions, or demands to a number of employers within an industry, although the employers act individually.

PEGGING—Attempting to keep a market within a certain range.

PENNY STOCKS—Low-priced issues, usually under $2 a share, and highly speculative.

PERSONAL INCOME—A measure of the current income of individuals, unincorporated businesses, and nonprofit institutions. It differs from national income in that it includes such payments as unemployment compensation, veterans' benefits, and interest payments by the government. It excludes corporate income and social security payments by employers and employees. It is published monthly. *Disposable personal income* is personal income from which are deducted taxes on individuals and customs receipts.

PILOT PLANT—An experimental plant where a new process is carried out on a small scale after it has left the research laboratory, but before it is attempted on a commercial scale in a manufacturing plant.

PINK SHEETS—The list of over-the-counter stock price quotations, issued daily and monthly. It is compiled by the National Quotation Bureau, a private corporation with headquarters in New York, owned by Commerce Clearing House, Inc., Chicago. It serves some 4,700 broker-dealers coast to coast who trade in an estimated 8,000 issues daily and are prepared to make markets in another 30,000 less active issues. The broker-dealers and their employees are under the strict jurisdiction of the National Association of Security Dealers, Inc., a self-policing organization, to which all OTC firms must belong.

PIT—The active trading center in a produce exchange.

PLUNGE—Reckless speculation on a large scale.

PM's—"Push money," paid to retail clerks during special sales as an incentive to dispose of slow-moving items.

POOL—A combination of persons organized for the purpose of exploiting the market in a certain stock or stocks. It is a joint venture of the participants, and during its existence the members usually agree not to trade separately for their own account.

PORTFOLIO—Loans and securities held by a corporation or an individual.

POSITION—Referring to whether a trader or corporation is long or short of securities or commodities and to what extent.

POUND STERLING—The British monetary unit.

PREFERRED STOCK—Stock which has a prior claim to earnings and dividends over the common stock, but is secondary to bonds and other floating debt.

PREMIUM—In the case of bonds or preferred stocks, it is the excess of the market price over par value. In new offerings of securities, it is the excess of the market price over the price at which the securities were offered by the underwriters. It can also refer to the redemption price of a preferred stock or a bond if that price is above the face value or par value. In a few very rare cases the word also applies to a charge made by the lender of shares to a short trader. This happens only when it becomes extremely difficult for the shorts to borrow.

PRICE-EARNINGS RATIO—The market price of a stock divided by its latest available or estimated earnings per share. The term is frequently abbreviated as P/E ratio. There is no set rule as to how high or low a stock's price-earnings ratio should be. A rule of thumb is that 10 to 15 times is normally justified. In times of confidence in the business outlook the ratio goes higher. Growth companies usually command a higher P/E ratio, and have gone to 70 or 80 in some speculative instances. The price-earnings ratio of the group of thirty stocks used in compiling the Dow-Jones average of industrial stocks is frequently referred to in the press.

PRIMARY RECEIPTS—Total receipts of a commodity at principal primary points, such as the major cities, which regularly receive the agricultural shipments from rural areas.

PRIME RATE—The fee banks charge their biggest borrowers, who have the best credit ratings.

PRIOR PREFERRED—A preferred stock that takes precedence over other preferreds both as to dividends and to assets in the event of liquidation.

PRIVATE-WIRE HOUSES—Brokerage firms that lease telegraph wires to distant cities to provide their out-of-town customers with faster service.

PROFESSIONAL—A market operator who makes a business of speculating.

PROFIT TAKING—Liquidating securities in which there is a paper profit in order to realize the cash profit.

PROMOTER—One who acts as a middleman in business in order to bring together those with money to risk and those who have a business proposition. His duties may include securing new funds for old or new business ventures, discovering new ventures, or merging established businesses.

PRORATE—In financial news the term is applied mostly to the oil industry. It is a method of limiting the oil production of each company. The potential production of a flush pool is estimated, and estimates are also made of the potential production of each unit. Then each company is assigned the amount it will be permitted to bring to the surface, the amount being based on the ratio of each company's potential to the potential of the entire field.

PROSPECTUS—A printed statement of the organization of a new enterprise or the expansion plans of an existing enterprise. The document contains detailed information on the nature of the business, the financial condition of the company, and such other facts as an investor in the enterprise would wish to know.

PROXY—Written authority given by a stockholder to some other party giving the latter the right to vote the stock at a stockholders' meeting.

PRUDENT MAN RULE—A term growing out of legislation in a number of states permitting fiduciaries to invest trusteed funds in securities which a man of discretion and intelligence might reasonably be expected to choose in his search for a fair return and the preservation of capital. Without such legislation the laws in certain states limit fiduciaries to an approved list of top-grade securities, known as the legal list.

PUBLIC UTILITY—A business organization which performs an essential service for the public. Usually the state grants it a monopoly in its particular territory and in return exerts a strict supervision or regulation of the company's rates and business practices.

PUDS—Abbreviation for the bonds of a public utility district.

PUT—An option to sell a certain amount of stock to the writer of the option at a specified price within an agreed-upon time. See CALL.

PYRAMIDING—Using paper profits as the basis of additional margin with which to finance the purchase of more stock. The term also applies to the piling of one holding company on top of another.

QUICK ASSETS—Assets that are readily marketable.

QUICKIE STRIKES—Work stoppages called without advance notice, usually because some practice is resented by the employees or the local union, and usually without authorization by the national or international union.

QUOTA—Some countries have limited the amount of imports of certain goods they will receive from other countries, this method being used to protect their home industries. The quota is established; and after it has been reached, no further imports of that article will be received during the year.

RAID—Active and heavy trading on either the buying or selling side of the market in order to shake out weakly margined traders. A bear raid would mean heavy selling to bring liquidation from small traders, while occasionally there is a bull raid to force shorts to cover.

RALLY—Expression denoting a short, but spirited, upturn in the market.

RAPID AMORTIZATION—A program which permits owners of facilities to write off all or a part of their cost for income tax purposes in a short space of time, usually five years. It was used extensively during World War II as an incentive to encourage companies to manufacture highly specialized materials needed by the Defense Department.

REACTION—The reversal of the previous trend in a stock or in a market as a whole.

REALIZING SALES—Sales to take profits on securities or commodities.

REAL WAGES—Amount of goods and services a worker may purchase with his pay.

RECIPROCAL TRADE—Trade between two countries under an agreement made for their mutual advantage.

REDISCOUNT—Discounting for a second time, as when one bank calls upon another bank or the Federal Reserve to discount paper which it had previously discounted for a customer.

REDISCOUNT RATE—The rate of interest charged by a Federal Reserve bank for rediscounting paper for its member banks.

REFUNDING—Refinancing a debt which cannot be paid off at maturity, or refinancing a debt prior to maturity, in order to secure better terms from the lenders.

REGIONAL BANK—Each of the twelve Federal Reserve banks.

REGISTERED BOND—A bond with the name of the owner written on its face. It is not negotiable until the owner has endorsed it, whereupon it can be transferred on the books of the issuing corporation.

REGISTERED REPRESENTATIVE—A securities salesman who has met certain standards established by stock exchanges and the National Association of Securities Dealers and thus, as an employee of a brokerage firm, is entitled to accept buy and sell orders from customers. He is sometimes referred to as a customer's man or an account executive.

REGULATION T—The Federal Reserve's regulation which prescribes the amount of credit which brokers and dealers may advance to their customers for the purchase of securities.

RENTES—The annual interest payable on the bonded debt of France, Austria, Italy, and a few other countries. The term is also applied to the bonds themselves.

RESERVE RATIO—The Federal Reserve ratio of reserves to deposit and Federal Reserve note liabilities.

RESISTANCE POINTS—A stock market term meaning the points at which a security slows up or stops after it has been moving definitely in one direction.

RESTRAINT OF TRADE—Interference with the normal activity of free trade. It is outlawed by the Sherman Anti-Trust Act.

RIGGING—Manipulating the market in any security.

RIGHTS—Privileges granted to stockholders to buy new stock or bonds at a concession below the prevailing market (*see* WARRANTS).

ROUND LOT—The unit of trading or a multiple thereof, established by a securities exchange for the various securities on its trading list.

RUNNER—Messenger for a bank or brokerage house.

SCAB—A worker who refuses to join coworkers in a strike.

SCALING—Trading in securities or commodities by placing orders at regular price intervals instead of placing the entire order all at once.

SCALPING—Taking a quick profit.

SCRIP—A provisional document certifying that the holder is entitled to receive something else, such as securities, dividends, interest, or back wages; paper currency of denominations of less than a dollar; a temporary certificate issued to be exchanged at a later date; the term also is frequently applied to fractional shares of stock, or to represent small dividends not payable in cash but deferred until a later date.

SEAT—A membership on an exchange.

SECONDARY BOYCOTT—Refusal of workers to handle or work on products made by an employer other than their own, in order to compel the boycotted employer to yield to union demands.

SECONDARY PICKETING—Picketing of an employer with whom the union has no direct dispute, in an attempt to cause him to refuse to deal with another employer who is having a dispute.

SECULAR TREND—The normal or long-term trend.

SECURED CREDITOR—A creditor who holds a claim on certain definite collateral or assets as a protection for a loan.

SEIGNIORAGE—Charge made by a government for minting coinage. It represents the difference between the bullion or metal price and the face value of the coins.

SELLING AGAINST THE BOX—A sale of securities which one owns but does not deliver. Technically the seller is short, although he may be holding the securities in his safe deposit box. He may cover his short position by buying, or he may get the securities from his box and make delivery.

SERIAL BONDS—An issue of bonds, portions of which fall due at regular periods, rather than the entire issue falling due at one time. Debt can be systematically reduced by this method, and the effect is much the same as a systematic setting up of a retirement fund for the issue through sinking fund payments.

SETTLEMENT—Payment of a debt to the creditor by the debtor; striking a balance between members of a clearing house association; balancing purchases and sales of securities or commodities between firms, including the payment of debits owed.

SETTLEMENT DAY—The date on which a buyer must pay for securities bought and the seller must deliver the securities he sold. In the United States this is the fourth business day following the transaction. On European exchanges there is a longer period between settlements, usually a fortnight, or twice a month. This is called the fortnightly settlement period, or account period.

SHADE—A slight concession in price.

SHAKING OUT—Forcing speculators who are undermargined to liquidate.

SHARE—Synonymous with stock.

SHOESTRING MARGIN—A small or inadequate margin.

SHORT COVERING—The buying back by a trader who has sold securities or commodities which he did not own.

SHORT SALE—The sale of securities or commodities which are not owned, in anticipation of being able to buy them later at a lower price. In the case of securities, the seller or his broker must borrow the securities with which to make delivery. In the case of commodities, the seller binds himself to deliver at some future date.

SINKING FUND—A fund created by a corporation into which it pays specified amounts of money at regular intervals in order to accumulate a sum of money with which to retire an obligation on maturity.

SIT-DOWN STRIKE—A strike in which the workers refuse to work but remain inside the employer's plant.

SLEEPER—A trading term applied to a security that is believed to be selling at far less than its value and which may easily "come awake" in the near future.

SLOWDOWN—A concerted and sustained refusal by workers to produce at a normal rate.

SOLDIERING—Deliberate failure to maintain ordinary work-performance standards.

S.O.P.—An abbreviation, meaning statement of policy.

SPECIALIST—A member of a stock exchange who, acting as a broker for other members, keeps a record of selling and buying orders of other members in certain specified stocks. He records the day orders and the G.T.C. (or good 'til countermanded) orders, and completes the transactions when possible.

SPECULATION—Putting of capital into an enterprise for quick or large returns, but with certain elements of risk which may impair the capital.

SPEED-UP—A system designed to increase worker productivity.

SPIN OFF—Distribution of real assets by a corporation. The distribution may be made as a reward to stockholders, as is a cash or stock dividend, or it may result from antitrust proceedings. If a company is guilty of restraining trade, or if it consents to distribute certain of its assets in order to avoid a long and costly trial, it divests itself of the disputed assets by issuing them to its stockholders. A spin off is the opposite of a merger.

SPLIT UP—Multiplying the number of shares of a corporation by dividing the present shares into two or more shares. The price of each share is thereby lowered but the value of the entire outstanding issue is not affected.

SPONSOR—To take an interest in a security issue and protect the market in it.

SPOT—Term used in commodities and in foreign exchange to denote something which can be delivered readily.

SPREAD—Difference between the bid and offer price of a security; a combination of a put and a call on a security. When applied to commodities, a spread or straddle constitutes the purchase of a futures contract in one month and a sale of the same commodity in another month, both commitments remaining open until closed at some later date.

SQUEEZE—Forcing shorts to cover their commitments due to rapidly rising prices; a money squeeze is a temporary shortage of available funds, accompanied by difficulty in borrowing and in advance in interest rates.

STAGGER SYSTEM—A practice whereby only a portion of a board of directors is elected in any one year. It is common among eleemosynary institutions, as it guarantees a continuity of service by directors or trustees who are familiar with the practice, aims, and ideals of the institution. In the case of corporations organized to make a profit, it has come under fire, as it may be responsible for perpetuating in office a group of directors who have lost the confidence of the holders of a majority of the stock. As an example, if a corporation has fifteen directors and only five of them stand for election in any one year, a new group might obtain control of a majority of the stock and yet be unable to name a majority to the board until it had held its stock into the second year.

STANDBY—Nonworking employee hired to satisfy featherbedding requirements.

STAPLE—The term is frequently applied to cotton and other major commodities. It also refers to the length of cotton fiber.

STATE BANK—A banking institution chartered by a state. These institutions may or may not join the Federal Reserve System.

STOCK—The junior security of a corporation, representing an equity interest in the business but entitled to earnings only after all prior obligations have been met. In business usage it means goods, merchandise, or finished products on hand.

STOCK DIVIDENDS—A payment made to stockholders in the form of additional shares instead of in cash.

STOCKHOLDERS OF RECORD—Stockholders whose names are registered in the stock ledger of the corporation.

STOP ORDER—An order given a broker by a customer in an effort to protect a profit or limit a loss. It instructs the broker to buy or sell at the market when the price of the security touches a certain point.

STRADDLE—A combination of a put and a call on the same security.

STRADDLING—The practice of buying a futures contract of a commodity for one month and selling a similar contract in another month, in the expectation that the price differential will be reduced and thus net a profit with comparatively little risk.

STREET—Popular name for the financial district of New York.

STREET NAME—In many cases an investor may prefer not to have his securities transferred to his own name. He leaves his securities with his broker or banker. This applies to those who trade in and out rapidly or who trade on margin. It may also apply to one who trades but rarely, and for cash, as it is usually more convenient for him to have his securities with a firm that is well known. In such cases the certificates do not contain the investor's name but that of a firm or bank. These are Street names, and the certificate is a Street certificate, well known to all, and the securities, when sold, can be transferred easily to the firm through whom the new buyer bought them.

SUPERPOWER—Interconnected electric power systems, tying in a number of generating plants.

SWAP AGREEMENT—A standby credit arrangement between two countries whereby a central bank stands ready, on request, to exchange a stated amount of its own currency for that of the other country in the agreement, throughout a set period. It is a reciprocal currency arrangement, within free world countries, designed to help protect the currency of any one party against undue pressure in the foreign exchange market.

SWEATSHOP—A factory where accepted standards of sanitation, safety, and working conditions are not met.

SWITCHING—Transferring one's interest in a future contract in a commodity from one month to another. Liquidating holdings of one security and purchasing another security.

SYNDICATE—Group of banks or investment firms formed to underwrite and distribute a new issue of securities.

TAKE-HOME PAY—The net of the pay envelope after deductions such as the withholding tax, pension charges, union dues, and insurance premiums.

TARIFF—Specified amount levied by the government on all imports. Tariffs are used for the purpose of collecting revenue and for the protection of home industries, as they make it more difficult for foreign manufacturers to sell here.

TAX EXEMPT BONDS—Securities of the federal government on the one hand, and of states and their political subdivisions on the other. Tax exemption arises from our dual form of government. It may be partial or complete.

TECHNICAL POSITION—Term used by operators in a market to indicate the circumstances, conditions, or controlling influences within the market itself, as distinguished from external factors which might have an influence on the price structure.

TENANCY-IN-COMMON—Ownership by two or more persons. Portions owned by the individuals may vary in size, and there can be any number of tenants. Income and expenses are shared by each in proportion to its ownership, and each tenant may dispose of his share as he wishes. On his death his portion passes to his heirs.

TENDERABLE—A commodity that meets the requirements as to grade and thus is a good delivery on a futures contract.

THIN MARGIN—A small, inadequate margin.

THIN MARKET—A market in which there are comparatively few offers to sell or bids to buy. It may come about because of lack of interest or because of limited supply. In such cases a little buying or selling can produce wide price swings.

THIRD MARKET—Nickname applied to over-the-counter, or off-board, trading in big blocks of listed securities. The 1963 SEC study of the securities industry devoted eighty-eight pages to this expanding market, and estimated it handles a volume of $2 billion a year. It exists largely to service the needs of institutional investors and definitely not the man in the street. Members of the New York Stock Exchange are barred from this trading except in special cases where they can secure an exemption, but the study found there are more than four hundred nonmember firms active in this third market, seven of which transact the bulk of the business.

TIME BILLS—A bill of exchange with a fixed payable date, thus contrasting with a demand or sight bill.

TIME DEPOSITS—Interest-bearing deposits, not subject to withdrawal before a fixed date.

TIME DRAFT—A draft with a definite period to run.

TIME LOANS—Loans made for a specified period.

TIME MONEY—Loans for a specified period, as contrasted with call money, which is payable on demand.

TIP—An unsupported statement regarding the possible movement of a security, given ostensibly in confidence without revealing the source of the information.

TOOK A BATH—A slang phrase applied to an underwriting or investment that turned sour.

TREASURY STOCK—Shares which have been issued by a corporation but later are reacquired by it. This stock has no vote and receives no dividends while held in the corporation's treasury. It may be held indefinitely, resold, or retired.

TURN—A completed transaction, involving a purchase and a sale.

TURNOVER—Term indicating the number of times and the rapidity with which capital, merchandise or accounts are moved within a given period. The term is also applied to the number of shares of stock, the total par value of bonds, or amount of commodities traded in on an exchange in a given period.

TWO-DOLLAR BROKERS—Members of the New York Stock Exchange who are not members of a commission house and do not trade for their own account, but handle business for other members at a specified charge.

UNDERLYING BONDS—Bonds secured by prior liens, having priority over other bonds.

UNDER THE RULE—If delivery of a security is not made by a member of an exchange in accordance with the terms of a contract, a designated official of the exchange may complete the transaction, buying the necessary stock at the market and thus buying in under the rule.

UNDERWRITER—One who insures for a compensation.

UNDERWRITING—Guaranteeing the sale of an issue of securities at a stated price to the issuing company.

UNDIGESTED SECURITIES—Securities issued in an amount too large to be absorbed by the investment market.

UNION SHOP—A form of union security under which the employer may hire nonunion workers, but they must then become members in order to retain their employee status.

UNLISTED SECURITIES—Securities not listed on an organized exchange.

UPSET PRICE—A previously fixed starting price in the auctioning of a piece of real estate. The prospective seller will not entertain a bid below that figure.

VELVET—An easily made profit or bonus.

VERTICAL UNION—A union which bargains for workers of different categories of employment, such as skilled, semiskilled and unskilled, or accepts into membership all workers of a bargaining unit irrespective of differences in their occupations.

VISIBLE SUPPLY—The amount of a commodity in store at leading points, which is reported regularly.

VOTING TRUST—An agreement under which stockholders deposit their shares with trustees who issue certificates in exchange. The stock thereupon retains all its rights except voting, which is lodged with the trustees for a specified length of time.

WALKING DELEGATE—Officer of a local union who acts as executive secretary for the union, handles its local business matters, enrolls members, investigates complaints, negotiates with employers, and generally handles the union's affairs.

WALL STREET—The street by that name in the financial district of New York. The term is now used to describe all the financial interests of the country.

WAREHOUSE RECEIPT—A receipt issued by a storage company to certify that a specific amount of goods has been placed in a tank, warehouse, barge, ship, or other storage facility. These receipts constitute one of the oldest and most trusted forms of financing as they may be used for loans at a bank or for payment of debts. They often pass from one corporation to another after their initial issuance.

WARRANTS—Rights to buy a stock at a specific price. Generally warrants run for longer periods of time than the ordinary subscription rights occasionally given stockholders when a corporation wishes to raise new capital. Some issues of warrants are perpetual. Aside from the time element, the chief difference between warrants and rights concerns the purpose of their issuance. A corporation issues rights to shares slightly below the market in order to raise capital.

Warrants, on the other hand, come into being for different reasons, two of which are common. In a reorganization the holders of a certain class of securities may be offered a new issue, with long-term or perpetual warrants attached, to induce them to relinquish the securities already owned. In the case of new financing, warrants may be attached to new issues of bonds, preferred stocks, or even common stocks, to make them more attractive to the investor. The warrants may be detached, and they are negotiable. Because of their long-term nature, certain warrants have a speculative appeal. In some cases they have increased in value by fantastic percentages. In a long bull market, in which the underlying security enjoys a major climb, the warrants, or privilege to buy the shares at a reduced price, can move from pennies to many dollars. The investor should realize, however, that a warrant is a privilege—nothing more—and it is not entitled to dividends nor backed by specific assets.

WASH SALES—Ostensibly the sale of a block of securities, but actually a transaction in which there is no real change of ownership. An individual may sell the securities from one of his accounts and buy the same securities for another of his accounts, or a closely knit group may trade the securities back and forth. The owners remain the same. As such transactions create a false impression of activity, usually at rising prices, they are forbidden by all the securities exchanges.

WATERED STOCK—Stock of a corporation issued to insiders for a nominal consideration and without a fair increase in the assets of the corporation, thus diluting the value behind each share of stock held by investors. The term dates back to a malpractice of feeding cattle salt and then letting them drink quantities of water just before selling them at so much a hundred pounds, on the hoof.

WHEN ISSUED—The term applies to a new issue of securities that has been duly authorized but which is not actually outstanding and in the hands of the purchasers. Such securities can be traded in, and may be listed, but transactions in them are settled only after the new securities are, in fact, issued. Trades are distinguished in newspaper tables by the label *wi*.

WHITE-COLLAR WORKERS—Clerical employees of an office.

WORKING CAPITAL—The excess of a corporation's total current assets over its total current liabilities.

WORKING CONTROL—Theoretically the ownership, or control, of more than half the outstanding shares of a corporation. In actual practice, especially in large corporations, a concentrated block, even though it represents but a small percentage of the outstanding shares, constitutes working control.

YIELD—The rate of return available on a security, expressed as a percentage of the current market price. If the security is owned by an investor, it is the percentage return he receives on his original purchase price.

INDEX